# HowExpert Guide to Brazilian Jiu-Jitsu

The Ultimate Handbook for Mastering Techniques, Developing Strategies, and Embracing the BJJ Lifestyle

## HowExpert

Copyright © 2024 Hot Methods, Inc. DBA HowExpert™
www.HowExpert.com

For more tips related to this topic, visit HowExpert.com/bjj.

# Recommended Resources

- HowExpert.com – How To Guides on All Topics from A to Z by Everyday Experts.
- HowExpert.com/free – Free HowExpert Email Newsletter.
- HowExpert.com/books – HowExpert Books
- HowExpert.com/courses – HowExpert Courses
- HowExpert.com/clothing – HowExpert Clothing
- HowExpert.com/membership – HowExpert Membership Site
- HowExpert.com/affiliates – HowExpert Affiliate Program
- HowExpert.com/jobs – HowExpert Jobs
- HowExpert.com/writers – Write About Your #1 Passion/Knowledge/Expertise & Become a HowExpert Author.
- HowExpert.com/resources – Additional HowExpert Recommended Resources
- YouTube.com/HowExpert – Subscribe to HowExpert YouTube.
- Instagram.com/HowExpert – Follow HowExpert on Instagram.
- Facebook.com/HowExpert – Follow HowExpert on Facebook.
- TikTok.com/@HowExpert – Follow HowExpert on TikTok.

# Publisher's Foreword

Dear HowExpert Reader,

HowExpert publishes quick 'how to' guides on all topics from A to Z by everyday experts.

At HowExpert, our mission is to discover, empower, and maximize everyday people's talents to ultimately make a positive impact in the world for all topics from A to Z…one everyday expert at a time!

HowExpert guides are written by everyday people just like you and me, who have a passion, knowledge, and expertise for a specific topic.

We take great pride in selecting everyday experts who have a passion, real-life experience in a topic, and excellent writing skills to teach you about the topic you are also passionate about and eager to learn.

We hope you get a lot of value from our HowExpert guides, and it can make a positive impact on your life in some way. All of our readers, including you, help us continue living our mission of positively impacting the world for all spheres of influences from A to Z.

If you enjoyed one of our HowExpert guides, then please take a moment to send us your feedback from wherever you got this book.

Thank you, and I wish you all the best in all aspects of life.

To your success,

Byungjoon "BJ" Min   민병준
Founder & Publisher of HowExpert
HowExpert.com

PS…If you are also interested in becoming a HowExpert author, then please visit our website at HowExpert.com/writers. Thank you & again, all the best! John 3:16

## COPYRIGHT, LEGAL NOTICE AND DISCLAIMER:

COPYRIGHT © 2024 HOT METHODS, INC. (DBA HOWEXPERT™). ALL RIGHTS RESERVED WORLDWIDE. NO PART OF THIS PUBLICATION MAY BE REPRODUCED IN ANY FORM OR BY ANY MEANS, INCLUDING SCANNING, PHOTOCOPYING, OR OTHERWISE WITHOUT PRIOR WRITTEN PERMISSION OF THE COPYRIGHT HOLDER.

DISCLAIMER AND TERMS OF USE: PLEASE NOTE THAT MUCH OF THIS PUBLICATION IS BASED ON PERSONAL EXPERIENCE AND ANECDOTAL EVIDENCE. ALTHOUGH THE AUTHOR AND PUBLISHER HAVE MADE EVERY REASONABLE ATTEMPT TO ACHIEVE COMPLETE ACCURACY OF THE CONTENT IN THIS GUIDE, THEY ASSUME NO RESPONSIBILITY FOR ERRORS OR OMISSIONS. ALSO, YOU SHOULD USE THIS INFORMATION AS YOU SEE FIT, AND AT YOUR OWN RISK. YOUR PARTICULAR SITUATION MAY NOT BE EXACTLY SUITED TO THE EXAMPLES ILLUSTRATED HERE; IN FACT, IT'S LIKELY THAT THEY WON'T BE THE SAME, AND YOU SHOULD ADJUST YOUR USE OF THE INFORMATION AND RECOMMENDATIONS ACCORDINGLY.

THE AUTHOR AND PUBLISHER DO NOT WARRANT THE PERFORMANCE, EFFECTIVENESS OR APPLICABILITY OF ANY SITES LISTED OR LINKED TO IN THIS BOOK. ALL LINKS ARE FOR INFORMATION PURPOSES ONLY AND ARE NOT WARRANTED FOR CONTENT, ACCURACY OR ANY OTHER IMPLIED OR EXPLICIT PURPOSE.

ANY TRADEMARKS, SERVICE MARKS, PRODUCT NAMES OR NAMED FEATURES ARE ASSUMED TO BE THE PROPERTY OF THEIR RESPECTIVE OWNERS, AND ARE USED ONLY FOR REFERENCE. THERE IS NO IMPLIED ENDORSEMENT IF WE USE ONE OF THESE TERMS.

NO PART OF THIS BOOK MAY BE REPRODUCED, STORED IN A RETRIEVAL SYSTEM, OR TRANSMITTED BY ANY OTHER MEANS: ELECTRONIC, MECHANICAL, PHOTOCOPYING, RECORDING, OR OTHERWISE, WITHOUT THE PRIOR WRITTEN PERMISSION OF THE AUTHOR.

ANY VIOLATION BY STEALING THIS BOOK OR DOWNLOADING OR SHARING IT ILLEGALLY WILL BE PROSECUTED BY LAWYERS TO THE FULLEST EXTENT. THIS PUBLICATION IS PROTECTED UNDER THE US COPYRIGHT ACT OF 1976 AND ALL OTHER APPLICABLE INTERNATIONAL, FEDERAL, STATE AND LOCAL LAWS AND ALL RIGHTS ARE RESERVED, INCLUDING RESALE RIGHTS: YOU ARE NOT ALLOWED TO GIVE OR SELL THIS GUIDE TO ANYONE ELSE.

THIS PUBLICATION IS DESIGNED TO PROVIDE ACCURATE AND AUTHORITATIVE INFORMATION WITH REGARD TO THE SUBJECT MATTER COVERED. IT IS SOLD WITH THE UNDERSTANDING THAT THE AUTHORS AND PUBLISHERS ARE NOT ENGAGED IN RENDERING LEGAL, FINANCIAL, OR OTHER PROFESSIONAL ADVICE. LAWS AND PRACTICES OFTEN VARY FROM STATE TO STATE AND IF LEGAL OR OTHER EXPERT ASSISTANCE IS REQUIRED, THE SERVICES OF A PROFESSIONAL SHOULD BE SOUGHT. THE AUTHORS AND PUBLISHER SPECIFICALLY DISCLAIM ANY LIABILITY THAT IS INCURRED FROM THE USE OR APPLICATION OF THE CONTENTS OF THIS BOOK.

HOT METHODS, INC. DBA HOWEXPERT
EMAIL: SUPPORT@HOWEXPERT.COM
WEBSITE: WWW.HOWEXPERT.COM

**COPYRIGHT © 2024 HOT METHODS, INC. (DBA HOWEXPERT™)
ALL RIGHTS RESERVED WORLDWIDE.**

# Table of Contents

Recommended Resources ................................................................................. 2
Publisher's Foreword ....................................................................................... 3
Book Overview ............................................................................................... 18
Part 1: Foundations of Brazilian Jiu-Jitsu ..................................................... 21
Chapter 1: The Origins and Evolution of BJJ ............................................... 21
   1.1 Japanese Jujutsu Roots ........................................................................ 21
   1.2 The Gracie Family and BJJ's Birth ..................................................... 22
   1.3 Global Spread and Influence ............................................................... 23
   Chapter 1 Review: The Origins and Evolution of BJJ ............................... 25
Chapter 2: Core Principles and Philosophy ................................................... 27
   2.1 The Gentle Art: Using Leverage and Technique ................................. 27
      A. Leverage ............................................................................................ 27
      B. Technique .......................................................................................... 28
      C. Practical Applications ....................................................................... 28
   2.2 Position Before Submission: Control Hierarchies .............................. 29
      A. The Importance of Control ............................................................... 29
      B. Hierarchy of Positions ...................................................................... 30
      C. Practical Applications ....................................................................... 30
   2.3 The Mindset: Discipline, Respect, and Continuous Growth ............... 31
      A. Discipline .......................................................................................... 31
      B. Respect ............................................................................................. 31
      C. Continuous Growth .......................................................................... 32
   Chapter 2 Review: Core Principles and Philosophy .................................. 32
Part 2: Getting Started .................................................................................... 35
Chapter 3: Choosing the Right Academy and Gear ....................................... 35
   3.1 Selecting a BJJ Academy ..................................................................... 35
      A. Research and Recommendations ...................................................... 35
      B. Visit Potential Academies ................................................................ 36
      C. Evaluate the Environment ................................................................ 36
      D. Practical Applications ...................................................................... 36
   3.2 Essential Gear and Equipment ............................................................ 37
      A. Gi and No-Gi Attire ......................................................................... 37

  B. Additional Gear .................................................................. 38

  C. Maintenance and Care ........................................................ 39

 3.3 BJJ Etiquette and Rules ........................................................ 39

  A. Respect and Humility ......................................................... 39

  B. Hygiene and Safety ............................................................ 40

  C. Academy Rules ................................................................... 40

 Chapter 3 Review: Choosing the Right Academy and Gear .......... 41

Chapter 4: Warm-Up and Conditioning ........................................... 43

 4.1 Importance of Warm-Ups ..................................................... 43

  A. Physical Preparation ........................................................... 43

  B. Mental Preparation ............................................................. 43

  C. Common Warm-Up Exercises ............................................ 44

 4.2 Stretching and Flexibility Exercises ..................................... 45

  A. Static Stretching ................................................................. 45

  B. Dynamic Stretching ............................................................ 45

  C. Yoga and Mobility Work .................................................... 46

 4.3 Strength and Conditioning for BJJ ....................................... 47

  A. Strength Training ............................................................... 47

  B. Cardiovascular Conditioning .............................................. 48

  C. Recovery and Injury Prevention ......................................... 48

 Chapter 4 Review: Warm-Up and Conditioning ........................... 49

Part 3: Essential Techniques and Movements .................................. 51

Chapter 5: Basic Movements and Drills ........................................... 51

 5.1 Stance and Posture ................................................................ 51

  A. Base and Balance ............................................................... 52

  B. Offensive and Defensive Postures ...................................... 52

  C. Movement and Adjustment ................................................ 52

 5.2 Shrimping, Bridging, and Rolling ......................................... 53

  A. Shrimping ........................................................................... 53

  B. Bridging .............................................................................. 54

  C. Rolling ................................................................................ 54

 5.3 Breakfalls and Safety Techniques ......................................... 55

  A. Back Breakfall .................................................................... 55

  B. Side Breakfall ..................................................................... 56

    C. Forward Roll Breakfall .................................................................. 56

  Chapter 5 Review: Basic Movements and Drills ....................................... 57

Chapter 6: Guard Positions and Variations ................................................... 59

  6.1 Closed Guard: Control and Submissions ............................................. 59

    A. Control ............................................................................................ 59

    B. Submissions .................................................................................... 60

    C. Sweeps ............................................................................................ 62

  6.2 Open Guard: Variations and Transitions .............................................. 63

    A. Variations ....................................................................................... 64

    B. Transitions ...................................................................................... 64

    C. Practical Techniques ....................................................................... 65

  6.3 Half Guard: Defense, Sweeps, and Attacks ......................................... 66

    A. Defense .......................................................................................... 66

    B. Sweeps ........................................................................................... 67

    C. Attacks ........................................................................................... 68

  Chapter 6 Review: Guard Positions and Variations .................................... 69

Chapter 7: Top Control and Dominance ....................................................... 71

  7.1 Mount: Attacks and Maintenance ......................................................... 71

    A. Attacks ........................................................................................... 71

    B. Maintenance ................................................................................... 72

  7.2 Side Control: Transitions and Submissions ......................................... 74

    A. Transitions ...................................................................................... 74

    B. Submissions .................................................................................... 75

  7.3 North-South: Control and Offensive Options ...................................... 76

    A. Control ........................................................................................... 77

    B. Offensive Options ........................................................................... 77

  7.4 Knee on Belly: Pressure and Movement .............................................. 79

    A. Pressure .......................................................................................... 79

    B. Movement ...................................................................................... 80

  Chapter 7 Review: Top Control and Dominance ........................................ 81

Chapter 8: Fundamental Submission Techniques ......................................... 84

  8.1 Chokes: Rear Naked Choke, Guillotine, Cross Collar ......................... 84

    A. Rear Naked Choke ......................................................................... 84

    B. Guillotine ........................................................................................ 85

    C. Cross Collar Choke ......................................................................... 86

  8.2 Joint Locks: Armbar, Kimura, Americana ............................................ 87

    A. Armbar ............................................................................................ 88

    B. Kimura ............................................................................................. 89

    C. Americana ....................................................................................... 90

  8.3 Leg Locks: Straight Ankle Lock, Heel Hook, Toe Hold ........................ 91

    A. Straight Ankle Lock ........................................................................ 91

    B. Heel Hook ....................................................................................... 92

    C. Toe Hold .......................................................................................... 93

  Chapter 8 Review: Fundamental Submission Techniques ........................... 94

Part 4: Intermediate Techniques and Strategies ............................................... 96

Chapter 9: Effective Sweeps and Reversals .................................................... 96

  9.1 Scissor Sweep ........................................................................................ 96

    A. Setup ................................................................................................ 97

    B. Execution ......................................................................................... 97

    C. Key Points ....................................................................................... 97

  9.2 Flower Sweep ........................................................................................ 98

    A. Setup ................................................................................................ 98

    B. Execution ......................................................................................... 99

    C. Key Points ....................................................................................... 99

  9.3 Hip Bump Sweep ................................................................................. 100

    A. Setup .............................................................................................. 100

    B. Execution ....................................................................................... 100

    C. Key Points ..................................................................................... 101

  9.4 Butterfly Guard Sweeps ....................................................................... 102

    A. Setup .............................................................................................. 102

    B. Execution ....................................................................................... 102

    C. Key Points ..................................................................................... 103

    D. Variations ...................................................................................... 103

  Chapter 9 Review: Effective Sweeps and Reversals .................................. 104

Chapter 10: Advanced Guard Techniques ..................................................... 107

  10.1 De La Riva Guard: Entries and Sweeps ............................................ 107

    A. Establishing the De La Riva Guard ............................................... 108

    B. Common Entries ............................................................................ 108

  C. Sweeps from De La Riva Guard .................................................. 108

 10.2 Spider Guard: Grip Control and Attacks .................................... 109

  A. Establishing the Spider Guard ..................................................... 109

  B. Common Entries ............................................................................ 109

  C. Attacks from Spider Guard .......................................................... 109

 10.3 X-Guard: Control and Transitions ............................................... 110

  A. Establishing the X-Guard ............................................................. 110

  B. Common Entries ............................................................................ 111

  C. Transitions from X-Guard ............................................................ 111

 10.4 Lasso Guard: Creating and Maintaining Control ......................... 111

  A. Establishing the Lasso Guard ...................................................... 112

  B. Common Entries ............................................................................ 112

  C. Techniques from Lasso Guard ..................................................... 112

 Chapter 10 Review: Advanced Guard Techniques ................................ 113

Chapter 11: Guard Passing Techniques ...................................................... 115

 11.1 Over-Under Pass: Pressure and Control ....................................... 115

  A. Establishing the Over-Under Pass ............................................... 115

  B. Key Steps ....................................................................................... 115

  C. Common Mistakes ........................................................................ 116

 11.2 Toreando Pass: Speed and Precision ............................................ 116

  A. Establishing the Toreando Pass ................................................... 116

  B. Key Steps ....................................................................................... 117

  C. Common Mistakes ........................................................................ 117

 11.3 Knee Slice Pass: Breaking Through Defenses .............................. 118

  A. Establishing the Knee Slice Pass ................................................. 118

  B. Key Steps ....................................................................................... 118

  C. Common Mistakes ........................................................................ 118

 11.4 Leg Drag Pass: Establishing Dominance ...................................... 119

  A. Establishing the Leg Drag Pass ................................................... 119

  B. Key Steps ....................................................................................... 119

  C. Common Mistakes ........................................................................ 120

 Chapter 11 Review: Guard Passing Techniques .................................... 120

Chapter 12: Escapes and Defense Mechanisms ......................................... 123

 12.1 Mount Escapes: Upa, Elbow Escape ............................................. 123

- A. Upa (Bridge) Escape ............................................................. 123
- B. Elbow Escape (Hip Escape) .................................................. 124
- 12.2 Side Control Escapes: Shrimping, Underhook Escape ........ 125
  - A. Shrimping Escape................................................................ 125
  - B. Underhook Escape............................................................... 126
- 12.3 Submission Defenses: Timing and Technique...................... 127
  - A. Timing.................................................................................. 127
  - B. Technique ............................................................................ 127
  - C. Specific Submission Defenses............................................. 128
- 12.4 Transitioning from Defense to Offense................................ 129
  - A. Creating Space .................................................................... 129
  - B. Reversals and Sweeps ........................................................ 129
  - C. Submission Counters........................................................... 130
- Chapter 12 Review: Escapes and Defense Mechanisms............. 131

Part 5: Advanced Techniques and Tactics ....................................... 134

Chapter 13: Advanced Submission Techniques.............................. 134
- 13.1 Advanced Chokes: Bow and Arrow, Loop Choke, Ezekiel Choke ....... 134
  - A. Bow and Arrow Choke......................................................... 134
  - B. Loop Choke ......................................................................... 135
  - C. Ezekiel Choke...................................................................... 135
- 13.2 Advanced Joint Locks: Omoplata, Wrist Lock ..................... 136
  - A. Omoplata............................................................................. 136
  - B. Wrist Lock............................................................................ 137
- 13.3 Advanced Leg Locks: Knee Bar, Calf Slicer, Heel Hook Variations .... 138
  - A. Knee Bar ............................................................................. 138
  - B. Calf Slicer............................................................................ 139
  - C. Heel Hook Variations .......................................................... 140
- Chapter 13 Review: Advanced Submission Techniques .............. 141

Chapter 14: Fluid Transitions and Flow Drills ................................ 143
- 14.1 Linking Techniques: Fluid Movement Strategies ................. 143
  - A. Understanding the Flow ...................................................... 143
  - B. Drilling Combinations.......................................................... 143
  - C. Adapting to Opponent Reactions......................................... 144
  - D. Examples of Linked Techniques.......................................... 144

14.2 Positional Transitions: Guard to Mount, etc. ..........................................145
    A. Guard to Mount ..........................................................................145
    B. Side Control to Mount ................................................................146
    C. Half Guard to Mount ..................................................................146
    D. Back Control to Mount ..............................................................146
    E. Guard to Side Control ................................................................146
    F. Mount to Back Control ..............................................................147
14.3 Flow Drills: Enhancing Coordination and Reflexes ..................147
    A. Benefits of Flow Drills ...............................................................147
    B. Examples of Flow Drills ............................................................148
    C. Implementing Flow Drills in Training ......................................149
    Chapter 14 Review: Fluid Transitions and Flow Drills ..................150
Chapter 15: Competition Strategies and Tactics ..............................................152
  15.1 Understanding Points and Scoring Systems ...........................................152
    A. Points System .............................................................................153
    B. Advantages .................................................................................154
    C. Penalties .....................................................................................154
  15.2 Gi vs. No-Gi Strategies ...........................................................155
    A. Gi Strategies ...............................................................................155
    B. No-Gi Strategies ........................................................................156
  15.3 Preparing for Tournaments: Mental and Physical Training ...................158
    A. Physical Training .......................................................................158
    B. Mental Training .........................................................................159
    C. Nutrition and Hydration ............................................................160
  Chapter 15 Review: Competition Strategies and Tactics ................................161
Part 6: Training, Conditioning, and Development ...........................................164
Chapter 16: Effective Training Methods ..........................................................164
  16.1 Solo Drills: Building Strength and Coordination ...................................164
    A. Bodyweight Exercises ................................................................164
    B. Movement Drills ........................................................................165
    C. Shadow Grappling .....................................................................167
  16.2 Partner Drills: Technique and Resistance Training ................................167
    A. Technique Drills ........................................................................168
    B. Resistance Training ...................................................................168

C. Implementation Tips..................................................................... 169
16.3 Sparring (Rolling): Applying Techniques in Real Time ................ 170
A. Types of Sparring ........................................................................ 170
B. Sparring Strategies ...................................................................... 171
C. Implementation Tips..................................................................... 172
Chapter 16 Review: Effective Training Methods ............................... 173
Chapter 17: Physical Conditioning for BJJ ............................................ 175
17.1 Strength Training: Building Functional Strength ......................... 175
A. Core Exercises............................................................................. 175
B. Accessory Exercises .................................................................... 176
C. Program Structure........................................................................ 177
17.2 Flexibility and Mobility: Essential Exercises ............................... 178
A. Dynamic Stretching..................................................................... 178
B. Static Stretching .......................................................................... 178
C. Mobility Drills............................................................................. 179
D. Implementation Tips ................................................................... 179
17.3 Cardiovascular Conditioning: Enhancing Endurance ................... 180
A. High-Intensity Interval Training (HIIT)...................................... 180
B. Steady-State Cardio .................................................................... 180
C. Sport-Specific Drills ................................................................... 181
D. Implementation Tips ................................................................... 181
Chapter 17 Review: Physical Conditioning for BJJ............................ 182
Chapter 18: Mental Preparation and Focus ........................................... 185
18.1 Goal Setting: Short-term and Long-term ..................................... 185
A. Short-term Goals ......................................................................... 186
B. Long-term Goals.......................................................................... 186
18.2 Visualization and Mental Rehearsal............................................. 187
A. Visualization Techniques ............................................................ 187
B. Mental Rehearsal ......................................................................... 188
C. Benefits of Visualization and Mental Rehearsal ......................... 189
18.3 Managing Stress and Competition Anxiety ................................. 189
A. Breathing Techniques.................................................................. 190
B. Mindfulness and Meditation........................................................ 190
C. Mental Strategies......................................................................... 191

D. Professional Support ................................................................. 192
  Chapter 18 Review: Mental Preparation and Focus ............................ 192
Part 7: Practical Applications and Self-Defense ..................................... 196
Chapter 19: Real-World Self-Defense Applications .............................. 196
  19.1 Techniques for Common Attacks ............................................... 196
    A. Headlock Defense ..................................................................... 196
    B. Bear Hug Escape ...................................................................... 197
    C. Choke Defense ......................................................................... 198
  19.2 Defending Against Strikes ........................................................ 198
    A. Cover and Clinch ...................................................................... 199
    B. Takedown Defense ................................................................... 199
    C. Ground Defense ....................................................................... 200
  19.3 Escaping Holds and Grabs ....................................................... 201
    A. Wrist Grab Escape .................................................................... 201
    B. Bear Hug Escape ...................................................................... 202
    C. Choke Hold Escape .................................................................. 202
    D. Full Nelson Escape ................................................................... 203
  Chapter 19 Review: Real-World Self-Defense Applications ................ 204
Chapter 20: BJJ for Law Enforcement and Military ............................... 206
  20.1 Control and Restraint Techniques ............................................. 206
    A. Positional Control ..................................................................... 206
    B. Restraint Techniques ................................................................ 207
    C. Implementation Tips ................................................................. 208
  20.2 Non-Lethal Force Application ................................................... 209
    A. Joint Locks ............................................................................... 209
    B. Control Holds ........................................................................... 210
    C. Implementation Tips ................................................................. 211
  20.3 Specialized Training Considerations ......................................... 212
    A. Scenario-Based Training .......................................................... 212
    B. Legal and Ethical Considerations ............................................. 213
    C. Continuous Learning and Improvement ................................... 214
  Chapter 20 Review: BJJ for Law Enforcement and Military ................ 215
Chapter 21: Empowering Women Through BJJ .................................... 218
  21.1 Building Confidence and Awareness ........................................ 218

    A. Physical Confidence ................................................................. 218
    B. Mental Confidence .................................................................. 219
  21.2 Techniques for Women's Self-Defense ..................................... 220
    A. Common Self-Defense Techniques .......................................... 220
    B. Specialized Techniques for Common Scenarios ...................... 221
  21.3 Real-World Scenarios and Prevention ....................................... 222
    A. Street Altercations .................................................................... 222
    B. Public Transport Incidents ....................................................... 223
    C. Domestic Violence Situations ................................................. 223
    D. Workplace Violence ................................................................ 224
    E. Anti-Bullying Defense for Youth ............................................. 224
    F. Women's Self-Defense ............................................................ 225
  Chapter 21 Review: Empowering Women Through BJJ ..................... 225
Chapter 22: The Culture and Community of BJJ ..................................... 228
  22.1 Dojo Etiquette and Traditions .................................................... 228
    A. Respect and Discipline ............................................................ 228
    B. Cleanliness ............................................................................... 228
    C. Punctuality ............................................................................... 229
    D. Hierarchy ................................................................................. 229
    E. Rituals ...................................................................................... 229
    F. Communication ........................................................................ 230
    G. Safety ....................................................................................... 230
  22.2 The Belt System: Progress and Milestones ............................... 231
    A. Ranking Structure .................................................................... 231
    B. Criteria for Advancement ........................................................ 231
    C. Milestones ................................................................................ 232
    D. The Journey of Continuous Growth ........................................ 232
    E. Cultural Significance ............................................................... 233
  22.3 Building and Participating in the BJJ Community .................... 233
    A. Fostering Connections ............................................................. 233
    B. Seminars and Workshops ........................................................ 234
    C. Competitions ............................................................................ 234
    D. Supporting Events ................................................................... 235
    E. Online Communities ................................................................ 235

- F. Contribution to the Community .................................................. 236
- Chapter 22 Review: The Culture and Community of BJJ .................... 236
- Chapter 23: Nutrition and Diet for Practitioners ................................. 239
  - 23.1 Nutritional Needs for Training and Recovery ............................ 239
    - A. Macronutrients ........................................................................ 239
    - B. Micronutrients ........................................................................ 240
    - C. Timing and Meal Composition ................................................ 241
    - D. Hydration ............................................................................... 242
  - 23.2 Weight Management and Competition Prep ............................. 242
    - A. Dietary Strategies ................................................................... 242
    - B. Weight Cutting ....................................................................... 243
    - C. Competition Day Nutrition ..................................................... 244
  - 23.3 Hydration and Supplementation ............................................... 244
    - A. Hydration ............................................................................... 245
    - B. Supplementation ..................................................................... 245
  - Chapter 23 Review: Nutrition and Diet for Practitioners .................. 247
- Chapter 24: Injury Prevention and Recovery ..................................... 250
  - 24.1 Common Injuries in BJJ and Their Prevention ......................... 250
    - A. Common Injuries .................................................................... 250
    - B. Prevention Strategies .............................................................. 251
  - 24.2 Effective Rehabilitation Strategies ........................................... 252
    - A. Immediate Response ............................................................... 253
    - B. Professional Care .................................................................... 253
    - C. Rehabilitation Exercises ......................................................... 254
  - 24.3 Maintaining Longevity in BJJ Practice .................................... 255
    - A. Consistent Conditioning ......................................................... 255
    - B. Listening to Your Body .......................................................... 256
    - C. Mental Health ......................................................................... 256
  - Chapter 24 Review: Injury Prevention and Recovery ...................... 257
- Part 9: The Future of Brazilian Jiu-Jitsu ............................................. 260
- Chapter 25: The Continuing Evolution of BJJ .................................... 260
  - 25.1 Modern Innovations and Techniques ....................................... 260
    - A. New Techniques and Strategies .............................................. 260
    - B. Technology in Training .......................................................... 261

25.2 The Impact of Mixed Martial Arts (MMA) .................................................. 262
    A. Integration of Techniques .................................................. 262
    B. MMA Influence on BJJ Competitions .................................................. 263
    C. Cultural and Perceptual Changes .................................................. 263
25.3 Future Trends in BJJ Training and Competition .................................................. 264
    A. Hybrid Training Models .................................................. 264
    B. Increased Accessibility .................................................. 265
    C. Advanced Training Methods .................................................. 265
    D. Competition Evolution .................................................. 266
Chapter 25 Review: The Continuing Evolution of BJJ .................................................. 267

Chapter 26: BJJ in Popular Culture .................................................. 270
  26.1 Representation in Movies and Media .................................................. 270
    A. Movies .................................................. 270
    B. Television Shows .................................................. 271
  26.2 Stories of Famous BJJ Practitioners .................................................. 272
    A. Pioneers and Legends .................................................. 272
    B. Modern Icons .................................................. 273
    C. Inspirational Figures .................................................. 274
  26.3 Influence in Video Games and Literature .................................................. 275
    A. Video Games .................................................. 276
    B. Literature .................................................. 276
  Chapter 26 Review: BJJ in Popular Culture .................................................. 278

Part 10: Resources and References .................................................. 281
Chapter 27: Glossary of BJJ Terms from A to Z .................................................. 281
Chapter 28: Recommended Reading and Viewing .................................................. 285
  A. Recommended Reading .................................................. 285
    1. Instructional Books .................................................. 285
    2. Biographies and Memoirs .................................................. 286
    3. Historical and Analytical Books .................................................. 286
  B. Recommended Viewing .................................................. 287
    1. Documentaries .................................................. 287
    2. Online Resources .................................................. 287
    3. Podcasts .................................................. 288
Chapter 29: BJJ Organizations and Competitions .................................................. 290

    A. Major BJJ Organizations ............................................................. 290
        1. International Brazilian Jiu-Jitsu Federation (IBJJF) ............................... 290
        2. United Arab Emirates Jiu-Jitsu Federation (UAEJJF) ........................ 290
        3. North American Grappling Association (NAGA) ............................. 291
        4. Abu Dhabi Combat Club (ADCC) ..................................................... 291
    B. Prestigious BJJ Competitions ........................................................ 291
        1. World Jiu-Jitsu Championship (Mundials) ........................................ 291
        2. Pan Jiu-Jitsu Championship ................................................................ 292
        3. Abu Dhabi World Professional Jiu-Jitsu Championship (ADWPJJC) .. 292
        4. ADCC Submission Fighting World Championship ............................ 292
        5. European Open Jiu-Jitsu Championship ............................................. 292
        6. Brasileiro (Brazilian National Jiu-Jitsu Championship) .................... 293
Chapter 30: Conclusion ......................................................................... 294
    Key Takeaways ................................................................................... 294
        1. Foundations of BJJ: ............................................................................ 294
        2. Techniques and Strategies: ................................................................. 294
        3. Practical Applications: ........................................................................ 294
        4. Cultural Impact: .................................................................................. 295
        5. Continuous Learning: ......................................................................... 295
    Final Thoughts .................................................................................... 295
About the Author .................................................................................. 296
About the Publisher ............................................................................... 297
Recommended Resources ..................................................................... 298

# Book Overview

If you're looking to master Brazilian Jiu-Jitsu, develop winning strategies, and embrace the BJJ lifestyle, then "HowExpert Guide to Brazilian Jiu-Jitsu" is your ultimate resource. This comprehensive guide covers everything from the rich history of BJJ and foundational principles to advanced techniques and competition strategies.

Chapter Descriptions:

1. The Origins and Evolution of BJJ - Discover the history and global impact of BJJ, from Japanese jujutsu roots to the Gracie family.
2. Core Principles and Philosophy - Learn essential principles of leverage, control, and mindset in BJJ.
3. Choosing the Right Academy and Gear - Get practical advice on selecting the best BJJ academy, gearing up, and understanding key etiquette.
4. Warm-Up and Conditioning - Explore effective warm-up routines, stretching exercises, and strength conditioning.
5. Basic Movements and Drills - Master fundamental movements like shrimping, bridging, and breakfalls.
6. Guard Positions and Variations - Delve into closed guard, open guard, and half guard techniques.
7. Top Control and Dominance - Learn to maintain mount, side control, and knee on belly positions.
8. Fundamental Submission Techniques - Develop your submission game with chokes, joint locks, and leg locks.
9. Effective Sweeps and Reversals - Enhance your sweeps and reversals with techniques like the scissor sweep.
10. Advanced Guard Techniques - Advance your guard game with De La Riva, spider guard, and X-guard.
11. Guard Passing Techniques - Master guard passes like the over-under, toreando, and knee slice.
12. Escapes and Defense Mechanisms - Escape mount and side control, and defend against submissions.
13. Advanced Submission Techniques - Explore advanced chokes, joint locks, and leg locks.

14. Fluid Transitions and Flow Drills - Improve fluidity with drills linking techniques and transitions.
15. Competition Strategies and Tactics - Prepare for tournaments with strategies for gi and no-gi competition.
16. Effective Training Methods - Optimize training with solo and partner drills.
17. Physical Conditioning for BJJ - Enhance conditioning with strength, flexibility, and cardio exercises.
18. Mental Preparation and Focus - Develop mental toughness with goal setting and visualization.
19. Real-World Self-Defense Applications - Apply BJJ to real-world self-defense scenarios.
20. BJJ for Law Enforcement and Military - Explore techniques for control and non-lethal force.
21. Empowering Women Through BJJ - Empower women with confidence-building self-defense techniques.
22. The Culture and Community of BJJ - Immerse in the BJJ community, understanding etiquette and the belt system.
23. Nutrition and Diet for Practitioners - Fuel training with nutritional advice and diet plans.
24. Injury Prevention and Recovery - Prevent and manage injuries with effective strategies.
25. The Continuing Evolution of BJJ - Stay updated on innovations and future trends in BJJ.
26. BJJ in Popular Culture - Discover BJJ's influence in media and the stories of famous practitioners.
27. Glossary of BJJ Terms - Reference essential BJJ terminology with a comprehensive glossary.
28. Recommended Reading and Viewing - Expand your knowledge with a curated list of books, documentaries, and online resources.
29. BJJ Organizations and Competitions - Connect with key BJJ organizations and major competitions.
30. Conclusion - Reflect on your BJJ journey and the importance of continuous learning and personal growth.

If you're ready to take your Brazilian Jiu-Jitsu skills to the next level and embrace a transformative journey, then access "HowExpert Guide to Brazilian

Jiu-Jitsu" today and start mastering the art of BJJ. This essential handbook will help you become the best version of yourself on and off the mat!

HowExpert publishes how to guides on all topics from A to Z. Visit [HowExpert.com](HowExpert.com) to learn more.

# Part 1: Foundations of Brazilian Jiu-Jitsu

The foundations of Brazilian Jiu-Jitsu (BJJ) are rooted in a rich history that spans continents and cultures. Understanding where BJJ comes from and how it has evolved over time provides practitioners with a deep appreciation of its techniques and philosophies. This part explores the origins of BJJ, tracing its lineage from Japanese Jujutsu to its development by the Gracie family and its eventual spread across the globe.

# Chapter 1: The Origins and Evolution of BJJ

Brazilian Jiu-Jitsu has a fascinating history that begins with its roots in Japanese Jujutsu and the adaptations made by the Gracie family. This chapter delves into the pivotal moments and key figures that shaped BJJ into the highly effective martial art it is today.

## *1.1 Japanese Jujutsu Roots*

Japanese Jujutsu, a traditional martial art, dates back to Japan's feudal era, when it was developed for samurai warriors. This combat system was designed to be effective against armored and armed opponents, focusing on techniques that emphasized leverage, balance, and timing rather than brute strength. The core techniques included throws, joint locks, pins, and strikes, which allowed practitioners to neutralize their adversaries by using their force against them.

The evolution of Jujutsu saw the emergence of various styles, each with unique techniques and philosophies. Despite these differences, all styles shared a common goal: to control or incapacitate an opponent with minimal effort. One of the most significant developments in Jujutsu history was the establishment of Kodokan Judo by Jigoro Kano in the late 19th century. Kano's system emphasized the principle of "maximum efficiency with minimum effort," which became a cornerstone in the practice of both Judo and, later, Brazilian Jiu-Jitsu.

Kano's Judo, which refined and organized traditional Jujutsu techniques, was introduced to the world through his students. One such student, Mitsuyo Maeda, played a pivotal role in the transmission of these techniques to Brazil. Maeda, also known as Count Koma, traveled extensively to demonstrate and teach Judo.

In 1914, he arrived in Brazil, where he met the Gracie family, marking the beginning of a new chapter in the evolution of Jujutsu.

Mitsuyo Maeda's teachings in Brazil laid the foundation for what would eventually become Brazilian Jiu-Jitsu. Maeda emphasized practical applications of Judo, including ground fighting techniques that were particularly effective in real combat situations. His teachings were embraced and further developed by Carlos Gracie and, later, Helio Gracie, who adapted the techniques to suit their physical limitations and the realities of unarmed combat. This adaptation process led to the creation of a new, distinct martial art that focused on leverage, technique, and the ability to control and submit opponents, regardless of size or strength.

Thus, Japanese Jujutsu's rich legacy and principles of leverage and technique provided the essential foundation for Brazilian Jiu-Jitsu, influencing its development and evolution into a globally recognized martial art.

## *1.2 The Gracie Family and BJJ's Birth*

The Gracie family is synonymous with Brazilian Jiu-Jitsu, having played a pivotal role in its creation and popularization. The story of BJJ's birth begins with Mitsuyo Maeda, a Japanese Judo expert and one of Jigoro Kano's top students. Maeda, also known as Count Koma, traveled extensively to demonstrate and teach Judo, which included a significant portion of ground-fighting techniques derived from traditional Jujutsu.

In 1914, Maeda arrived in Brazil and began teaching Judo to a small group of students. Among them was Carlos Gracie, the eldest son of a large Brazilian family. Carlos was captivated by Maeda's teachings and became his devoted student. After several years of rigorous training, Carlos began teaching the art to his brothers, including Helio Gracie.

Helio Gracie, despite being smaller and physically weaker than his brothers, showed immense dedication and ingenuity. He found that certain techniques were difficult to execute due to his size and strength. To overcome this, Helio began modifying the techniques to rely more on leverage, timing, and technique rather than brute force. These modifications were crucial in making the martial art accessible and effective for individuals of all sizes and strengths.

The Gracie family started to test their new system of Jiu-Jitsu in various no-holds-barred challenge matches. These matches, known as "Vale Tudo" fights in Brazil, showcased the effectiveness of their techniques against practitioners of other martial arts. The Gracies emerged victorious in many of these encounters, cementing their reputation and demonstrating the superiority of their system.

To further promote Brazilian Jiu-Jitsu, the Gracie family opened the first BJJ academy in Rio de Janeiro. They continued to refine their techniques and teach a new generation of practitioners. The family's dedication to the art and their willingness to test their skills in real combat situations helped to rapidly spread the popularity of BJJ.

The Gracie family's most significant contribution to the global recognition of BJJ came in the 1990s with the advent of the Ultimate Fighting Championship (UFC). Royce Gracie, one of Helio's sons, competed in the early UFC events, where he successfully used BJJ techniques to defeat much larger and stronger opponents from various martial arts backgrounds. His victories in the UFC brought international attention to Brazilian Jiu-Jitsu and proved its effectiveness in mixed martial arts (MMA) competition.

Through their innovative adaptations and relentless promotion, the Gracie family established Brazilian Jiu-Jitsu as a unique and highly effective martial art. Their legacy continues to influence and inspire practitioners around the world.

## *1.3 Global Spread and Influence*

The global spread and influence of Brazilian Jiu-Jitsu (BJJ) are a testament to its effectiveness and adaptability. The Gracie family's tireless efforts to promote the art played a crucial role in its international expansion, but several key events and figures further catalyzed BJJ's rise to worldwide prominence.

In the early 1990s, the creation of the Ultimate Fighting Championship (UFC) by Rorion Gracie and Art Davie marked a pivotal moment for BJJ. Royce Gracie, representing his family's martial art, entered the UFC's first tournament in 1993. Despite being smaller and seemingly less physically imposing than many of his opponents, Royce used BJJ techniques to defeat competitors from various martial arts backgrounds, winning the tournament. His success in the UFC's early events showcased the effectiveness of BJJ in real combat situations, capturing the attention of martial artists and combat sports enthusiasts globally.

This exposure led to a surge in interest and demand for BJJ training. Martial artists from around the world traveled to Brazil to learn the techniques from the Gracie family and other prominent BJJ practitioners. Recognizing the growing international interest, many Brazilian BJJ masters, including members of the Gracie family, began opening academies outside of Brazil, particularly in the United States.

The establishment of these academies played a critical role in spreading BJJ. Notable figures such as Rickson Gracie, Renzo Gracie, and Marcelo Garcia opened schools in major cities around the world, each bringing their unique approaches and techniques. These academies became hubs for learning and development, attracting students eager to master BJJ.

In addition to the expansion of academies, the inclusion of BJJ in mixed martial arts (MMA) competitions further accelerated its global spread. As MMA grew in popularity, so did the recognition of BJJ as a foundational element of a well-rounded fighter's skill set. Fighters with a background in BJJ, such as Anderson Silva and Demian Maia, achieved great success in MMA, further validating the art's effectiveness.

BJJ also found its way into law enforcement and military training programs worldwide. Its techniques for controlling and subduing opponents without relying on strikes made it particularly suitable for non-lethal force applications. Many police departments and military units adopted BJJ training to enhance their personnel's hand-to-hand combat skills.

The influence of BJJ extends beyond combat sports and self-defense. The art has fostered a global community characterized by mutual respect, camaraderie, and continuous learning. BJJ practitioners often participate in international competitions, seminars, and workshops, further strengthening the bonds within the community.

Today, BJJ academies can be found in virtually every corner of the globe, from small towns to major metropolitan areas. The art continues to evolve, with practitioners constantly refining techniques and developing new strategies. The global spread and enduring influence of BJJ highlight its versatility, practicality, and universal appeal, making it one of the most respected and widely practiced martial arts in the world.

# *Chapter 1 Review: The Origins and Evolution of BJJ*

**- 1.1 Japanese Jujutsu Roots:**

  - Japanese Jujutsu, developed during Japan's feudal era, emphasized leverage and technique over brute strength.

  - Key techniques included throws, joint locks, and strikes, designed to neutralize armored opponents.

  - Jigoro Kano refined Jujutsu techniques, leading to the establishment of Kodokan Judo, which influenced BJJ's development.


**- 1.2 The Gracie Family and BJJ's Birth:**

  - Mitsuyo Maeda, a Japanese Judo expert, taught Judo in Brazil, where Carlos Gracie became his student.

  - Helio Gracie adapted the techniques to suit his smaller stature, focusing on leverage and technique.

  - The Gracie family proved BJJ's effectiveness through public challenge matches, leading to the opening of the first BJJ academy in Rio de Janeiro.

  - Royce Gracie's success in the early UFC events brought international attention to BJJ, proving its superiority in mixed martial arts competition.


**- 1.3 Global Spread and Influence:**

  - Royce Gracie's victories in the UFC showcased BJJ's effectiveness, sparking global interest.

  - Brazilian BJJ masters, including members of the Gracie family, opened academies worldwide, spreading the art.

  - BJJ became a foundational element in MMA, with fighters achieving success using its techniques.

  - Law enforcement and military units adopted BJJ for its effective control and non-lethal force techniques.

  - BJJ fostered a global community characterized by respect, camaraderie, and continuous learning, with international competitions and seminars strengthening these bonds.

Understanding the origins and evolution of Brazilian Jiu-Jitsu provides a deeper appreciation for its techniques and philosophies. From its roots in Japanese Jujutsu to its global spread, BJJ has proven to be a versatile and effective martial art, influencing combat sports, self-defense, and fostering a worldwide community.

# Chapter 2: Core Principles and Philosophy

The core principles and philosophy of Brazilian Jiu-Jitsu (BJJ) are what set it apart from other martial arts. Understanding these foundational concepts is crucial for any practitioner, as they provide the framework for all techniques and strategies in BJJ. This chapter delves into the essential elements that define BJJ, emphasizing leverage, control, and a growth-oriented mindset.

## *2.1 The Gentle Art: Using Leverage and Technique*

Brazilian Jiu-Jitsu (BJJ) is often referred to as "The Gentle Art" because it prioritizes the use of leverage and technique over brute strength. This principle is foundational to BJJ and allows practitioners of all sizes and physical capabilities to effectively defend themselves against larger and stronger opponents. The essence of BJJ lies in its ability to neutralize an opponent's strength through precise movements and strategic use of the body.

### *A. Leverage*

Leverage is the cornerstone of BJJ. It involves using the body's natural mechanics to gain an advantage over an opponent. By positioning the body in specific ways, a practitioner can maximize their force while minimizing the effort required. This concept is applied in various techniques, such as joint locks and chokes, where small adjustments in positioning can significantly increase the effectiveness of the technique.

1. Example: Armbar - In an armbar, the practitioner uses their legs and hips to apply pressure to the opponent's arm. The legs, being much stronger than the arms, provide the necessary leverage to extend and hyperextend the opponent's elbow joint, leading to a submission.

2. Example: Triangle Choke - In the triangle choke, the practitioner uses their legs to encircle the opponent's neck and arm, cutting off blood flow to the brain and forcing the opponent to submit.

## *B. Technique*

Technique in BJJ refers to the precise and practiced execution of movements designed to control and submit an opponent. Techniques are developed through repetition and drilling, allowing practitioners to perform them instinctively under pressure. Proper technique ensures that the practitioner can apply maximum force with minimal effort, making BJJ an art that relies on skill and strategy rather than physical attributes.

- Creating Angles - One of the key aspects of BJJ technique is the concept of "creating angles." Instead of facing an opponent head-on, practitioners often move to the side or behind their opponent to gain a superior position. This not only reduces the opponent's ability to defend but also allows the practitioner to use leverage more effectively.

   - Example: Guard Position - In the guard position, rather than trying to push an opponent directly away, a practitioner might use a hip escape (shrimping) to create space and angles for sweeps or submissions.

## *C. Practical Applications*

The principles of leverage and technique are not limited to submissions; they are also essential for controlling an opponent and escaping disadvantageous positions. In escapes, leverage is used to create space and break free from holds.

- Example: Bridge and Roll (Upa) Escape - From mount, the bridge and roll escape uses the practitioner's entire body to generate the force needed to dislodge an opponent sitting on their chest.

In addition to physical applications, the focus on leverage and technique fosters a strategic mindset in practitioners. BJJ practitioners learn to assess situations, anticipate opponents' moves, and respond with calculated techniques. This strategic thinking extends beyond the mat, encouraging problem-solving and adaptability in everyday life.

By mastering the use of leverage and technique, BJJ practitioners can overcome physical limitations and effectively control and submit opponents. These principles are what make BJJ accessible to people of all sizes and strengths, embodying the true essence of "The Gentle Art." Understanding and applying these concepts are fundamental steps in a practitioner's journey towards proficiency in Brazilian Jiu-Jitsu.

## *2.2 Position Before Submission: Control Hierarchies*

The principle of "position before submission" is a cornerstone of Brazilian Jiu-Jitsu (BJJ). This concept emphasizes the importance of establishing and maintaining dominant positions before attempting to submit an opponent. By prioritizing control, practitioners can effectively limit their opponent's movements and increase the likelihood of successful submissions.

### *A. The Importance of Control*

Control is the foundation of effective BJJ practice. Establishing control involves securing a position that restricts the opponent's ability to move or escape while providing the practitioner with a stable platform from which to launch attacks. The ability to control an opponent is crucial for both offensive and defensive strategies.

1. Mount Position - The mount is one of the most dominant positions in BJJ. By sitting on top of the opponent's chest, the practitioner can control their movements, apply pressure, and execute various submissions. The mount provides a high level of control, making it difficult for the opponent to escape.

2. Side Control - Side control involves pinning the opponent to the mat while lying perpendicular to them. This position allows the practitioner to control the opponent's upper body, limit their mobility, and set up submissions or transitions to other dominant positions.

3. Back Control - Taking the opponent's back is considered the ultimate position of control in BJJ. With hooks in (legs wrapped around the opponent's waist) and seatbelt grip (one arm over the shoulder and the other under the armpit), the practitioner can control the opponent's torso and execute powerful submissions like the rear-naked choke.

## B. Hierarchy of Positions

BJJ employs a hierarchy of positions that guides practitioners in achieving and maintaining control. Understanding this hierarchy helps practitioners prioritize their movements and strategies during a match.

1. Dominant Positions - These positions provide the highest level of control and include the mount, back control, and knee-on-belly. Practitioners in these positions have a significant advantage and can effectively apply pressure and submissions.

2. Neutral Positions - Positions such as guard and half guard are considered neutral. Both the practitioner and the opponent have opportunities to attack and defend. The goal is to transition from a neutral position to a dominant one.

3. Defensive Positions - Positions where the practitioner is at a disadvantage, such as being in the opponent's mount or side control. The primary objective in these positions is to escape and regain a neutral or dominant position.

## C. Practical Applications

Applying the principle of "position before submission" in practice ensures that practitioners maintain control and increase their chances of success when attempting submissions.

1. Example: Armbar from Mount - By first establishing the mount position, the practitioner can control the opponent's upper body and limit their ability to defend. From this position, the practitioner can isolate an arm and transition to an armbar with greater efficiency and success.

2. Example: Rear-Naked Choke from Back Control - When taking the opponent's back, the practitioner secures the position with hooks and a seatbelt grip. With control established, the practitioner can patiently work to sink in the rear-naked choke, minimizing the risk of escape.

The principle of "position before submission" is fundamental to BJJ. By prioritizing control and understanding the hierarchy of positions, practitioners can effectively limit their opponent's movements and increase their chances of successful submissions. Mastery of this principle is essential for achieving proficiency and success in Brazilian Jiu-Jitsu.

# 2.3 The Mindset: Discipline, Respect, and Continuous Growth

The mindset in Brazilian Jiu-Jitsu (BJJ) extends beyond physical techniques and includes a strong emphasis on mental and emotional development. Practitioners are encouraged to cultivate a mindset of discipline, respect, and continuous growth, which not only enhances their practice but also positively impacts their personal lives.

## *A. Discipline*

Discipline is a fundamental aspect of BJJ, necessary for consistent training and improvement. It involves dedication, perseverance, and the ability to push through challenges.

1. Consistent Training - Regular practice is crucial for mastering techniques and developing muscle memory. Discipline ensures that practitioners attend classes consistently, even when motivation wanes.

2. Perseverance - BJJ is a demanding martial art that requires perseverance. Practitioners must be willing to endure setbacks, such as injuries or plateauing progress, and continue training with determination.

3. Self-Control - Discipline also involves self-control, particularly in sparring sessions. Practitioners must exercise restraint to ensure the safety of their training partners while maintaining focus and composure.

## *B. Respect*

Respect is a core value in the BJJ community, encompassing respect for oneself, training partners, instructors, and the art itself.

1. Respect for Training Partners - Mutual respect among training partners is essential for a positive training environment. Practitioners should approach each session with humility, recognizing that everyone is there to learn and improve.

2. Respect for Instructors - Instructors impart valuable knowledge and guidance. Showing respect to instructors involves listening attentively, following their instructions, and appreciating their expertise.

3. Respect for the Art - Respecting BJJ means upholding its traditions, rules, and values. Practitioners should strive to preserve the integrity of the art by training ethically and promoting a positive image of BJJ.

## *C. Continuous Growth*

The concept of continuous growth is central to BJJ, where practitioners are encouraged to view challenges and setbacks as opportunities for learning and improvement.

1. Lifelong Learning - BJJ is a lifelong journey where there is always something new to learn. Practitioners should remain open to new techniques, strategies, and perspectives, constantly seeking to expand their knowledge.

2. Adapting to Challenges - Setbacks and failures are inevitable in BJJ. A growth-oriented mindset involves embracing these challenges, learning from mistakes, and adapting strategies to overcome obstacles.

3. Personal Development - The principles of continuous growth in BJJ extend beyond the mat. Practitioners often find that the resilience, problem-solving skills, and humility developed through BJJ contribute to their personal and professional lives.

The mindset of discipline, respect, and continuous growth is essential for success in Brazilian Jiu-Jitsu. By cultivating these values, practitioners can enhance their training, build strong relationships within the BJJ community, and achieve personal development both on and off the mat. Embracing this mindset leads to a fulfilling and transformative journey in the art of BJJ.

# *Chapter 2 Review: Core Principles and Philosophy*

Understanding the core principles and philosophy of Brazilian Jiu-Jitsu is crucial for any practitioner. This chapter delves into the foundational concepts that guide

BJJ practice, emphasizing the importance of leverage, control, and a growth-oriented mindset.

### - 2.1 The Gentle Art: Using Leverage and Technique:

- BJJ prioritizes leverage and technique over brute strength, allowing practitioners to neutralize larger and stronger opponents.

- Techniques like the armbar and triangle choke demonstrate the effectiveness of leverage.

- Creating angles and proper positioning are key aspects of technique, enhancing control and submission efficiency.

### - 2.2 Position Before Submission: Control Hierarchies:

- The principle of "position before submission" emphasizes establishing control before attempting submissions.

- Control is achieved through dominant positions such as mount, side control, and back control.

- Understanding the hierarchy of positions—dominant, neutral, and defensive—guides practitioners in their movements and strategies.

- Practical applications, like the armbar from mount and rear-naked choke from back control, illustrate the importance of control in successful submissions.

### - 2.3 The Mindset: Discipline, Respect, and Continuous Growth:

- Discipline is essential for consistent training, perseverance through challenges, and self-control during sparring.

- Respect for training partners, instructors, and the art itself fosters a positive and ethical training environment.

- Continuous growth involves lifelong learning, adapting to challenges, and personal development, both on and off the mat.

By focusing on leverage and technique, prioritizing position before submission, and embracing a mindset of discipline, respect, and continuous growth, BJJ practitioners can achieve mastery in the art and personal development. These principles provide the foundation for effective practice, fostering a supportive community, and encouraging lifelong learning and improvement.

# Part 2: Getting Started

Starting your journey in Brazilian Jiu-Jitsu (BJJ) requires careful consideration and preparation. This part provides guidance on how to choose the right academy, select the necessary gear, and understand the essential etiquette and rules to ensure a smooth and rewarding experience.

# Chapter 3: Choosing the Right Academy and Gear

Choosing the right academy and gear is crucial for a positive and productive BJJ experience. This chapter offers practical advice on how to select a suitable training environment, acquire the essential equipment, and adhere to the etiquette and rules that govern the BJJ community.

## *3.1 Selecting a BJJ Academy*

Choosing the right Brazilian Jiu-Jitsu (BJJ) academy is a crucial step in your journey as a practitioner. The right academy provides a supportive environment, skilled instructors, and a positive culture that fosters learning and growth. Here's how to make an informed decision when selecting a BJJ academy.

### *A. Research and Recommendations*

1. Research Online - Begin by researching local BJJ academies online. Look for reviews, testimonials, and detailed information about the instructors and their credentials. Websites and social media pages can offer insights into the academy's philosophy, class structure, and community.

2. Seek Recommendations - Personal recommendations from friends, family, or colleagues who practice BJJ can be invaluable. They can provide firsthand accounts of their experiences, helping you gauge the quality of instruction and the atmosphere of the academy.

## B. Visit Potential Academies

1. Observe Classes - Visiting potential academies to observe classes is essential. Pay attention to the teaching style, the structure of the classes, and how engaged the students are. Note the instructor's ability to communicate techniques clearly and effectively.

2. Meet the Instructors - Introduce yourself to the instructors. Ask questions about their experience, teaching philosophy, and the variety of classes offered. A good instructor should be approachable, knowledgeable, and willing to answer your questions.

## C. Evaluate the Environment

1. Assess the Facilities - Evaluate the cleanliness, safety, and overall condition of the facilities. A well-maintained academy reflects a professional and caring environment. Look for clean mats, adequate space, and proper training equipment.

2. Consider the Community - The community within the academy is just as important as the instruction. Observe the interactions among students and between students and instructors. Look for a welcoming and respectful atmosphere that aligns with your personal values and goals.

## D. Practical Applications

Applying these steps in your search will help ensure that you find an academy that meets your needs and provides a positive learning environment.

1. Example: Online Research - If you find an academy with numerous positive reviews and testimonials highlighting the supportive community and skilled instructors, it's a good sign that the academy is reputable.

2. Example: Class Observation - During a visit, if you observe that the instructor is attentive, students are engaged, and the atmosphere is encouraging, it indicates a conducive learning environment.

3. Example: Meeting Instructors - A conversation with the instructor that leaves you feeling informed and welcomed can be a strong indicator of the academy's commitment to student success.

Selecting the right BJJ academy involves thorough research, visiting potential academies, and evaluating the facilities and community. By following these steps, you can ensure that you find a supportive environment that promotes your growth and development in Brazilian Jiu-Jitsu. The right academy will not only enhance your skills but also provide a positive and enriching experience throughout your BJJ journey.

## *3.2 Essential Gear and Equipment*

Having the right gear is essential for training effectively and safely in Brazilian Jiu-Jitsu (BJJ). This section outlines the basic equipment needed for beginners and provides guidance on selecting and maintaining your gear.

*Brazilian Jiu-Jitsu Gi and Belts*

## *A. Gi and No-Gi Attire*

1. Gi - A Gi (kimono) is the traditional uniform worn in BJJ. It consists of a jacket, pants, and a belt. When choosing a Gi, ensure it fits well and is made of

durable material. Proper fit is crucial for comfort and performance during training. Many practitioners have multiple Gis to rotate between training sessions.

- Material and Weave - Gis come in various materials and weaves, such as single weave, double weave, and gold weave. Single weave is lighter and cooler, while double weave is more durable and suitable for intense training. Choose based on your training frequency and comfort preference.

- Fit and Size - Ensure the Gi fits properly, allowing for a full range of motion without being too loose or tight. Consult size charts provided by manufacturers and consider shrinking if necessary.

2. No-Gi Attire - No-Gi training requires a rash guard and shorts. Rash guards are typically made of moisture-wicking materials that keep you dry and prevent mat burns. No-Gi shorts should be comfortable, flexible, and durable.

- Rash Guard - A good rash guard should fit snugly and be made of breathable material. Long-sleeve and short-sleeve options are available, and some practitioners prefer compression fit for added muscle support.

- Shorts - No-Gi shorts should have a secure waistband and be made from flexible materials to allow for a wide range of motion. Avoid shorts with pockets or zippers to prevent injuries.

## *B. Additional Gear*

1. Belt - The belt signifies your rank in BJJ. Beginners start with a white belt and progress through various colors as they advance. Ensure the belt is the correct length and tied securely during training.

2. Protective Gear - Consider wearing protective gear for added safety during training.

- Mouthguard - A mouthguard protects your teeth and jaw during sparring sessions. Custom-fit mouthguards offer the best protection and comfort.

- Knee Pads - Knee pads provide extra cushioning and support, especially during techniques that put pressure on the knees. They can help prevent injuries and prolong your training career.

## _C. Maintenance and Care_

1. Gi Care - Proper care of your Gi is essential to maintain hygiene and prolong its lifespan. Wash your Gi after each use to prevent the buildup of bacteria and odors. Follow the manufacturer's care instructions, typically involving cold water washes and air drying to prevent shrinkage.

2. Gear Storage - Store your gear in a clean, dry place to prevent mold and odors. Use a dedicated gear bag to keep your equipment organized and easily accessible. Ensure your rash guards and shorts are thoroughly dried before storing.

3. Regular Inspection - Regularly inspect your gear for signs of wear and tear. Replace any damaged or worn-out items to maintain safety and performance. Check seams, zippers, and fabric integrity to ensure everything is in good condition.

Acquiring the essential gear and equipment for BJJ is crucial for effective and safe training. A well-fitted Gi or No-Gi attire, along with necessary protective gear, ensures comfort and performance on the mat. Proper maintenance and care of your equipment will extend its lifespan and keep you prepared for consistent training sessions. By investing in quality gear and taking good care of it, you'll enhance your BJJ experience and progress more effectively in your journey.

## *3.3 BJJ Etiquette and Rules*

Understanding and adhering to the etiquette and rules of Brazilian Jiu-Jitsu (BJJ) is essential for maintaining a respectful and safe training environment. This section covers the basic guidelines that all practitioners should follow to ensure a positive experience for everyone involved.

## _A. Respect and Humility_

1. Respect Your Instructors - Always show respect to your instructors by listening attentively and following their guidance. Acknowledge their expertise and experience by addressing them appropriately and demonstrating appreciation for their efforts in teaching you.

2. Respect Your Training Partners - Treat your training partners with respect and consideration. Avoid using excessive force and communicate openly to ensure a safe practice. Recognize that everyone is at different levels of experience and skill, and approach each training session with humility and a willingness to learn from others.

3. Respect the Academy - Show respect for the training environment by keeping it clean and orderly. Follow the academy's specific rules and guidelines, such as bowing when entering and leaving the mat, and taking care of the facilities and equipment.

## *B. Hygiene and Safety*

1. Personal Hygiene - Maintain good personal hygiene by showering before class, wearing clean gear, and keeping your nails trimmed. This helps prevent the spread of infections and ensures a more pleasant training experience for everyone.

2. Safety Practices - Practice safety by tapping out when necessary, controlling your movements, and being aware of your surroundings. Always prioritize your safety and the safety of your training partners. Avoid techniques that you are not confident in performing safely.

3. Avoid Training When Sick or Injured - If you are feeling unwell or have an injury, it is best to sit out and recover rather than risk spreading illness or exacerbating an injury. Communicate with your instructor about any concerns regarding your health and safety.

## *C. Academy Rules*

1. Follow Academy Rules - Adhere to the specific rules and guidelines set by your academy. This may include protocols for attendance, class behavior, and use of facilities. Understanding and following these rules helps maintain order and respect within the academy.

2. Be Punctual - Arrive on time for classes and events, demonstrating respect for the instructors and fellow students. Punctuality shows your commitment and readiness to learn. If you are late, wait for the instructor's permission to join the class to avoid disrupting the session.

3. Proper Attire and Equipment - Wear the appropriate attire for each class, whether it is Gi or No-Gi. Ensure that your gear is in good condition and that you have all necessary equipment. Remove any jewelry or accessories that could cause injury during training.

Understanding and practicing BJJ etiquette and rules are essential for creating a respectful, safe, and positive training environment. Respecting instructors, training partners, and the academy, maintaining good hygiene and safety practices, and adhering to academy rules will enhance your experience and contribute to a supportive BJJ community. By following these guidelines, you will build strong relationships and foster a culture of mutual respect and continuous learning.

# *Chapter 3 Review: Choosing the Right Academy and Gear*

Selecting the right Brazilian Jiu-Jitsu (BJJ) academy and gear is crucial for a positive and productive experience. This chapter provides practical advice on how to choose a suitable training environment, acquire the essential equipment, and understand the etiquette and rules that govern the BJJ community.

- **3.1 Selecting a BJJ Academy:**

  - Research and Recommendations: Start by researching local academies online, looking for reviews and testimonials, and seek recommendations from friends or colleagues.

  - Visit Potential Academies: Observe classes and meet instructors to gauge the teaching style, class structure, and community.

  - Evaluate the Environment: Assess the facilities for cleanliness and safety, and consider the community's atmosphere to ensure it aligns with your values and goals.

- **3.2 Essential Gear and Equipment:**

- Gi and No-Gi Attire: Choose a well-fitted, durable Gi and appropriate No-Gi attire, such as rash guards and shorts.

  - Additional Gear: Use a proper belt to signify your rank, and consider protective gear like mouthguards and knee pads for safety.

  - Maintenance and Care: Maintain hygiene by washing your Gi after each use and storing your gear properly. Regularly inspect and replace any worn-out equipment.

**- 3.3 BJJ Etiquette and Rules:**

  - Respect and Humility: Show respect to instructors and training partners, and maintain a humble attitude.

  - Hygiene and Safety: Practice good personal hygiene, ensure safety by tapping out when necessary, and avoid training when sick or injured.

  - Academy Rules: Follow specific academy rules, be punctual, and wear proper attire and equipment during classes.

Choosing the right BJJ academy, acquiring essential gear, and understanding the etiquette and rules are foundational steps in your BJJ journey. These elements ensure a positive, respectful, and productive training experience, setting the stage for continuous learning and growth in the art of Brazilian Jiu-Jitsu.

# Chapter 4: Warm-Up and Conditioning

Warm-up and conditioning are essential components of a successful Brazilian Jiu-Jitsu (BJJ) training regimen. Proper preparation helps prevent injuries, improves performance, and ensures longevity in the sport. This chapter explores the importance of warm-ups, effective stretching and flexibility exercises, and strength and conditioning routines tailored for BJJ practitioners.

## *4.1 Importance of Warm-Ups*

Warm-ups are a crucial part of any Brazilian Jiu-Jitsu (BJJ) training session. They prepare the body for intense physical activity, increase blood flow to muscles, and reduce the risk of injury. A well-structured warm-up enhances overall performance and ensures that practitioners are physically and mentally ready for training.

### *A. Physical Preparation*

1. Increased Blood Flow - Warm-ups increase blood flow to the muscles, improving oxygen delivery and preparing the body for the physical demands of BJJ. This helps reduce the risk of muscle strains and injuries.

   - Example: Light jogging or jumping jacks can elevate heart rate and stimulate circulation, effectively warming up the muscles.

2. Improved Muscle Elasticity - Gradually increasing the intensity of physical activity during warm-ups improves muscle elasticity and joint flexibility, reducing the likelihood of strains and sprains.

   - Example: Dynamic stretches like leg swings and arm circles help enhance muscle flexibility and joint mobility.

### *B. Mental Preparation*

1. Focus and Concentration - Warm-ups help practitioners transition from their daily routines to the focused environment of the training mat. This mental shift enhances concentration and readiness for learning and sparring.

- Example: Incorporating breathing exercises and mindfulness techniques during warm-ups can help center the mind and improve focus.

2. Routine and Consistency - Establishing a consistent warm-up routine helps build discipline and sets the tone for the rest of the training session.

   - Example: Performing the same set of warm-up exercises at the beginning of each session creates a sense of familiarity and routine.

## *C. Common Warm-Up Exercises*

1. Joint Rotations - Perform gentle rotations of the neck, shoulders, elbows, wrists, hips, knees, and ankles to increase joint mobility and lubricate the joints.

   - Example: Neck rolls, shoulder circles, and ankle rotations are simple exercises to start with.

2. Light Cardiovascular Activity - Engage in light cardiovascular exercises such as jogging, jumping jacks, or jump rope to elevate heart rate and increase blood flow.

   - Example: A few minutes of jumping jacks or skipping rope can effectively get the heart pumping.

3. Dynamic Stretching - Incorporate dynamic stretching exercises that mimic the movements of BJJ, such as leg swings, arm circles, and hip openers.

   - Example: Leg swings (both front-to-back and side-to-side) help prepare the hips and legs for the dynamic movements in BJJ.

Warm-ups are essential for preparing both the body and mind for the physical and mental demands of Brazilian Jiu-Jitsu. By increasing blood flow, improving muscle elasticity, and enhancing focus and concentration, a well-structured warm-up routine can significantly reduce the risk of injury and improve overall performance. Consistency in warm-up routines helps build discipline and sets the foundation for effective training sessions.

## *4.2 Stretching and Flexibility Exercises*

Flexibility is a key component of Brazilian Jiu-Jitsu (BJJ), allowing practitioners to execute techniques more effectively and reduce the risk of injuries. Incorporating regular stretching and flexibility exercises into your training routine is essential for optimal performance and overall physical health.

## *A. Static Stretching*

Static stretching involves holding a stretch for a period of time to lengthen and relax the muscles. This type of stretching is most effective after training sessions when the muscles are warm.

1. Post-Training Stretching - Static stretching helps improve flexibility and aids in muscle recovery after training. Hold each stretch for 15-30 seconds and focus on major muscle groups used in BJJ.

   - Example: Perform a hamstring stretch by sitting on the floor with one leg extended and reaching towards your toes.

2. Common Static Stretches - Include stretches for major muscle groups such as the hamstrings, quadriceps, hip flexors, and shoulders.

   - Hamstring Stretch: Sit on the floor with one leg extended and reach towards your toes, holding the position.

   - Quadriceps Stretch: Stand on one leg, pull your opposite foot towards your buttocks, and hold the stretch.

   - Hip Flexor Stretch: Kneel on one knee, push your hips forward, and hold the stretch.

   - Shoulder Stretch: Bring one arm across your chest and use the opposite hand to hold it in place.

## *B. Dynamic Stretching*

Dynamic stretching involves moving parts of your body and gradually increasing reach, speed, or both. This type of stretching is ideal before training sessions to prepare the muscles and joints for movement.

1. Pre-Training Stretching - Dynamic stretching helps increase range of motion and reduce stiffness before training. Perform dynamic stretches for 5-10 minutes to activate muscles and improve mobility.

   - Example: Leg swings, where you swing your legs forward and backward or side to side, can effectively loosen up the hips and legs.

2. Common Dynamic Stretches - Incorporate exercises like leg swings, torso twists, and lunge walks to activate muscles and improve mobility.

   - Leg Swings: Swing your leg forward and backward or side to side to loosen up the hip joints.

   - Torso Twists: Stand with your feet shoulder-width apart and twist your torso from side to side.

   - Lunge Walks: Perform walking lunges, focusing on a deep stretch in the hip flexors and quadriceps.

## *C. Yoga and Mobility Work*

Yoga and mobility exercises can significantly enhance flexibility, balance, and body awareness, making them excellent additions to a BJJ training regimen.

1. Yoga for BJJ - Practicing yoga can improve flexibility, balance, and mental focus. Incorporate yoga poses that target areas commonly used in BJJ.

   - Example: Downward dog, pigeon pose, and warrior poses are effective for stretching and strengthening muscles used in BJJ.

   - Downward Dog: Stretches the hamstrings, calves, and shoulders while strengthening the arms and legs.

   - Pigeon Pose: Stretches the hip rotators and flexors, helping to increase hip flexibility.

   - Warrior Poses: Improve strength and flexibility in the legs, hips, and shoulders.

2. Mobility Drills - Use mobility drills to improve joint health and functional movement. These exercises can include foam rolling, resistance band exercises, and proprioceptive neuromuscular facilitation (PNF) stretching.

   - Foam Rolling: Use a foam roller to massage and release tension in the muscles, improving blood flow and flexibility.

- Resistance Band Exercises: Use resistance bands to perform stretches that enhance mobility and flexibility.

- PNF Stretching: This advanced stretching technique involves contracting and relaxing muscles to increase range of motion.

Incorporating stretching and flexibility exercises into your BJJ training routine is essential for optimal performance and injury prevention. Static stretching after training, dynamic stretching before training, and incorporating yoga and mobility work can significantly enhance your flexibility, balance, and overall physical health. Consistent practice of these exercises will help you execute techniques more effectively and maintain a healthy, injury-free training regimen.

## *4.3 Strength and Conditioning for BJJ*

Strength and conditioning are vital for improving overall athleticism and enhancing Brazilian Jiu-Jitsu (BJJ) performance. A well-rounded program should include exercises that build strength, endurance, and power while focusing on functional movements relevant to BJJ.

### *A. Strength Training*

Strength training helps build muscle, improve joint stability, and enhance overall power, which are crucial for BJJ practitioners.

1. Compound Movements - Focus on compound movements that engage multiple muscle groups, such as squats, deadlifts, bench presses, and pull-ups. These exercises build overall strength and power.

- Squats: Strengthen the legs and core, providing a strong base for movements in BJJ.

- Deadlifts: Develop lower back, glute, and hamstring strength, crucial for explosive movements and maintaining posture.

- Bench Press: Enhance upper body strength, important for pushing and controlling opponents.

- Pull-Ups: Improve back and grip strength, aiding in control and submissions.

2. Functional Strength - Incorporate functional strength exercises that mimic the movements of BJJ, such as kettlebell swings, Turkish get-ups, and medicine ball slams.

- Kettlebell Swings: Build explosive hip power and endurance.

- Turkish Get-Ups: Enhance overall body coordination, stability, and strength.

- Medicine Ball Slams: Improve core strength and explosive power.

## *B. Cardiovascular Conditioning*

Cardiovascular conditioning is essential for maintaining stamina and endurance during prolonged BJJ training sessions and competitions.

1. High-Intensity Interval Training (HIIT) - HIIT involves short bursts of intense exercise followed by brief rest periods. This type of training improves cardiovascular fitness and mimics the intensity of BJJ matches.

- Example: Perform sprints for 30 seconds, followed by 30 seconds of rest, repeating for 10-15 minutes.

2. Steady-State Cardio - Include steady-state cardio exercises like running, cycling, or swimming to build endurance and improve overall cardiovascular health.

- Example: Jog or cycle at a moderate pace for 30-45 minutes.

## *C. Recovery and Injury Prevention*

Proper recovery and injury prevention strategies are essential for maintaining longevity in BJJ training.

1. Rest and Recovery - Ensure adequate rest and recovery between training sessions to prevent overtraining and reduce the risk of injuries. Prioritize sleep, nutrition, and hydration.

- Example: Incorporate rest days into your training schedule and focus on getting 7-9 hours of sleep per night.

2. Injury Prevention - Incorporate exercises that strengthen stabilizing muscles and improve joint stability, such as rotator cuff exercises, balance drills, and proprioceptive training.

- Rotator Cuff Exercises: Strengthen the shoulder muscles to prevent common shoulder injuries.

  - Balance Drills: Improve proprioception and joint stability, reducing the risk of falls and injuries.

  - Proprioceptive Training: Use balance boards or stability balls to enhance joint awareness and stability.

Strength and conditioning are crucial components of a comprehensive BJJ training regimen. By incorporating compound movements, functional strength exercises, cardiovascular conditioning, and injury prevention strategies, practitioners can enhance their performance and maintain a healthy, injury-free training routine. Consistent strength and conditioning work will ensure that you are physically prepared for the demands of Brazilian Jiu-Jitsu, leading to improved performance on the mat.

# *Chapter 4 Review: Warm-Up and Conditioning*

Warm-up and conditioning routines are essential for preparing the body and mind for the demands of Brazilian Jiu-Jitsu (BJJ). This chapter covers the importance of warm-ups, effective stretching and flexibility exercises, and strength and conditioning programs tailored for BJJ practitioners.

- **4.1 Importance of Warm-Ups:**

  - Physical Preparation: Warm-ups increase blood flow to muscles, improving oxygen delivery and muscle elasticity, which reduces the risk of injury.

    - Example: Light jogging and dynamic stretches like leg swings and arm circles enhance muscle flexibility and joint mobility.

  - Mental Preparation: Warm-ups help practitioners transition from daily routines to a focused training environment, enhancing concentration and readiness.

    - Example: Breathing exercises and mindfulness techniques during warm-ups can improve mental focus.

  - Common Warm-Up Exercises: Include joint rotations, light cardiovascular activity, and dynamic stretching to prepare the body for training.

## - 4.2 Stretching and Flexibility Exercises:

- Static Stretching: Best performed after training to improve flexibility and aid in muscle recovery.
  - Example: Hamstring, quadriceps, hip flexor, and shoulder stretches.
- Dynamic Stretching: Ideal before training to increase range of motion and reduce stiffness.
  - Example: Leg swings, torso twists, and lunge walks.
- Yoga and Mobility Work: Enhance flexibility, balance, and body awareness through yoga poses and mobility drills.
  - Example: Downward dog, pigeon pose, and foam rolling for muscle release and improved joint health.

## - 4.3 Strength and Conditioning for BJJ:

- Strength Training: Focus on compound movements and functional strength exercises to build overall strength and power.
  - Example: Squats, deadlifts, kettlebell swings, and Turkish get-ups.
- Cardiovascular Conditioning: Maintain stamina and endurance with high-intensity interval training (HIIT) and steady-state cardio exercises.
  - Example: Sprints for HIIT and jogging or cycling for steady-state cardio.
- Recovery and Injury Prevention: Ensure adequate rest and recovery, and incorporate exercises that strengthen stabilizing muscles and improve joint stability.
  - Example: Rotator cuff exercises, balance drills, and proprioceptive training.

Understanding and incorporating warm-ups, stretching, and conditioning routines are essential for effective BJJ training. These practices not only enhance performance but also reduce the risk of injuries and ensure longevity in the sport. Consistent preparation and conditioning will help practitioners achieve success and maintain a healthy training regimen.

# Part 3: Essential Techniques and Movements

Mastering the essential techniques and movements is fundamental to excelling in Brazilian Jiu-Jitsu (BJJ). This part provides a comprehensive guide to the basic movements and drills that form the foundation of BJJ practice.

# Chapter 5: Basic Movements and Drills

Understanding and practicing basic movements and drills are crucial for developing the coordination, balance, and agility needed in BJJ. This chapter covers the fundamental aspects of stance and posture, key movement drills like shrimping, bridging, and rolling, and essential breakfall techniques for safety.

## *5.1 Stance and Posture*

Stance and posture are the building blocks of effective Brazilian Jiu-Jitsu (BJJ) technique. Proper stance and posture provide stability, balance, and the ability to move efficiently, which are crucial for both offensive and defensive actions.

*Brazilian Jiu-Jitsu Sparring Stance*

## *A. Base and Balance*

1. Foundation of Movement - A strong base and good balance are essential for maintaining your position and responding effectively to your opponent's movements.

   - Example: Stand with your feet shoulder-width apart, knees slightly bent, and weight evenly distributed to create a stable foundation.

2. Weight Distribution - Proper weight distribution helps maintain balance and prevents you from being easily swept or taken down.

   - Example: Lean slightly forward with your weight on the balls of your feet, ready to move in any direction.

## *B. Offensive and Defensive Postures*

1. Defensive Posture - A defensive posture helps protect against attacks and prepares you to defend against takedowns or sweeps.

   - Example: Keep your elbows close to your body, hands up to protect your face, and chin tucked.

2. Offensive Posture - An offensive posture enables you to initiate attacks and apply pressure on your opponent.

   - Example: Lean slightly forward, ready to engage, with your hands positioned to grip or strike.

## *C. Movement and Adjustment*

1. Maintaining Stance - Practice maintaining your stance while moving to ensure you can keep your balance and stability.

   - Example: Move in small, controlled steps, keeping your stance intact, to avoid compromising your balance.

2. Adjusting to Opponent - Adjust your stance and posture based on your opponent's movements to maintain a strong position.

   - Example: Pivot on your feet and adjust your body angle to face your opponent directly, ensuring you're always in a position to defend or attack.

Mastering stance and posture is fundamental in Brazilian Jiu-Jitsu. A solid stance provides the necessary foundation for balance and movement, while proper posture allows you to efficiently transition between offensive and defensive actions. Practicing these elements regularly ensures you are prepared to handle various situations on the mat, enhancing your overall performance and effectiveness in BJJ.

## *5.2 Shrimping, Bridging, and Rolling*

Shrimping, bridging, and rolling are fundamental drills in Brazilian Jiu-Jitsu (BJJ) that develop essential movement skills, help escape bad positions, and improve overall agility. Mastering these techniques is crucial for building a strong foundation in BJJ.

### *A. Shrimping*

Shrimping, or hip escaping, is a vital movement used to create space and escape from underneath an opponent.

1. Purpose - Shrimping is used to move your hips away from your opponent, creating space for escapes and transitions.

   - Example: When trapped in side control, shrimping can help you regain guard or move to a more advantageous position.

2. Technique - Proper shrimping technique involves pushing off with your foot, lifting your hips, and sliding your body away.

   - Step-by-Step:

     1. Lie on your back with one foot planted firmly on the mat.
     2. Push off with your foot, lift your hips, and turn to your side.
     3. Slide your hips away from your planted foot, extending your body.
     4. Repeat on the other side, continuously moving and creating space.

## *B. Bridging*

Bridging is used to generate power and create space, often employed in escapes from dominant positions like mount.

1. Purpose - Bridging helps you use your legs and hips to lift and move your opponent, creating opportunities to escape.

   - Example: When mounted, bridging can help you disrupt your opponent's balance and create space for an escape.

2. Technique - Drive through your heels, lift your hips, and twist your body to the side to create movement and leverage.

   - Step-by-Step:

     1. Lie on your back with your feet flat on the mat and close to your hips.

     2. Push through your heels, lifting your hips off the ground.

     3. Twist your body to one side, aiming to roll your opponent off balance.

     4. Combine the bridge with other movements, like shrimping, to create an effective escape.

## *C. Rolling*

Rolling drills improve body awareness, balance, and the ability to transition smoothly between positions.

1. Purpose - Rolling enhances agility and coordination, allowing you to move fluidly between different positions and recover from falls.

   - Example: Forward and backward rolls help you transition smoothly between techniques and recover from being thrown.

2. Technique - Keep your body tight, tuck your chin, and roll over your shoulder to protect your neck and spine.

   - Step-by-Step:

     1. For a forward roll, start from a kneeling or standing position.

     2. Tuck your chin to your chest and place one hand on the mat.

     3. Roll over your shoulder (not your head) and continue the motion smoothly.

4. For a backward roll, sit down, tuck your chin, and roll over one shoulder, ensuring a smooth transition.

Mastering shrimping, bridging, and rolling is essential for effective movement in Brazilian Jiu-Jitsu. These foundational drills enhance your ability to create space, escape bad positions, and transition smoothly between techniques. Consistent practice of these movements will improve your agility, balance, and overall effectiveness on the mat, providing a strong base for further development in BJJ.

## *5.3 Breakfalls and Safety Techniques*

Learning how to fall safely is crucial in Brazilian Jiu-Jitsu (BJJ) to prevent injuries. Breakfalls teach you to absorb impact and protect vital areas of your body, ensuring that you can train and compete safely. This section covers essential breakfall techniques for various directions of falls.

### *A. Back Breakfall*

A back breakfall helps you safely fall backward without injuring your head or spine.

1. Purpose - Protect the head, neck, and spine by distributing the impact of the fall across a larger surface area.

  - Example: Falling backward during a throw or sweep.

2. Technique - Tuck your chin to your chest, roll back, and slap the mat with your arms extended to dissipate the impact.

  - Step-by-Step:

    1. Start in a seated position with your knees bent and feet flat on the mat.

    2. Tuck your chin to your chest to protect your head.

    3. Roll backward, keeping your chin tucked and your back rounded.

    4. As your back touches the mat, slap the mat with both arms extended out to the sides at a 45-degree angle, palms down.

## *B. Side Breakfall*

A side breakfall helps you safely fall to the side, protecting your head and ribs.

1. Purpose - Protect the head and ribs by dispersing the impact along the arm and side of the body.

   - Example: Falling to the side during a sweep or trip.

2. Technique - Tuck your chin, roll onto your side, and slap the mat with your arm and leg extended.

   - Step-by-Step:

     1. Start in a standing or kneeling position.

     2. Tuck your chin to your chest and lean to one side.

     3. Roll onto your side, keeping your chin tucked and your back rounded.

     4. Slap the mat with your arm and leg extended on the side you are falling to, dispersing the impact.

## *C. Forward Roll Breakfall*

A forward roll breakfall helps you safely roll forward and absorb the impact with your arms and shoulders.

1. Purpose - Protect the head and spine by rolling through the impact and dispersing it across the arms and shoulders.

   - Example: Falling forward during a throw or trip.

2. Technique - Tuck your chin, roll over one shoulder, and slap the mat with your arms extended to break the fall.

   - Step-by-Step:

     1. Start in a kneeling or standing position.

     2. Tuck your chin to your chest and place one hand on the mat.

     3. Roll over your shoulder (not your head) and continue the motion smoothly.

     4. Extend your arms and slap the mat to break the fall as you complete the roll.

Mastering breakfalls and safety techniques is essential for preventing injuries in Brazilian Jiu-Jitsu. By learning how to fall safely and effectively, practitioners can train and compete with confidence, knowing they can protect themselves during unexpected falls or throws. Consistent practice of back breakfalls, side breakfalls, and forward roll breakfalls will enhance your safety on the mat and contribute to a long and healthy BJJ journey.

## *Chapter 5 Review: Basic Movements and Drills*

Mastering the basic movements and drills is crucial for developing the foundational skills needed in Brazilian Jiu-Jitsu (BJJ). This chapter covers the fundamental aspects of stance and posture, key movement drills like shrimping, bridging, and rolling, and essential breakfall techniques for safety.

**- 5.1 Stance and Posture:**

  - Base and Balance: A strong base and good balance are essential for maintaining your position and responding effectively to your opponent's movements.

    - Example: Stand with your feet shoulder-width apart, knees slightly bent, and weight evenly distributed.

  - Offensive and Defensive Postures: Proper posture enables both effective defense and the ability to initiate attacks.

    - Example: Defensive posture with elbows close and hands up; offensive posture leaning slightly forward.

  - Movement and Adjustment: Practice maintaining and adjusting your stance while moving to keep balance and stability.

    - Example: Move in small, controlled steps, pivoting on your feet to face your opponent directly.

**- 5.2 Shrimping, Bridging, and Rolling:**

  - Shrimping: Used to create space and escape from underneath an opponent.

- Example: Push off with your foot, lift your hips, and slide your body away to create space.

  - Bridging: Generates power to create space, often used to escape from dominant positions like mount.

  - Example: Push through your heels, lift your hips, and twist your body to roll your opponent off balance.

  - Rolling: Improves body awareness, balance, and smooth transitions between positions.

  - Example: Perform forward and backward rolls to enhance agility and coordination.

- 5.3 Breakfalls and Safety Techniques:

  - Back Breakfall: Protects the head, neck, and spine by distributing the impact across a larger surface area.

  - Example: Tuck your chin, roll back, and slap the mat with both arms to dissipate the impact.

  - Side Breakfall: Protects the head and ribs by dispersing the impact along the arm and side of the body.

  - Example: Tuck your chin, roll onto your side, and slap the mat with your arm and leg extended.

  - Forward Roll Breakfall: Absorbs impact with the arms and shoulders while rolling forward.

  - Example: Tuck your chin, roll over one shoulder, and slap the mat with your arms extended to break the fall.

Understanding and practicing these basic movements and drills are fundamental for success in Brazilian Jiu-Jitsu. Proper stance and posture provide the foundation for balance and effective movement, while shrimping, bridging, and rolling enhance your ability to create space and transition smoothly. Learning to breakfall safely is crucial for injury prevention and building confidence in training. Consistent practice of these basic skills sets the stage for continuous improvement and success in BJJ.

# Chapter 6: Guard Positions and Variations

Guard positions are a fundamental aspect of Brazilian Jiu-Jitsu (BJJ), providing both defensive and offensive options. Mastering different guard positions and their variations allows practitioners to control their opponents, set up submissions, and execute sweeps and attacks. This chapter covers the essential guard positions, including closed guard, open guard, and half guard.

*Brazilian Jiu-Jitsu Guard Position*

## *6.1 Closed Guard: Control and Submissions*

The closed guard is one of the most fundamental and secure positions in Brazilian Jiu-Jitsu (BJJ). It involves wrapping your legs around your opponent's waist, effectively controlling their posture and limiting their movement. This position offers numerous opportunities for control and submissions.

### *A. Control*

Control in the closed guard is essential for setting up submissions and preventing your opponent from passing your guard.

1. Maintaining Control - The primary goal of the closed guard is to control your opponent's posture and movement, making it difficult for them to mount an effective offense.

- Example: Keep your legs locked around your opponent's waist and use your arms to control their upper body by gripping their collar or sleeve.

2. Breaking Posture - Use your legs and arms to break your opponent's posture, pulling them down and making it hard for them to sit up and strike or pass.

- Example: Pull your opponent's head or collar down while using your legs to squeeze and control their hips.

## *B. Submissions*

From the closed guard, you have several powerful submission options that can be applied when you effectively control your opponent's posture and movement.

*Brazilian Jiu Jitsu Arm Bar*

1. Armbar - The armbar is a powerful submission that targets the elbow joint.

- Technique:

1. Control your opponent's arm by gripping their wrist and controlling their elbow.

2. Pivot your hips, bringing one leg across your opponent's face and the other across their back.

3. Extend your hips and pull down on the arm to apply pressure to the elbow joint.

*Brazilian Jiu-Jitsu Triangle Choke*

2. Triangle Choke - The triangle choke is a blood choke that restricts blood flow to the brain.

- Technique:

1. Trap one of your opponent's arms while pushing the other arm across their body.

2. Shoot your legs up, creating a triangle shape around their neck and trapped arm.

3. Lock your legs, pull down on your opponent's head, and squeeze your legs to apply the choke.

3. Guillotine Choke - The guillotine choke targets the neck, applying pressure to induce a tap.

- Technique:

1. Control your opponent's head by wrapping your arm around their neck.

2. Sit back, bringing their head into your chest, and use your legs to control their body.

3. Squeeze your arm and lift your hips to apply pressure to the neck.

## *C. Sweeps*

*Brazilian Jiu Jitsu Sweep*

In addition to submissions, the closed guard offers several effective sweeps that can help you transition to a more dominant position.

1. Scissor Sweep - This sweep off-balances your opponent and allows you to transition to the mount position.

   - Technique:

   1. Control your opponent's sleeve and collar.

   2. Open your guard, placing one shin across their abdomen and the other leg behind their knee.

   3. Scissor your legs while pulling on their sleeve and collar, sweeping them to their back.

2. Hip Bump Sweep - This sweep utilizes your hips to off-balance your opponent and take the top position.

- Technique:

1. Sit up quickly, controlling your opponent's arm and posting one hand behind you.

2. Bump your hips into your opponent's chest, using the momentum to roll them over.

Mastering the closed guard is crucial for any BJJ practitioner. By learning to maintain control, break your opponent's posture, and execute effective submissions and sweeps, you can dominate from the closed guard position. Consistent practice of these techniques will enhance your ability to control and submit opponents, making the closed guard a vital part of your BJJ arsenal.

## *6.2 Open Guard: Variations and Transitions*

The open guard offers a wide range of variations and transitions, providing flexibility and numerous offensive and defensive options. Unlike the closed guard, where the legs are locked around the opponent, the open guard involves using the legs to control and manipulate the opponent's movements while keeping the guard open. This section explores the essential variations of the open guard and the transitions that can be performed from these positions.

*Brazilian Jiu-Jitsu Open Guard*

## *A. Variations*

The open guard encompasses several key variations, each with unique control and attack opportunities.

1. De La Riva Guard - The De La Riva guard involves hooking one leg around the opponent's leg while controlling their other leg or collar.

  - Technique:

    1. Hook your outside leg around the opponent's leg, with your foot on their thigh.

    2. Control their opposite sleeve or collar with your hand.

    3. Use your free leg to push against their hip or thigh to create distance and off-balance them.

2. Spider Guard - The spider guard uses your feet on the opponent's biceps to control their arms and posture.

  - Technique:

    1. Place your feet on your opponent's biceps, extending your legs to control their arms.

    2. Grip their sleeves with your hands for added control.

    3. Use your legs to create tension and manipulate their movement.

3. X-Guard - The X-Guard positions your legs in an "X" shape around the opponent's leg, providing strong control and sweep opportunities.

  - Technique:

    1. From a seated position, place one leg behind your opponent's knee and the other across their waist.

    2. Hook your feet around their legs to form an "X" shape.

    3. Control their far leg with your hands to set up sweeps.

## *B. Transitions*

Effective transitions from the open guard allow you to maintain control, execute sweeps, and move to more dominant positions.

1. Guard Retention - Transition between different open guard variations to maintain control and prevent your opponent from passing.

   - Example: If your opponent starts to break your spider guard, transition to De La Riva guard to retain control and continue your attack.

2. Sweeps and Attacks - Use the open guard to set up sweeps and attacks by creating angles and leveraging your opponent's movement.

   - Example: From De La Riva guard, execute a hook sweep to off-balance your opponent and transition to a top position.

## *C. Practical Techniques*

1. Berimbolo - A rolling back take often set up from De La Riva guard.

   - Technique:

     1. From De La Riva guard, grip your opponent's belt or pants.

     2. Invert your body, rolling underneath them while maintaining the hook.

     3. Use the momentum to take their back or transition to another dominant position.

2. Lasso Guard - A variation where one leg wraps around the opponent's arm, providing strong control.

   - Technique:

     1. Insert one leg deep under your opponent's armpit, wrapping it around their arm.

     2. Grip their sleeve and use your other foot to control their hip.

     3. Manipulate their posture and set up sweeps or submissions from this position.

3. Butterfly Guard - A versatile open guard where both feet are placed on the opponent's inner thighs.

   - Technique:

     1. Sit up with both feet hooked inside your opponent's thighs.

     2. Control their arms or collar to keep them close.

     3. Use your hooks to lift and sweep them, transitioning to a dominant position.

Mastering the open guard and its variations is essential for a well-rounded BJJ game. The De La Riva guard, spider guard, X-guard, and other variations provide numerous opportunities for control, sweeps, and submissions. Understanding how to transition effectively between these guards and execute practical techniques like the Berimbolo, lasso guard, and butterfly guard will significantly enhance your ability to control and dominate your opponent. Consistent practice and exploration of these positions will deepen your understanding and effectiveness in Brazilian Jiu-Jitsu.

## *6.3 Half Guard: Defense, Sweeps, and Attacks*

The half guard is a versatile position in Brazilian Jiu-Jitsu (BJJ) that offers both defensive and offensive strategies. In this position, you trap one of your opponent's legs between your legs while maintaining control of their upper body. Mastering the half guard allows you to defend against passes, execute sweeps, and set up attacks effectively.

### *A. Defense*

1. Maintaining Distance - Use your legs and arms to create distance and prevent your opponent from advancing to a more dominant position.

   - Example: Use a knee shield to keep your opponent's weight off you and maintain space.

   - Technique:

     1. Place your knee across your opponent's chest or hip.

     2. Use your arms to control their upper body and keep them from closing the distance.

2. Recovering Guard - Transition from half guard to full guard or another guard position to regain control.

   - Example: Use your free leg to shrimp and recover to closed guard or an open guard variation.

   - Technique:

1. Use your bottom foot to push off the mat and create space.

2. Shrimp your hips away and slide your top leg across your opponent's waist to recover guard.

## *B. Sweeps*

1. Old School Sweep - This sweep involves trapping your opponent's leg and using your body to off-balance and roll them over.

- Technique:

1. Control your opponent's far leg with your hands.

2. Underhook their near leg with your arm and roll onto your shoulder.

3. Drive with your legs to roll them over and secure the top position.

2. Deep Half Guard Sweep - From deep half guard, you can sweep your opponent by controlling their leg and using leverage to roll them over.

- Technique:

1. Get underneath your opponent, trapping their leg between yours.

2. Control their far leg with your hands and use your legs to lift and off-balance them.

3. Roll them over to secure a more dominant position.

## *C. Attacks*

*Brazilian Jiu-Jitsu Kimura*

1. Kimura - The Kimura is a powerful shoulder lock that can be set up from half guard.

   - Technique:

     1. Control your opponent's wrist with a two-on-one grip.

     2. Sit up and reach over their back to grab your own wrist, creating a figure-four grip.

     3. Use your hips to drive forward and apply pressure on their shoulder joint.

2. Back Take - Use the half guard to transition to your opponent's back, gaining a dominant position.

   - Technique:

     1. Create space by using a knee shield or underhooking their arm.

     2. Shrimp out to the side and use your free leg to hook their far leg.

     3. Pull yourself up to their back, securing hooks with your legs and establishing control.

3. Sweep to Mount - Sweep your opponent from half guard directly to the mount position.

- Technique:

1. Use an underhook to control your opponent's far side.

2. Bridge and roll towards your underhook side, using your legs to elevate and sweep.

3. Follow through to secure the mount position.

Mastering the half guard provides a robust platform for both defense and offense in Brazilian Jiu-Jitsu. By learning to maintain distance, recover guard, execute sweeps like the old school and deep half guard sweeps, and set up attacks such as the Kimura and back take, you can effectively control and dominate your opponent from the half guard position. Consistent practice of these techniques will enhance your ability to transition smoothly between defense and offense, making the half guard a critical component of your BJJ arsenal.

# *Chapter 6 Review: Guard Positions and Variations*

Mastering different guard positions and their variations is essential for a well-rounded Brazilian Jiu-Jitsu (BJJ) game. This chapter covers the essential guard positions, including closed guard, open guard, and half guard, providing a comprehensive understanding of how to control opponents, set up submissions, and execute sweeps and attacks.

### - 6.1 Closed Guard: Control and Submissions:

- Control: The closed guard is fundamental for controlling an opponent's posture and movement.

- Example: Keep your legs locked around your opponent's waist and use your arms to control their upper body.

- Submissions: From the closed guard, you can execute powerful submissions like the armbar, triangle choke, and guillotine choke.

- Example: For the armbar, control your opponent's arm, pivot your hips, and extend your legs to apply pressure on the elbow.

### - 6.2 Open Guard: Variations and Transitions:

- Variations: The open guard includes several key variations, each offering unique control and attack opportunities.

- Example: The De La Riva guard involves hooking one leg around the opponent's leg while controlling their other leg or collar.

- Transitions: Effective transitions between open guard variations allow you to maintain control and set up sweeps and attacks.

- Example: Transition from the spider guard to the De La Riva guard to retain control and continue your attack.

### - 6.3 Half Guard: Defense, Sweeps, and Attacks:

- Defense: The half guard allows you to create distance and prevent your opponent from advancing to a more dominant position.

- Example: Use a knee shield to keep your opponent's weight off you and maintain space.

- Sweeps: Execute effective sweeps like the old school sweep and deep half guard sweep to transition to a dominant position.

- Example: For the old school sweep, control your opponent's far leg, underhook their near leg, and roll them over.

- Attacks: Set up powerful attacks such as the Kimura and back take from the half guard.

- Example: For the Kimura, control your opponent's wrist, sit up to create a figure-four grip, and use your hips to apply pressure on their shoulder joint.

Understanding and practicing these guard positions and their variations are crucial for success in Brazilian Jiu-Jitsu. The closed guard offers control and submission opportunities, the open guard provides flexibility and numerous offensive options, and the half guard allows for both defense and powerful sweeps and attacks. Consistent practice and understanding of these positions will enhance your ability to control and dominate your opponent, setting the stage for continuous improvement and success in BJJ.

# Chapter 7: Top Control and Dominance

Top control is a critical aspect of Brazilian Jiu-Jitsu (BJJ), allowing practitioners to dominate their opponents, apply pressure, and set up submissions. This chapter explores various top control positions, including mount, side control, north-south, and knee on belly, providing strategies for maintaining control and executing attacks.

## *7.1 Mount: Attacks and Maintenance*

The mount position is one of the most dominant positions in Brazilian Jiu-Jitsu (BJJ). It provides excellent control over your opponent and offers numerous opportunities for attacks and submissions. This section focuses on the key aspects of maintaining the mount position and executing effective attacks from there.

*Brazilian Jiu-Jitsu Mount Position*

### *A. Attacks*

1. Armbar - The armbar is a powerful submission that targets the elbow joint.

   - Technique:

     1. Isolate your opponent's arm by pinning it to the mat or controlling it with both hands.

2. Slide your knee up towards their head on the same side as the trapped arm.

3. Swing your other leg over their head, ensuring your knees are tight to their body.

4. Lean back and extend your hips to apply pressure on the elbow joint, forcing a tap.

2. Americana - The Americana is a shoulder lock that leverages the opponent's arm into an unnatural position.

- Technique:

1. Pin your opponent's wrist to the mat with one hand.

2. Slide your other hand under their arm, grasping your own wrist to create a figure-four grip.

3. Lift their elbow while keeping their wrist pinned, applying pressure to the shoulder joint.

3. Mounted Triangle - The mounted triangle is a choke that involves using your legs to trap the opponent's neck and one arm.

- Technique:

1. Isolate one of your opponent's arms by pushing it across their body.

2. Swing your leg over their shoulder and lock your legs in a triangle shape around their neck and arm.

3. Squeeze your legs and pull down on their head to tighten the choke and induce a tap.

## *B. Maintenance*

1. Base and Balance - Maintaining a low center of gravity and wide base is crucial to prevent being rolled or bucked off.

- Example: Spread your knees wide and keep your hips low, constantly adjusting your weight in response to your opponent's movements.

- Technique:

1. Keep your feet active and toes engaged to adjust your balance.

2. Distribute your weight evenly and stay flexible to react to your opponent's attempts to escape.

2. Pressure and Control - Use your body weight to apply pressure and control your opponent's upper body, limiting their ability to escape or counter.

- Example: Apply chest-to-chest pressure and grip your opponent's head or arms to limit their movement.

- Technique:

1. Keep your chest low and maintain a tight connection with your opponent.

2. Use your hands to control their head or collar, preventing them from creating space.

3. Transitions - Move fluidly between high mount, low mount, and technical mount to maintain control and set up attacks.

- Example: Shift to technical mount by placing one knee next to your opponent's head and the other near their hips.

- Technique:

1. Move to high mount by sliding your knees up towards their armpits, making it harder for them to bridge.

2. Transition to low mount by sliding your knees back and applying pressure on their hips.

3. Use technical mount to control their upper body and set up submissions, keeping your knee near their head and the other foot posted.

Mastering the mount position is essential for any BJJ practitioner. The mount offers numerous opportunities for control and attacks, including submissions like the armbar, Americana, and mounted triangle. Maintaining a strong base and balance, applying pressure and control, and transitioning fluidly between different mount variations will enhance your ability to dominate your opponent. Consistent practice and understanding of these techniques will significantly improve your effectiveness in the mount position, making it a key part of your BJJ arsenal.

## *7.2 Side Control: Transitions and Submissions*

Side control, also known as side mount, is a dominant position in Brazilian Jiu-Jitsu (BJJ) that offers strong control over your opponent and numerous opportunities for transitions and submissions. This section focuses on maintaining side control, executing effective transitions, and applying submissions.

*Brazilian Jiu-Jitsu Side Control*

## **<u>*A. Transitions*</u>**

1. Knee on Belly - Transitioning to knee on belly can increase pressure and create submission opportunities.

   - Technique:

   1. From side control, slide your knee across your opponent's abdomen, placing it firmly on their belly.

   2. Keep your other leg posted for balance, and your hands controlling their collar or head.

   3. Use this position to apply pressure, control their movements, and set up attacks.

2. Mount - Transitioning from side control to mount secures an even more dominant position.

- Technique:

1. From side control, slide your knee across your opponent's abdomen or hips.

2. Use your hands to control their far arm or collar to stabilize yourself.

3. As you shift your weight, bring your other leg over their body to establish the mount position.

3. North-South - Transition to north-south to maintain control and set up different submissions.

- Technique:

1. From side control, pivot your body around your opponent's head.

2. Maintain chest-to-chest pressure while moving your hips and legs to align with their head.

3. Keep your weight centered to prevent escapes and prepare for submissions like the north-south choke.

## *B. Submissions*

1. Kimura - A powerful shoulder lock applied from side control.

- Technique:

1. Isolate your opponent's far arm by pinning their wrist to the mat.

2. Slide your hand under their arm, grasping your own wrist to create a figure-four grip.

3. Lift their elbow while keeping their wrist pinned, applying pressure to the shoulder joint.

2. Arm Triangle - A choke that compresses the opponent's carotid arteries.

- Technique:

1. From side control, slide your arm under your opponent's neck and across their far arm.

2. Join your hands and apply chest pressure, driving your shoulder into their neck.

3. Walk towards their head to tighten the choke and force a tap.

3. Americana - Similar to the Americana from mount, this shoulder lock can be applied from side control.

   - Technique:

   1. Pin your opponent's wrist to the mat with one hand.

   2. Slide your other hand under their arm, grasping your own wrist to create a figure-four grip.

   3. Lift their elbow while keeping their wrist pinned, applying pressure to the shoulder joint.

4. Baseball Bat Choke - A choke that uses a gi grip similar to holding a baseball bat.

   - Technique:

   1. From side control, grip your opponent's collar with both hands, one palm up and the other palm down, like holding a baseball bat.

   2. Slide your elbows to the mat while maintaining the grip.

   3. Apply pressure by dropping your weight and squeezing your hands together to tighten the choke.

Mastering side control is essential for any BJJ practitioner. It provides a stable platform for applying pressure, executing transitions, and setting up a variety of submissions. By learning to maintain control, perform effective transitions to positions like knee on belly, mount, and north-south, and apply submissions like the Kimura, arm triangle, Americana, and baseball bat choke, you can dominate your opponent from side control. Consistent practice and understanding of these techniques will enhance your ability to control and submit opponents, making side control a key part of your BJJ arsenal.

## *7.3 North-South: Control and Offensive Options*

The north-south position in Brazilian Jiu-Jitsu (BJJ) is a dominant top control position that provides excellent control over your opponent and offers various offensive options. This section focuses on maintaining control in the north-south position and executing effective submissions and transitions from there.

## *A. Control*

1. Head and Arm Control - Maintaining control of your opponent's head and arms is crucial in the north-south position.

- Technique:

1. Position your chest over your opponent's head, ensuring your weight is centered.

2. Use your arms to control their arms by gripping their elbows or wrists, preventing them from creating space or escaping.

3. Keep your hips low and legs wide for a stable base.

2. Maintaining Position - Use your legs and hips to balance and adjust your position in response to your opponent's movements.

- Technique:

1. Stay on your toes, ready to shift your weight and adjust your position.

2. Use small movements to counter your opponent's attempts to escape, maintaining tight control over their upper body.

## *B. Offensive Options*

1. North-South Choke - A choke that uses your arms and body weight to apply pressure to the opponent's neck.

- Technique:

1. From the north-south position, wrap your arm around your opponent's neck, with your bicep on one side and forearm on the other.

2. Grip your hands together, with your free hand grabbing your wrist.

3. Apply pressure by lowering your body and squeezing your arms together, compressing their neck.

2. Kimura - Transition to a Kimura from north-south for a powerful shoulder lock.

- Technique:

    1. Control your opponent's far arm by pinning their wrist to the mat.

    2. Slide your hand under their arm, creating a figure-four grip by grasping your own wrist.

    3. Lift their elbow while keeping their wrist pinned, applying pressure to the shoulder joint.

3. Armbar - Set up an armbar from north-south by isolating one of your opponent's arms.

    - Technique:

    1. Control your opponent's far arm, positioning it across your body.

    2. Transition to one side, sliding your knee over their head and sitting back.

    3. Extend your hips to apply pressure to the elbow joint, forcing a tap.

4. Transition to Side Control - Move back to side control to maintain top dominance and continue your attack.

    - Technique:

    1. Pivot around your opponent's head, keeping your chest low and maintaining control of their arm.

    2. Settle back into side control, ready to apply submissions like the Kimura or Americana.

5. Reverse Triangle Choke - Apply a reverse triangle choke by trapping your opponent's head and arm with your legs.

    - Technique:

    1. From the north-south position, use your legs to encircle your opponent's head and one arm.

    2. Lock your legs together in a triangle shape, squeezing to apply the choke.

    3. Adjust your body position to increase pressure and ensure a secure choke.

Mastering the north-south position is essential for any BJJ practitioner seeking to dominate their opponent and apply effective submissions. By maintaining control through head and arm control, and using your legs and hips to balance, you can effectively neutralize your opponent's movements. The north-south position offers various offensive options, including the north-south choke, Kimura, armbar, and reverse triangle choke, providing numerous opportunities to submit your opponent. Consistent practice and understanding of these techniques will enhance your ability to control and finish your opponent from the north-south position, making it a valuable addition to your BJJ arsenal.

## *7.4 Knee on Belly: Pressure and Movement*

The knee on belly position in Brazilian Jiu-Jitsu (BJJ) is a versatile top control position that applies significant pressure on your opponent and allows for quick transitions and attacks. This section focuses on applying and maintaining pressure in the knee on belly position, as well as executing effective movements and attacks from this position.

*Brazilian Jiu-Jitsu Knee on Belly*

## *A. Pressure*

1. Applying Pressure - The primary goal of the knee on belly position is to apply pressure to your opponent's abdomen, causing discomfort and limiting their breathing.

   - Technique:

1. From side control, slide your knee across your opponent's abdomen, placing it firmly on their belly.

2. Keep your other leg posted out to the side for balance.

3. Use your hands to control their collar or head, maintaining pressure and stability.

2. Maintaining Control - Balance your weight to prevent your opponent from escaping or rolling.

- Technique:

1. Keep your weight centered on your knee, using your hands to control your opponent's upper body.

2. Adjust your position in response to your opponent's movements, shifting your weight as needed to maintain pressure.

3. Be ready to move your knee or adjust your base to counter their escape attempts.

## *B. Movement*

1. Transitions - Use knee on belly to transition to mount, side control, or back control.

- Technique:

1. To transition to mount, slide your knee across your opponent's body and bring your other leg over their hips, securing the mount position.

2. To transition back to side control, slide your knee off their abdomen and settle into side control, maintaining pressure.

3. To transition to back control, create space and slide your knee off their body, moving around to their back and securing hooks.

2. Attacks - Set up submissions like armbars, chokes, and other attacks from the knee on belly position.

- Technique:

1. Armbar:

- Control your opponent's far arm, pulling it towards you.

   - Slide your knee over their head and sit back, securing the armbar.

   2. Baseball Bat Choke:

   - Grip your opponent's collar with one hand palm up and the other palm down, like holding a baseball bat.

   - Slide your knee across their body and apply pressure to tighten the choke.

   3. Cross Choke:

   - Grip your opponent's collar with both hands, one on each side.

   - Use your knee to apply pressure while tightening the choke with your hands.

3. Dynamic Movement - Use the knee on belly position to move dynamically, keeping your opponent off balance and unable to mount an effective defense.

   - Technique:

   1. Constantly shift your weight and adjust your knee position to keep your opponent uncomfortable.

   2. Move fluidly between knee on belly, mount, and side control to maintain dominance and create opportunities for attacks.

Mastering the knee on belly position is essential for any BJJ practitioner seeking to dominate their opponent and apply effective pressure and attacks. By learning to apply and maintain pressure, execute transitions to other dominant positions, and set up submissions like armbars and chokes, you can effectively control and submit your opponent from the knee on belly position. Consistent practice and understanding of these techniques will enhance your ability to use the knee on belly position to your advantage, making it a valuable part of your BJJ skill set.

# *Chapter 7 Review: Top Control and Dominance*

Mastering top control positions is essential for dominating your opponent in Brazilian Jiu-Jitsu (BJJ). This chapter covers various top control positions, including mount, side control, north-south, and knee on belly, providing strategies for maintaining control and executing effective attacks.

## - 7.1 Mount: Attacks and Maintenance:

- Attacks: The mount position offers numerous submission opportunities, such as the armbar, Americana, and mounted triangle.

- Example: Isolate your opponent's arm for an armbar by sliding your knee up and swinging your leg over their head.

- Maintenance: Maintain a low center of gravity and wide base to prevent being rolled off.

- Example: Spread your knees and keep your hips low, adjusting your weight in response to your opponent's movements.

- Pressure and Control: Use your body weight to apply pressure and control your opponent's upper body.

- Example: Apply chest-to-chest pressure and grip your opponent's head or arms to limit their movement.

## - 7.2 Side Control: Transitions and Submissions:

- Transitions: Move fluidly between positions like knee on belly, mount, and north-south to maintain control and set up attacks.

- Example: Slide your knee across your opponent's abdomen to transition to knee on belly.

- Submissions: Execute submissions such as the Kimura, arm triangle, and Americana from side control.

- Example: Pin your opponent's wrist to the mat, slide your hand under their arm, and lift their elbow to apply the Americana.

## - 7.3 North-South: Control and Offensive Options:

- Control: Maintain control by keeping your chest over your opponent's head and using your arms to control their arms.

- Example: Stay on your toes, ready to shift your weight and adjust your position.

- Offensive Options: Apply submissions like the north-south choke, Kimura, and armbar from the north-south position.

   - Example: Wrap your arm around your opponent's neck and apply pressure to execute the north-south choke.

**- 7.4 Knee on Belly: Pressure and Movement:**

   - Pressure: Apply pressure to your opponent's abdomen, causing discomfort and limiting their breathing.

   - Example: Place your knee on their belly and keep your other leg posted for balance.

   - Movement: Use the knee on belly position to transition to mount, side control, or back control.

   - Example: Slide your knee across their body to move into the mount position.

   - Attacks: Set up submissions like armbars and chokes from the knee on belly position.

   - Example: Control your opponent's far arm and swing your leg over their head to secure the armbar.

Understanding and practicing these top control positions are crucial for success in Brazilian Jiu-Jitsu. The mount, side control, north-south, and knee on belly positions provide strong control and numerous submission opportunities. By maintaining control, applying pressure, and executing effective transitions and attacks, you can dominate your opponent from these positions. Consistent practice and understanding of these techniques will enhance your ability to control and submit opponents, making top control a key part of your BJJ arsenal.

# Chapter 8: Fundamental Submission Techniques

Mastering fundamental submission techniques is essential for any Brazilian Jiu-Jitsu (BJJ) practitioner. This chapter covers the essential chokes, joint locks, and leg locks that form the core of BJJ's offensive arsenal.

## *8.1 Chokes: Rear Naked Choke, Guillotine, Cross Collar*

Chokes are fundamental techniques in Brazilian Jiu-Jitsu (BJJ) that can render an opponent unconscious by restricting blood flow or air. This section covers three essential chokes: the rear naked choke, the guillotine choke, and the cross collar choke.

### *A. Rear Naked Choke*

*Brazilian Jiu-Jitsu Rear Naked Choke*

1. Setup - Secure back control with hooks in place.

   - Example: Position yourself behind your opponent, with your legs wrapped around their waist and hooks secured.

2. Technique - Slide one arm around their neck, securing a figure-four lock with your other arm.

   - Steps:

      1. Slide your choking arm under your opponent's chin, with your hand reaching towards your own bicep.

      2. Use your free hand to push their head forward while locking your hands in a figure-four grip.

      3. Squeeze your arms and apply pressure to their neck, forcing a tap or rendering them unconscious.

3. Key Points:

   - Ensure your choking arm is deep under the chin to apply maximum pressure.

   - Maintain a tight figure-four grip to prevent your opponent from escaping.

   - Use your chest and back muscles to increase the pressure of the choke.

## *B. Guillotine*

1. Setup - Control your opponent's head and neck from a standing position or guard.

   - Example: Grip their neck and pull it down while securing a grip with your arms.

2. Technique - Wrap your arm around their neck, applying pressure to the throat.

   - Steps:

      1. Wrap your arm around your opponent's neck, with your hand reaching towards your opposite armpit.

      2. Secure your grip by locking your hands together.

      3. Sit back and apply pressure by pulling up with your arms and squeezing, cutting off their airway or blood flow.

3. Key Points:

- Ensure your arm is deep around the neck to effectively cut off airflow or blood flow.

- Use your legs to stabilize your position and prevent your opponent from escaping.

- Lean back and use your body weight to increase the pressure of the choke.

## *C. Cross Collar Choke*

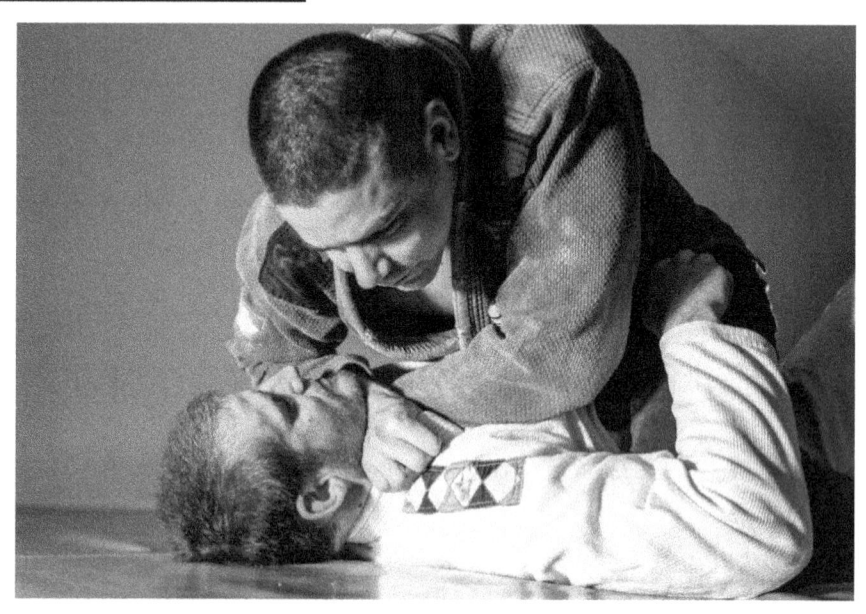

*Brazilian Jiu-Jitsu Cross Collar Choke*

1. Setup - Secure a grip on your opponent's collar from the guard position.

  - Example: Grip their collar with one hand, inserting your thumb inside.

2. Technique - Use your other hand to grab the opposite side of their collar, creating a choking effect.

  - Steps:

    1. Insert your second hand across their neck, gripping the opposite collar.

    2. Cross your arms and pull their collar towards you, tightening the choke.

    3. Apply pressure by pulling your elbows back and squeezing, restricting their blood flow.

3. Key Points:

- Ensure your grips on the collar are deep and secure to apply effective pressure.

- Cross your arms tightly to maximize the choking effect.

- Use your legs to stabilize your position and prevent your opponent from escaping.

Mastering chokes is essential for any BJJ practitioner. The rear naked choke, guillotine, and cross collar choke are fundamental techniques that provide powerful submission options. By learning the setups, techniques, and key points for each choke, you can effectively control and submit your opponents. Consistent practice and understanding of these techniques will enhance your ability to apply chokes in various situations, making them a critical part of your BJJ skill set.

## *8.2 Joint Locks: Armbar, Kimura, Americana*

Joint locks are essential techniques in Brazilian Jiu-Jitsu (BJJ) that target specific joints, applying pressure to force a submission. This section covers three fundamental joint locks: the armbar, Kimura, and Americana.

## *A. Armbar*

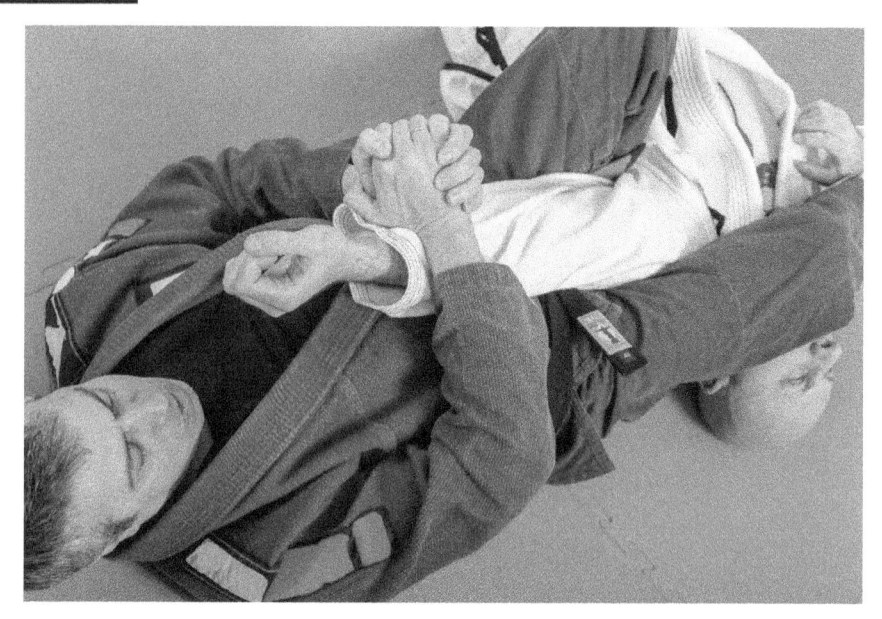

*Brazilian Jiu-Jitsu Armbar*

1. Setup - Isolate your opponent's arm from the guard or mount position.

   - Example: Control their wrist and elbow, positioning your legs to trap their arm.

2. Technique - Extend your hips to apply pressure to the elbow joint.

   - Steps:

     1. Control your opponent's arm by gripping their wrist with one hand and their elbow with the other.

     2. Place one of your legs across their chest while the other leg swings over their head.

     3. Pinch your knees together to trap their arm and prevent escape.

     4. Lean back and extend your hips to apply pressure to the elbow joint, forcing a tap.

3. Key Points:

   - Ensure your knees are tight around their arm to maintain control.

   - Keep your opponent's thumb pointing upwards to maximize the pressure on their elbow.

- Use your hips, not just your arms, to apply the finishing pressure.

## *B. Kimura*

*Brazilian Jiu-Jitsu Kimura*

1. Setup - Control your opponent's wrist and elbow from the guard or side control position.

   - Example: Secure a figure-four grip on their arm.

2. Technique - Use your hips to apply pressure to their shoulder joint.

   - Steps:

      1. Control your opponent's wrist with one hand while reaching over their arm to grab your own wrist, creating a figure-four grip.

      2. From guard, sit up to bring your opponent's arm behind their back. From side control, use your body weight to lift their elbow.

      3. Rotate your hips and apply pressure to their shoulder joint by lifting their elbow while keeping their wrist pinned, forcing a tap.

3. Key Points:

   - Maintain a tight figure-four grip to prevent your opponent from escaping.

   - Use your entire body to apply pressure, not just your arms.

- Ensure your opponent's arm is bent at a 90-degree angle to maximize the pressure on their shoulder.

## *C. Americana*

*Brazilian Jiu-Jitsu Americana Americana Arm Lock*

1. Setup - Pin your opponent's wrist to the mat from the mount or side control position.

　- Example: Control their arm, securing a figure-four grip.

2. Technique - Lift their elbow while keeping their wrist pinned to apply pressure to the shoulder joint.

　- Steps:

　　1. Pin your opponent's wrist to the mat with one hand while sliding your other hand under their arm, grabbing your own wrist to create a figure-four grip.

　　2. From mount, use your body weight to pin their wrist. From side control, maintain control with your upper body.

　　3. Lift their elbow while keeping their wrist pinned to the mat, applying pressure to their shoulder joint, forcing a tap.

3. Key Points:

- Ensure a strong figure-four grip to maintain control of your opponent's arm.

- Use your body weight to keep their wrist pinned while lifting their elbow.

- Keep their arm bent at a 90-degree angle to effectively apply pressure to their shoulder.

Mastering joint locks is crucial for any BJJ practitioner. The armbar, Kimura, and Americana are fundamental techniques that provide powerful submission options. By learning the setups, techniques, and key points for each joint lock, you can effectively control and submit your opponents. Consistent practice and understanding of these techniques will enhance your ability to apply joint locks in various situations, making them a critical part of your BJJ skill set.

## 8.3 Leg Locks: Straight Ankle Lock, Heel Hook, Toe Hold

Leg locks are powerful techniques in Brazilian Jiu-Jitsu (BJJ) that target the lower extremities, applying pressure to the joints to force a submission. This section covers three fundamental leg locks: the straight ankle lock, heel hook, and toe hold.

### *A. Straight Ankle Lock*

1. Setup - Control your opponent's leg, securing their ankle from the guard or leg entanglement position.

   - Example: Wrap your arm around their ankle, gripping it tightly.

2. Technique - Extend your hips to apply pressure to the ankle joint.

   - Steps:

     1. Control their ankle by wrapping your arm around it, with your hand gripping their shin.

     2. Place your other hand on your own wrist to secure the grip.

     3. Position your foot on their hip to create leverage.

4. Extend your hips while pulling back with your arms, applying pressure to the ankle joint and forcing a tap.

3. Key Points:

   - Ensure a tight grip on your opponent's ankle and shin to maintain control.

   - Use your hips to apply pressure, not just your arms.

   - Keep your opponent's leg extended and control their movement with your legs.

## *B. Heel Hook*

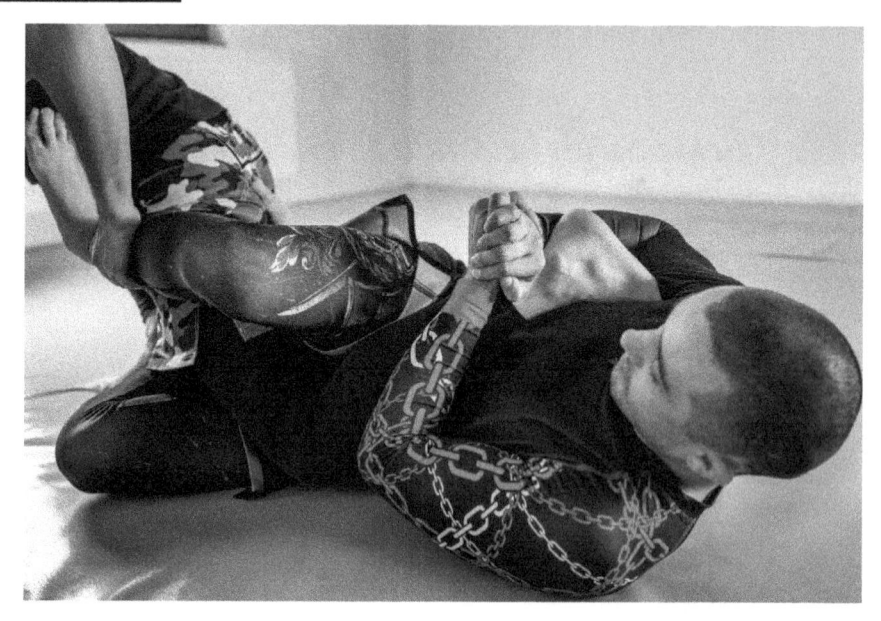

*Brazilian Jiu-Jitsu Heel Hook*

1. Setup - Control your opponent's leg, securing their heel from the guard or leg entanglement position.

   - Example: Wrap your arm around their heel, gripping it tightly.

2. Technique - Rotate your hips to apply pressure to the knee joint.

   - Steps:

     1. Control their heel by wrapping your arm around it, with your hand gripping their foot.

     2. Secure your grip by locking your hands together.

3. Position your legs to control their movement and prevent escape.

4. Rotate your hips while twisting your body, applying pressure to their knee joint and forcing a tap.

3. Key Points:

   - Ensure a secure grip on your opponent's heel to prevent them from escaping.

   - Use your entire body to apply pressure, not just your arms.

   - Be cautious with the heel hook, as it can cause severe knee injuries.

## *C. Toe Hold*

*Brazilian Jiu-Jitsu Toe Hold*

1. Setup - Control your opponent's foot, securing their toes from the guard or leg entanglement position.

   - Example: Wrap your arm around their foot, gripping their toes tightly.

2. Technique - Use your hips to apply pressure to the ankle and toe joints.

   - Steps:

   1. Control their foot by wrapping your arm around it, with your hand gripping their toes.

2. Secure your grip by locking your hands together.

   3. Position your legs to control their movement and prevent escape.

   4. Twist your body while pushing your hips forward, applying pressure to their ankle and toe joints and forcing a tap.

3. Key Points:

   - Ensure a tight grip on your opponent's foot and toes to maintain control.

   - Use your hips to apply pressure, not just your arms.

   - Maintain control of their leg to prevent them from escaping or countering.

Mastering leg locks is crucial for any BJJ practitioner. The straight ankle lock, heel hook, and toe hold are fundamental techniques that provide powerful submission options. By learning the setups, techniques, and key points for each leg lock, you can effectively control and submit your opponents. Consistent practice and understanding of these techniques will enhance your ability to apply leg locks in various situations, making them a critical part of your BJJ skill set.

# *Chapter 8 Review: Fundamental Submission Techniques*

Mastering fundamental submission techniques is essential for any Brazilian Jiu-Jitsu (BJJ) practitioner. This chapter covers the essential chokes, joint locks, and leg locks that form the core of BJJ's offensive arsenal.

**- 8.1 Chokes: Rear Naked Choke, Guillotine, Cross Collar:**

   - Rear Naked Choke: Secure back control with hooks in place, slide one arm around the opponent's neck, and apply pressure by locking your hands in a figure-four grip, forcing a tap or rendering them unconscious.

   - Guillotine: Control the opponent's head and neck, wrap your arm around their neck, secure your grip, and apply pressure by pulling up and squeezing to cut off airflow or blood flow.

- Cross Collar Choke: From the guard, grip the opponent's collar, insert your second hand across their neck to grab the opposite collar, and apply pressure by pulling your elbows back and squeezing.

### - 8.2 Joint Locks: Armbar, Kimura, Americana:

- Armbar: Isolate the opponent's arm from guard or mount, control their wrist and elbow, swing your leg over their head, and extend your hips to apply pressure to the elbow joint.

- Kimura: Control the opponent's wrist and elbow from guard or side control, secure a figure-four grip, rotate your hips, and apply pressure to their shoulder joint.

- Americana: Pin the opponent's wrist to the mat from mount or side control, secure a figure-four grip, lift their elbow while keeping their wrist pinned, and apply pressure to their shoulder joint.

### - 8.3 Leg Locks: Straight Ankle Lock, Heel Hook, Toe Hold:

- Straight Ankle Lock: Control the opponent's leg, secure their ankle, extend your hips, and apply pressure to the ankle joint to force a tap.

- Heel Hook: Control the opponent's leg, secure their heel, rotate your hips, and apply pressure to the knee joint.

- Toe Hold: Control the opponent's foot, secure their toes, use your hips to apply pressure to the ankle and toe joints, and force a tap.

Understanding and practicing these fundamental submission techniques are crucial for success in Brazilian Jiu-Jitsu. Chokes like the rear naked choke, guillotine, and cross collar choke, joint locks like the armbar, Kimura, and Americana, and leg locks like the straight ankle lock, heel hook, and toe hold form the core of BJJ's offensive arsenal. By mastering the setups, techniques, and key points for each submission, you can effectively control and submit your opponents. Consistent practice and understanding of these techniques will enhance your ability to apply submissions in various situations, making them a critical part of your BJJ skill set.

# Part 4: Intermediate Techniques and Strategies

Advancing in Brazilian Jiu-Jitsu (BJJ) requires a solid understanding of intermediate techniques and strategies. This part delves into effective sweeps and reversals, which are crucial for transitioning from defensive to offensive positions.

# Chapter 9: Effective Sweeps and Reversals

Sweeps and reversals allow you to transition from a defensive position to a dominant one, giving you the upper hand in a match. This chapter covers several fundamental sweeps that every BJJ practitioner should master.

*Brazilian Jiu-Jitsu Sweep*

## 9.1 Scissor Sweep

The scissor sweep is a fundamental and effective technique in Brazilian Jiu-Jitsu (BJJ) that uses a scissoring motion of the legs to off-balance and topple your opponent. It is an essential sweep that every practitioner should master, as it combines leverage, timing, and technique to transition from a defensive position to a dominant one.

## A. Setup

1. Guard Position - Begin in closed guard and establish grips on your opponent's collar and sleeve.

   - Example: Secure your opponent's collar with your right hand and their opposite sleeve with your left hand.

2. Create Angle - Open your guard and shift your hips to create an angle.

   - Example: Open your legs, pivot your hips to the side, and position your right shin across your opponent's abdomen while your left leg is positioned to sweep.

## B. Execution

1. Scissor Motion - Use a scissoring motion with your legs to off-balance and sweep your opponent.

   - Steps:

     1. Pull: Pull your opponent towards you using your grips on their collar and sleeve, breaking their posture.

     2. Push and Pull with Legs: Simultaneously, push with your right shin against their abdomen while pulling your left leg towards you, creating a scissoring motion.

     3. Sweep: Use the momentum generated by the scissor motion to sweep your opponent over your left leg.

     4. Transition: As your opponent falls, follow through by coming up into the mount position or another dominant position.

## C. Key Points

1. Grip Control - Maintain strong grips on your opponent's collar and sleeve to control their posture and direction.

- Example: Keep your grips tight and use them to pull your opponent towards you, breaking their balance.

2. Hip Movement - Pivot your hips effectively to create the necessary angle for the sweep.

- Example: Use your hips to generate leverage and power for the scissoring motion.

3. Leg Coordination - Coordinate the push and pull of your legs to create the scissoring motion.

- Example: Ensure that your pushing leg (right shin) and pulling leg (left leg) work together to off-balance your opponent.

4. Follow Through - Transition smoothly into a dominant position after completing the sweep.

- Example: As your opponent falls, use the momentum to come up into mount, securing a dominant position and preparing for further attacks or control.

The scissor sweep is a vital technique in BJJ that allows practitioners to transition from a defensive guard position to a dominant top position. By mastering the setup, execution, and key points of the scissor sweep, you can effectively off-balance and sweep your opponent, gaining a significant advantage. Consistent practice of the scissor sweep will enhance your ability to control and dominate opponents, making it a crucial part of your BJJ skill set.

## *9.2 Flower Sweep*

The flower sweep, also known as the pendulum sweep, is a powerful technique in Brazilian Jiu-Jitsu (BJJ) that uses a pendulum-like motion to destabilize and sweep your opponent. It is an effective way to transition from the guard to a dominant top position.

### *A. Setup*

1. Guard Position - Begin in closed guard and control one of your opponent's arms and the opposite leg.

- Example: Grip your opponent's right sleeve with your left hand and their left pant leg with your right hand.

2. Create Angle - Open your guard and create an angle to initiate the sweep.

   - Example: Open your legs and swing your body to the right, positioning your left leg under your opponent's right armpit while your right leg is ready to swing.

## *B. Execution*

1. Pendulum Motion - Swing your leg like a pendulum to generate momentum and off-balance your opponent.

   - Steps:

     1. Pull and Lift: Pull your opponent's right arm towards you while lifting their left leg with your grip.

     2. Swing: Swing your right leg in a wide arc to create momentum, using it as a pendulum to off-balance your opponent.

     3. Sweep: As your right leg swings down, use the momentum to lift your opponent's hips and sweep them over your left leg.

     4. Transition: Follow through by coming up into the mount position or another dominant position.

## *C. Key Points*

1. Grip Control - Maintain strong grips on your opponent's sleeve and pant leg to control their posture and movement.

   - Example: Keep your grips tight and use them to pull your opponent towards you, breaking their balance.

2. Angle Creation - Create a sharp angle by pivoting your hips to generate the necessary leverage for the sweep.

   - Example: Swing your body to the side, positioning your leg under your opponent's armpit to enhance the pendulum motion.

3. Leg Swing - Use your leg swing to generate momentum and off-balance your opponent.

- Example: Ensure your swinging leg moves in a wide arc to create the necessary force for the sweep.

4. Follow Through - Transition smoothly into a dominant position after completing the sweep.

   - Example: As your opponent falls, use the momentum to come up into mount, securing a dominant position and preparing for further attacks or control.

The flower sweep is a versatile and powerful technique in BJJ that allows practitioners to transition from a defensive guard position to a dominant top position. By mastering the setup, execution, and key points of the flower sweep, you can effectively off-balance and sweep your opponent, gaining a significant advantage. Consistent practice of the flower sweep will enhance your ability to control and dominate opponents, making it a crucial part of your BJJ skill set.

## *9.3 Hip Bump Sweep*

The hip bump sweep is a dynamic and effective technique in Brazilian Jiu-Jitsu (BJJ) that uses the power of your hips to off-balance and sweep your opponent. It is particularly useful when your opponent is postured up or attempting to pass your guard.

### *A. Setup*

1. Guard Position - Begin in closed guard and sit up, securing a grip on your opponent's waist or shoulder.

   - Example: Open your guard and post on one hand to sit up, reaching over your opponent's shoulder or gripping their waist.

2. Create Angle - Position your hips close to your opponent's body.

   - Example: Scoot your hips closer to your opponent to ensure your body is aligned for the sweep.

### *B. Execution*

1. Hip Bump - Use your hips to bump and off-balance your opponent.

- Steps:

1. Post and Reach: Open your guard, plant one foot on the mat, and post on your opposite hand to sit up.

2. Grip and Lift: Reach over your opponent's shoulder with your free hand, gripping their waist or shoulder to control their upper body.

3. Drive Hips: Drive your hips forward into your opponent's chest or shoulder, using the momentum to lift them.

4. Follow Through: Follow through with the motion, sweeping your opponent to their back and transitioning to mount or a dominant position.

## *C. Key Points*

1. Grip Control - Maintain strong grips on your opponent's waist or shoulder to control their posture and movement.

- Example: Use your grip to pull your opponent towards you, breaking their balance.

2. Hip Movement - Use explosive hip movement to generate the necessary force for the sweep.

- Example: Drive your hips forward with power, using the planted foot on the mat to push off and lift your opponent.

3. Follow Through - Transition smoothly into a dominant position after completing the sweep.

- Example: As your opponent falls, use the momentum to come up into mount, securing a dominant position and preparing for further attacks or control.

4. Timing and Leverage - Execute the sweep when your opponent is postured up or attempting to pass your guard, using their momentum against them.

- Example: Time your hip bump as your opponent starts to rise or shift their weight forward, making it easier to off-balance them.

The hip bump sweep is a versatile and effective technique in BJJ that allows practitioners to transition from a defensive guard position to a dominant top position. By mastering the setup, execution, and key points of the hip bump sweep, you can effectively off-balance and sweep your opponent, gaining a significant advantage. Consistent practice of the hip bump sweep will enhance your ability to control and dominate opponents, making it a crucial part of your BJJ skill set.

## *9.4 Butterfly Guard Sweeps*

The butterfly guard is a versatile and dynamic position in Brazilian Jiu-Jitsu (BJJ) that allows for effective sweeps by using hooks and leverage to off-balance the opponent. Mastering butterfly guard sweeps can significantly enhance your ability to transition from a defensive to an offensive position.

### *A. Setup*

1. Butterfly Guard Position - Sit up with your legs hooked inside your opponent's thighs.

   - Example: Sit with an upright posture, your feet placed as hooks inside your opponent's inner thighs, and your hands controlling their arms or collars.

2. Control Grips - Secure grips on your opponent's arms or collars to control their upper body.

   - Example: Grip your opponent's sleeves or collar to maintain control and prevent them from posturing up.

### *B. Execution*

1. Lifting Motion - Use your hooks to lift and off-balance your opponent.

   - Steps:

     1. Establish Hooks and Grips: Ensure your feet are firmly hooked inside your opponent's thighs and your grips on their arms or collars are secure.

     2. Create Angle: Lean back slightly to create space and pull your opponent forward.

     3. Lift and Sweep: Use your hooks to lift your opponent's legs while simultaneously pulling with your grips to off-balance them. Sweep your opponent to the side or over your head, using the momentum to come on top.

## *C. Key Points*

1. Grip Control - Maintain strong grips on your opponent's arms or collars to control their posture and direction.

   - Example: Use your grips to pull your opponent forward, breaking their balance and setting up the sweep.

2. Hook Placement - Ensure your hooks are deep inside your opponent's thighs for maximum control and leverage.

   - Example: Position your feet to effectively lift your opponent's legs and disrupt their base.

3. Body Movement - Use your body weight and momentum to enhance the effectiveness of the sweep.

   - Example: Lean back to create space and generate momentum, then drive forward and up with your hooks to complete the sweep.

4. Follow Through - Transition smoothly into a dominant position after completing the sweep.

   - Example: As your opponent falls, follow through by coming up into mount or side control, securing a dominant position and preparing for further attacks or control.

## *D. Variations*

1. Standard Butterfly Sweep - A basic sweep using the butterfly guard position.

   - Steps:

     1. Lean back slightly and pull your opponent forward with your grips.

     2. Use your hooks to lift their legs while sweeping them to the side.

     3. Follow through by transitioning to a dominant top position.

2. Reverse Butterfly Sweep - A variation where you sweep your opponent in the opposite direction.

   - Steps:

     1. Secure grips and hooks as in the standard butterfly sweep.

2. Instead of sweeping to the side, use your hooks to lift and direct your opponent in the opposite direction.

3. Follow through by transitioning to a dominant top position.

3. Butterfly Sweep to Arm Drag - Combining an arm drag with a butterfly sweep for added control.

 - Steps:

1. Secure grips and hooks, then perform an arm drag to pull your opponent's arm across your body.

2. Use the momentum from the arm drag to initiate the sweep, lifting with your hooks.

3. Follow through by taking your opponent's back or transitioning to a dominant top position.

Mastering butterfly guard sweeps is essential for any BJJ practitioner looking to enhance their offensive capabilities from the guard position. By learning the setup, execution, key points, and variations of butterfly guard sweeps, you can effectively off-balance and sweep your opponent, gaining a significant advantage. Consistent practice of these techniques will enhance your ability to control and dominate opponents, making butterfly guard sweeps a crucial part of your BJJ skill set.

## Chapter 9 Review: Effective Sweeps and Reversals

Mastering sweeps and reversals is crucial for advancing in Brazilian Jiu-Jitsu (BJJ). This chapter covers several fundamental sweeps that every practitioner should master, allowing you to transition from a defensive position to a dominant one.

- **9.1 Scissor Sweep:**

  - Setup: Start in closed guard, establish grips on your opponent's collar and sleeve, and create an angle by shifting your hips.

- Example: Secure your opponent's collar with your right hand and their opposite sleeve with your left hand. Open your legs and pivot your hips to the side.

- Execution: Use a scissoring motion with your legs to off-balance and sweep your opponent.

- Example: Pull your opponent towards you with your grips, push with your right shin against their abdomen while pulling your left leg towards you, and use the momentum to sweep your opponent to their back, transitioning to mount.

### - 9.2 Flower Sweep:

- Setup: Start in closed guard, control one of your opponent's arms and the opposite leg, and create an angle by swinging your body to the side.

- Example: Grip your opponent's right sleeve with your left hand and their left pant leg with your right hand. Open your legs and swing your body to the right.

- Execution: Use a pendulum-like motion with your leg to generate momentum and off-balance your opponent.

- Example: Pull your opponent's right arm towards you while lifting their left leg with your grip. Swing your right leg in a wide arc, using the momentum to lift your opponent's hips and sweep them over your left leg, transitioning to mount.

### - 9.3 Hip Bump Sweep:

- Setup: Start in closed guard, sit up by posting on one hand, and secure a grip on your opponent's waist or shoulder.

- Example: Open your guard, post on your left hand to sit up, and reach over your opponent's right shoulder with your right hand.

- Execution: Use your hips to bump and off-balance your opponent.

- Example: Drive your hips forward into your opponent's chest or shoulder, using the momentum to lift them and sweep them to their back, transitioning to mount or a dominant position.

### - 9.4 Butterfly Guard Sweeps:

- Setup: Sit up with your legs hooked inside your opponent's thighs, securing grips on their arms or collars.

    - Example: Position your feet as hooks inside your opponent's legs while maintaining an upright posture and gripping their sleeves or collar.

- Execution: Use your hooks to lift and off-balance your opponent.

    - Example: Lean back to create space and pull your opponent forward, then use your hooks to lift their legs while pulling with your grips to sweep your opponent to the side or over your head, transitioning to a dominant position.

Understanding and practicing these fundamental sweeps are crucial for success in Brazilian Jiu-Jitsu. Techniques like the scissor sweep, flower sweep, hip bump sweep, and butterfly guard sweeps allow you to transition from defense to offense, gaining dominant positions. Consistent practice and understanding of these techniques will enhance your ability to control and dominate your opponents, making these sweeps a vital part of your BJJ repertoire.

# Chapter 10: Advanced Guard Techniques

The advanced guard techniques in Brazilian Jiu-Jitsu offer practitioners a wide array of options for controlling, sweeping, and submitting opponents. This chapter delves into four highly effective and versatile guard positions: the De La Riva Guard, Spider Guard, X-Guard, and Lasso Guard. Each section will provide detailed instruction on how to establish these guards, maintain control, and execute successful sweeps and attacks. By mastering these advanced techniques, practitioners can significantly enhance their guard game, creating a formidable defense and a dynamic offense.

## *10.1 De La Riva Guard: Entries and Sweeps*

The De La Riva Guard, named after Ricardo de la Riva, is a highly versatile and dynamic guard position in Brazilian Jiu-Jitsu. It focuses on using the legs to create distance, control, and leverage to set up sweeps and transitions.

*Brazilian Jiu-Jitsu De La Riva Guard*

## *A. Establishing the De La Riva Guard*

1. Basic Entry: Start from an open guard with your opponent standing. Hook your outside leg around the back of their knee, using your foot to create leverage. Position your other leg to control their movements.

2. Control Points: Secure a grip on the opponent's ankle with the same side hand as your hooked leg, and use your opposite hand to grip their sleeve or collar. These grips are crucial for maintaining balance and manipulating your opponent's posture.

## *B. Common Entries*

1. From Standing Position: Utilize a lasso guard entry or transition from an open guard as your opponent attempts to pass.

2. From Guard Retention: When your opponent tries to pass your open guard, quickly establish the De La Riva hook to regain control and prevent their progress.

## *C. Sweeps from De La Riva Guard*

**1. Classic De La Riva Sweep:**

   - Control the opponent's far sleeve with your opposite hand and their near ankle with the hand on the same side as your hooked leg.

   - Off-balance your opponent by pulling with your grips while lifting with your De La Riva hook.

   - As your opponent falls, follow through by maintaining your grips and transitioning to a dominant position, such as side control or mount.

**2. Berimbolo Transition:**

   - From the De La Riva Guard, use your hook to invert your body, spinning underneath your opponent.

   - Leverage the momentum to take your opponent's back or sweep them to the ground, securing a dominant position.

Mastering the De La Riva Guard can significantly enhance your ability to control and manipulate your opponent. By effectively utilizing entries and sweeps, you can create opportunities for transitions and submissions, making this advanced guard an essential part of your BJJ arsenal.

## *10.2 Spider Guard: Grip Control and Attacks*

The Spider Guard is a powerful and flexible guard position in Brazilian Jiu-Jitsu that emphasizes controlling your opponent's posture and movements using your legs and grips. Mastering this guard involves precise grip control and effective attacks to keep your opponent off balance and create opportunities for submissions.

### *A. Establishing the Spider Guard*

1. Basic Entry: Start from the open guard with both feet on your opponent's hips. Use your grips on their sleeves to pull them forward while simultaneously placing your feet on their biceps.

2. Control Points: Maintain tension in your legs to control your opponent's arms and posture. Your grips on their sleeves are crucial for manipulating their movements and setting up attacks.

### *B. Common Entries*

1. From Closed Guard: Open your guard and transition to Spider Guard by placing your feet on your opponent's hips and then moving them to their biceps.

2. From Open Guard: Establish grips on your opponent's sleeves and place your feet on their biceps as they attempt to pass or advance.

### *C. Attacks from Spider Guard*

**1. Triangle Choke:**

- Use your legs to pull one of your opponent's arms across your body.

- Transition your legs to lock around their neck and opposite shoulder, securing the choke by squeezing your knees together and pulling their head down.

**2. Armbar:**

- Control one of your opponent's arms with a strong grip on their sleeve.

- Swing your hips out to the side and use your legs to isolate their arm, locking your knees together to secure the armbar.

**3. Omoplata:**

- From the Spider Guard, control one of your opponent's arms and swing your leg over their shoulder.

- Use your hips to rotate, locking their arm and shoulder in a powerful submission.

Mastering the Spider Guard allows you to control and dominate your opponent's movements while setting up a variety of submissions and attacks. By effectively using your grips and legs, you can create numerous opportunities for offensive maneuvers, making the Spider Guard an essential tool in your BJJ repertoire.

## *10.3 X-Guard: Control and Transitions*

The X-Guard is a dynamic and highly effective guard position that emphasizes controlling your opponent's balance and creating opportunities for sweeps and transitions. This guard position allows for excellent leverage and can disrupt even the most stable opponents.

## *A. Establishing the X-Guard*

1. Basic Entry: Start from the open guard or as your opponent stands. Slide under their base and position your legs in an X configuration, with one leg hooking their far leg and the other leg pushing against their near leg.

2. Control Points: Use your hands to grip your opponent's far ankle or knee to stabilize their posture and maintain control.

## B. Common Entries

1. From Single Leg X-Guard: Transition to the full X-Guard by hooking both legs around your opponent's legs, creating the X configuration.

2. From Half Guard: Sweep your opponent and use the momentum to slide into the X-Guard position as they attempt to regain their balance.

## C. Transitions from X-Guard

### 1. Technical Stand-Up:

  - Control your opponent's far ankle and use your legs to off-balance them.

  - Perform a technical stand-up by bringing your base leg underneath you and standing up while maintaining control of their leg.

### 2. Back Take:

  - Use the X-Guard to disrupt your opponent's balance and create space.

  - Transition to their back by releasing your leg hooks and moving around to secure back control.

### 3. Sweep to Mount:

  - Control your opponent's far leg and use your legs to lift and off-balance them.

  - Sweep them to the ground and transition to a dominant mount position, maintaining control throughout the movement.

Mastering the X-Guard provides you with a powerful tool for controlling your opponent's balance and creating numerous opportunities for sweeps and transitions. By effectively using your legs and grips, you can dominate from the bottom and transition to advantageous positions.

## *10.4 Lasso Guard: Creating and Maintaining Control*

The Lasso Guard is a versatile and controlling guard position that allows you to immobilize your opponent and set up various sweeps and submissions. By effectively using your legs and grips, you can control your opponent's posture and create opportunities for attacks.

## *A. Establishing the Lasso Guard*

1. Basic Entry: From the open guard, establish grips on your opponent's sleeves. Thread one of your legs around their arm, hooking their bicep with your leg and maintaining tension.

2. Control Points: Use your lassoed leg to control your opponent's arm and posture. Your grips on their sleeves are vital for maintaining control and setting up attacks.

## *B. Common Entries*

1. From Spider Guard: Transition to the Lasso Guard by threading your leg around your opponent's arm while maintaining your grips.

2. From Closed Guard: Open your guard and establish grips on your opponent's sleeves. Thread your leg around their arm to create the lasso.

## *C. Techniques from Lasso Guard*

### 1. Lasso Sweep:

- Use your lassoed leg to control and off-balance your opponent.

- Sweep them to the side by using your free leg to push against their knee, toppling them over.

### 2. Triangle Setup:

- Use your lassoed leg to pull one of your opponent's arms across your body.

- Transition to a triangle choke by locking your legs around their neck and opposite shoulder.

### 3. Omoplata:

- From the Lasso Guard, control your opponent's arm and swing your leg over their shoulder.

- Rotate your hips to lock their arm and shoulder, securing the omoplata submission.

Mastering the Lasso Guard allows you to effectively control and manipulate your opponent's posture and movements. By utilizing your legs and grips, you can create numerous opportunities for sweeps and submissions, making the Lasso Guard a valuable addition to your BJJ skill set.

# *Chapter 10 Review: Advanced Guard Techniques*

Chapter 10: Advanced Guard Techniques covers four highly effective and versatile guard positions that are essential for any Brazilian Jiu-Jitsu practitioner looking to elevate their guard game. Here's a summary of the key points from each section:


**- 10.1 De La Riva Guard: Entries and Sweeps**

 - The De La Riva Guard, named after Ricardo de la Riva, uses the legs to create distance, control, and leverage.

 - Establish the guard by hooking your outside leg around the opponent's knee and securing grips on their ankle and sleeve.

 - Common entries include transitioning from standing or guard retention.

 - Effective sweeps include the Classic De La Riva Sweep and the Berimbolo Transition.


**- 10.2 Spider Guard: Grip Control and Attacks**

 - The Spider Guard emphasizes controlling the opponent's posture using legs and grips.

 - Establish the guard by placing feet on the opponent's biceps and maintaining strong sleeve grips.

 - Common entries include transitioning from closed guard or open guard.

 - Effective attacks include the Triangle Choke, Armbar, and Omoplata.


**- 10.3 X-Guard: Control and Transitions**

- The X-Guard focuses on controlling the opponent's balance and creating opportunities for sweeps.

- Establish the guard by sliding under the opponent and positioning legs in an X configuration.

- Common entries include transitioning from Single Leg X-Guard or Half Guard.

- Effective transitions include the Technical Stand-Up, Back Take, and Sweep to Mount.

**- 10.4 Lasso Guard: Creating and Maintaining Control**

- The Lasso Guard immobilizes the opponent using a leg threaded around their arm.

- Establish the guard by hooking the opponent's bicep with your leg and maintaining sleeve grips.

- Common entries include transitioning from Spider Guard or Closed Guard.

- Effective techniques include the Lasso Sweep, Triangle Setup, and Omoplata.

Mastering these advanced guard techniques enhances a practitioner's ability to control and manipulate their opponent from the bottom, creating numerous opportunities for sweeps, transitions, and submissions. These techniques are essential for developing a comprehensive and effective guard game in Brazilian Jiu-Jitsu.

# Chapter 11: Guard Passing Techniques

Guard passing is a crucial skill in Brazilian Jiu-Jitsu, allowing practitioners to transition from a defensive position to a dominant one. This chapter covers four essential guard passing techniques: the Over-Under Pass, Toreando Pass, Knee Slice Pass, and Leg Drag Pass. Each technique emphasizes different aspects of pressure, control, speed, and precision, providing a comprehensive approach to overcoming an opponent's guard.

## *11.1 Over-Under Pass: Pressure and Control*

The Over-Under Pass is a fundamental guard passing technique in Brazilian Jiu-Jitsu that relies on pressure and control to effectively break through an opponent's defenses. This pass is highly effective against various guard types and provides a secure way to transition to a dominant position.

### *A. Establishing the Over-Under Pass*

1. Initial Setup: Begin by controlling one of your opponent's legs with an underhook, threading your arm underneath their thigh. With your other hand, control their opposite leg by gripping it from above, applying downward pressure.

2. Pressure Points: Apply significant downward pressure with your shoulder on the opponent's torso while keeping their leg elevated with your underhook. This pressure immobilizes their hips and restricts their movement.

### *B. Key Steps*

1. Drive Forward: Use your body weight to drive forward, maintaining constant pressure on your opponent's torso and hips. Your head should be positioned close to their hip on the side of the underhook, maximizing control.

2. Leg Clearance: Step around the opponent's leg that you are controlling with the overhook. Keep your hips low and maintain pressure to prevent them from re-establishing their guard.

3. **Secure Side Control**: As you pass their legs, transition into side control by sliding your body across their torso, ensuring you keep pressure on them to maintain control.

## *C. Common Mistakes*

1. **Insufficient Pressure**: Failing to apply enough pressure can allow the opponent to recover guard or counter your pass. Ensure you maintain constant downward pressure with your shoulder and underhook.

2. **Poor Head Positioning**: Incorrect head placement can lead to losing control and getting caught in submissions such as triangles or guillotines. Keep your head close to their hip on the side of the underhook to prevent these counters.

3. **Rushing the Pass**: Attempting to pass too quickly without securing control can result in losing balance and position. Focus on maintaining pressure and control before moving to side control.

Mastering the Over-Under Pass involves understanding the importance of pressure and control. By effectively applying pressure with your shoulder and underhook, and maintaining proper head positioning, you can successfully pass your opponent's guard and transition to a dominant position. This technique is essential for building a solid guard passing game in Brazilian Jiu-Jitsu.

## *11.2 Toreando Pass: Speed and Precision*

The Toreando Pass, also known as the Bullfighter Pass, is a dynamic guard passing technique that emphasizes speed and precision. By swiftly maneuvering around your opponent's legs, you can bypass their guard and secure a dominant position. This pass is effective against various types of guards and is a valuable addition to any BJJ practitioner's repertoire.

## *A. Establishing the Toreando Pass*

1. **Initial Grips**: Begin by gripping both of your opponent's pant legs at the knees. Ensure your grips are firm and secure to control their legs effectively.

2. Control Points: Use your grips to lift and manipulate your opponent's legs, creating an opening for the pass. Maintain a strong stance to ensure balance and stability.

## *B. Key Steps*

1. Leg Movement: Swing your opponent's legs to one side while simultaneously moving your body in the opposite direction. This creates a clear path to pass their guard.

2. Footwork: Employ quick and precise footwork to circle around your opponent's legs. Keep your hips low and stay balanced as you move to avoid getting swept or countered.

3. Upper Body Control: As you bypass their legs, transition your grips from their knees to their shoulders or chest, driving forward to secure control. This prevents your opponent from re-establishing their guard.

## *C. Common Mistakes*

1. Slow Movement: Hesitation or slow movement can give your opponent time to counter or recover their guard. Execute the pass with speed and confidence to minimize their reaction time.

2. Poor Footwork: Inefficient or sloppy footwork can lead to losing balance or failing to pass the guard. Focus on maintaining a low stance and using precise steps to navigate around your opponent's legs.

3. Inadequate Upper Body Control: Failing to transition your grips effectively can allow your opponent to re-establish their guard or counter your pass. Ensure you secure control of their upper body as you complete the pass.

Mastering the Toreando Pass involves honing your speed, precision, and timing. By effectively controlling your opponent's legs and employing quick footwork, you can successfully bypass their guard and establish a dominant position. This technique is essential for developing a dynamic and effective guard passing game in Brazilian Jiu-Jitsu.

# 11.3 Knee Slice Pass: Breaking Through Defenses

The Knee Slice Pass, also known as the Knee Cut Pass, is a highly effective guard passing technique that focuses on slicing your knee through your opponent's defenses. This pass is particularly useful against half guard and open guard, allowing you to establish a dominant position with precision and control.

## *A. Establishing the Knee Slice Pass*

1. Initial Setup: Start by controlling the opponent's leg with an underhook, positioning your knee between their legs. Your other hand should grip their collar or shoulder for upper body control.

2. Pressure Points: Apply downward pressure with your knee on the opponent's inner thigh while maintaining control of their upper body. This pressure disrupts their balance and prevents them from effectively defending the pass.

## *B. Key Steps*

1. Slice Motion: Drive your knee across the opponent's thigh, aiming to pin their leg to the mat. Your knee should move diagonally, slicing through their guard.

2. Upper Body Control: Maintain a strong underhook and grip on their collar or shoulder. This control prevents your opponent from countering or recovering guard.

3. Transition to Side Control: As your knee slices through, slide your body into side control while keeping pressure on the opponent. Ensure your hips stay low to maintain control and prevent escapes.

## *C. Common Mistakes*

1. Weak Pressure: Failing to apply sufficient pressure with your knee and upper body can allow the opponent to counter or recover guard. Ensure consistent pressure throughout the pass.

2. Incorrect Knee Positioning: Poor knee placement can result in losing control and getting swept. Aim your knee diagonally across the opponent's thigh to effectively slice through their guard.

3. Rushing the Pass: Attempting to pass too quickly without securing control can lead to losing balance and position. Focus on maintaining pressure and control before transitioning to side control.

Mastering the Knee Slice Pass involves understanding the importance of pressure and precise movement. By effectively driving your knee through your opponent's defenses and maintaining upper body control, you can successfully pass their guard and establish a dominant position. This technique is essential for developing a robust guard passing game in Brazilian Jiu-Jitsu.

## *11.4 Leg Drag Pass: Establishing Dominance*

The Leg Drag Pass is a versatile and highly effective guard passing technique that emphasizes control and positioning to bypass your opponent's guard and establish dominance. This pass is particularly effective against open guard and spider guard, allowing you to transition smoothly into a superior position.

### *A. Establishing the Leg Drag Pass*

1. Initial Grips: Start by gripping your opponent's leg at the ankle and knee. Ensure your grips are firm and secure to manipulate their leg effectively.

2. Control Points: Use your grips to pull the opponent's leg across their body, creating an angle that disrupts their guard and limits their mobility.

### *B. Key Steps*

1. Drag Motion: Pull the opponent's leg across their body while stepping to the side. This motion off-balances them and creates an opening for you to pass.

2. Upper Body Control: As you drag the leg, use your upper body to pin their hips and prevent them from recovering guard. Place your chest on their hip and use your grips to maintain control.

3. Transition to Side Control: Secure the pass by moving into side control while keeping pressure on the opponent. Ensure your hips stay low and maintain control of their leg to prevent escapes.

## C. Common Mistakes

1. Insufficient Control: Failing to control the opponent's leg and hips can allow them to recover guard or counter the pass. Ensure your grips are secure and maintain pressure throughout the pass.

2. Poor Timing: Incorrect timing can lead to getting caught in submissions or losing balance. Execute the pass with precision and confidence to minimize your opponent's reaction time.

3. Inadequate Upper Body Pressure: Failing to apply sufficient pressure with your upper body can allow the opponent to regain control. Ensure you pin their hips effectively and maintain pressure as you transition to side control.

Mastering the Leg Drag Pass involves understanding the importance of control and precise movement. By effectively dragging your opponent's leg across their body and maintaining upper body pressure, you can successfully pass their guard and establish a dominant position. This technique is essential for developing a comprehensive and effective guard passing game in Brazilian Jiu-Jitsu.

# Chapter 11 Review: Guard Passing Techniques

Chapter 11: Guard Passing Techniques covers four essential methods for overcoming your opponent's guard, each emphasizing different aspects of pressure, control, speed, and precision. Here's a summary of the key points from each section:

**- 11.1 Over-Under Pass: Pressure and Control**

  - The Over-Under Pass relies on pressure and control, using an underhook to manipulate your opponent's legs while applying shoulder pressure to immobilize their hips.

  - Key steps include driving forward with body weight, maintaining head positioning close to the opponent's hip, and clearing the leg to transition into side control.

- Common mistakes include insufficient pressure, poor head positioning, and rushing the pass without securing control.

### - 11.2 Toreando Pass: Speed and Precision

- The Toreando Pass, or Bullfighter Pass, utilizes speed and precision to maneuver around the opponent's legs.

- Key steps involve gripping the opponent's pant legs, swinging their legs to one side, employing quick footwork to circle around, and securing upper body control.

- Common mistakes include slow movement, poor footwork, and inadequate upper body control, which can allow the opponent to recover guard or counter.

### - 11.3 Knee Slice Pass: Breaking Through Defenses

- The Knee Slice Pass focuses on slicing the knee through the opponent's defenses, effectively breaking through their guard.

- Key steps involve driving the knee diagonally across the opponent's thigh, maintaining strong underhook and collar grips, and transitioning to side control.

- Common mistakes include weak pressure, incorrect knee positioning, and attempting to pass too quickly without securing control.

### - 11.4 Leg Drag Pass: Establishing Dominance

- The Leg Drag Pass emphasizes control and positioning by dragging the opponent's leg across their body.

- Key steps include gripping the opponent's leg at the ankle and knee, pulling their leg across their body while stepping to the side, and using upper body pressure to pin their hips and transition to side control.

- Common mistakes include insufficient control, poor timing, and inadequate upper body pressure, which can allow the opponent to recover guard or counter the pass.

Mastering these guard passing techniques enhances a practitioner's ability to transition from a defensive position to a dominant one, creating numerous opportunities for controlling and submitting their opponent. Each technique offers unique advantages and can be effectively used in various situations, making them essential tools for any Brazilian Jiu-Jitsu practitioner.

# Chapter 12: Escapes and Defense Mechanisms

In Brazilian Jiu-Jitsu, being able to escape from bad positions and defend against submissions is crucial for survival and success on the mat. This chapter focuses on essential escapes and defense mechanisms, providing you with the tools needed to turn a defensive situation into an offensive opportunity.

## *12.1 Mount Escapes: Upa, Elbow Escape*

Mount escapes are crucial techniques in Brazilian Jiu-Jitsu for regaining a neutral or dominant position when an opponent has established mount control. This section covers two fundamental mount escapes: the Upa escape and the Elbow escape.

### *A. Upa (Bridge) Escape*

The Upa escape, also known as the Bridge escape, is a powerful technique that uses leverage and momentum to reverse the position.

**1. Initial Position:**

- Start with your opponent in the mount position.

- Keep your elbows close to your body and your feet flat on the mat.

**2. Control Points:**

- Secure one of your opponent's arms by trapping it against your chest. Use your same side hand to grip their wrist, and your other hand to control their elbow or sleeve.

- Trap the same side leg by hooking your foot over their ankle.

**3. Bridge Motion:**

- Bridge your hips explosively upward while pushing their trapped arm across your body.

- Use the momentum from the bridge to roll your opponent over to the side, reversing the position and landing in their guard or on top in a more dominant position.

## *B. Elbow Escape (Hip Escape)*

The Elbow escape, or Hip escape, is an essential technique that uses hip movement to create space and escape the mount position.

### 1. Initial Position:

- Begin with your opponent in the mount position.

- Keep your elbows close to your body and your hands positioned near your hips.

### 2. Shrimping Motion:

- Turn onto your side and use a shrimping motion to push your hips away from your opponent.

- Use your elbow to push against the opponent's knee and create space between your hips and their legs.

### 3. Knee Insert:

- Slide your knee into the space created between your hips and your opponent's leg.

- Once your knee is inserted, use it to pry their leg off your hip.

### 4. Escape to Guard:

- Continue the shrimping motion with your hips to free your other leg.

- Transition to a guard position, such as closed guard or half guard, by bringing both legs around your opponent.


Mastering the Upa and Elbow escapes allows you to effectively defend against the mount position and regain control in a match. These techniques are foundational skills that every Brazilian Jiu-Jitsu practitioner should practice and refine to improve their overall defensive capabilities.

# *12.2 Side Control Escapes: Shrimping, Underhook Escape*

Escaping from side control is essential in Brazilian Jiu-Jitsu to avoid being dominated and to regain a neutral or advantageous position. This section covers two effective techniques for escaping side control: the Shrimping escape and the Underhook escape.

## *A. Shrimping Escape*

The Shrimping escape, also known as the Hip Escape, is a fundamental technique that uses hip movement to create space and recover guard.

**1. Initial Position:**

 - Start with your opponent in side control.

 - Keep your arms framed against their hips and shoulders, maintaining a tight and protective posture.

**2. Shrimping Motion:**

 - Use your legs to push your hips away from your opponent, creating space between your bodies.

 - Turn onto your side, facing your opponent, and push off the mat with your feet to move your hips out.

**3. Knee Insert:**

 - Slide your knee into the space created between your hips and your opponent's body.

 - Use your knee to pry their body away, continuing to create space.

**4. Escape to Guard:**

 - Once you have created enough space, bring your other leg through and recover guard.

 - You can transition to a closed guard, half guard, or another defensive position, maintaining control and preventing further attacks.

## *B. Underhook Escape*

The Underhook escape is a powerful technique that utilizes an underhook to create leverage and space, allowing you to transition to a safer position.

### 1. Initial Position:

- Start with your opponent in side control.

- Frame against their hips and shoulders with your arms to protect yourself and create a base.

### 2. Underhook Motion:

- Use your far arm (the arm furthest from your opponent) to create an underhook by slipping it under their armpit.

- As you establish the underhook, turn onto your side, facing your opponent.

### 3. Hip Escape:

- Combine the underhook with a shrimping motion to create space and move your hips out from under your opponent.

- Use your legs to push off the mat and move your hips away from your opponent, increasing the space between you.

### 4. Transition to Knees:

- With the space created, use the underhook to elevate your opponent slightly and bring your bottom knee through.

- Transition to your knees, using the underhook to maintain control and regain a neutral or dominant position, such as turtle or standing up.

Mastering the Shrimping and Underhook escapes is crucial for any Brazilian Jiu-Jitsu practitioner. These techniques allow you to effectively defend against side control and create opportunities to regain control and transition to advantageous positions. Practice these escapes regularly to improve your defensive capabilities and overall game.

# 12.3 Submission Defenses: Timing and Technique

Defending against submissions is a critical skill in Brazilian Jiu-Jitsu, requiring precise timing and effective technique. This section covers fundamental principles and specific strategies for defending common submissions such as chokes and joint locks.

## *A. Timing*

**1. Early Recognition:**

- The earlier you recognize a submission attempt, the better your chances of defending against it.

- Stay aware of your opponent's movements and grips to identify submission setups before they fully develop.

**2. Immediate Action:**

- Act immediately to counter the submission attempt before it becomes fully locked in.

- Hesitation can lead to the submission being fully applied, making escape much more difficult.

## *B. Technique*

**1. Posture and Base:**

- Maintain a strong posture and solid base to prevent your opponent from effectively applying submissions.

- For example, when defending against a triangle choke, posture up and keep your back straight to alleviate pressure on your neck.

**2. Grip Fighting:**

- Disrupt your opponent's grips and control points to weaken their submission attempt.

- Break grips and control their hands to prevent them from securing key positions for submissions.

## 3. Counter Movements:

- Use specific counter movements to escape or alleviate the pressure of the submission.

- For example, when defending an armbar, turn your thumb towards the mat and stack your opponent to relieve pressure and create space for escape.

## *C. Specific Submission Defenses*

### 1. Choke Defenses:

- Rear Naked Choke: Tuck your chin and use your hands to control the attacking arm. Turn towards the choking arm and try to escape your hips to the side.

- Guillotine Choke: Defend by controlling the choking arm and creating space by driving your shoulder into their chest. Use your other hand to push on their hips and work to escape your head.

### 2. Armbar Defenses:

- Stack Escape: When caught in an armbar, turn your thumb down and stack your opponent by driving your weight forward. Use your other hand to push their legs down and create space to pull your arm out.

- Hitchhiker Escape: Rotate your arm so your thumb points up, then turn your body away from your opponent while kicking your legs over their head to escape the armbar.

### 3. Leg Lock Defenses:

- Straight Ankle Lock: Defend by straightening your leg and pushing your opponent's grip down towards your foot. Create space by scooting your hips away and freeing your ankle.

- Heel Hook: Control your opponent's hands to prevent them from fully securing the grip. Rotate your foot in the direction of the pressure and work to free your knee line from their control.

Mastering submission defenses requires consistent practice and an understanding of the principles of timing and technique. By maintaining a strong posture, disrupting your opponent's grips, and using specific counter movements, you can effectively defend against a variety of submissions. This will improve your overall game and increase your ability to survive and thrive in challenging positions.

## 12.4 *Transitioning from Defense to Offense*

Effective defense in Brazilian Jiu-Jitsu not only involves escaping from bad positions and defending against submissions but also creating opportunities to transition to offensive techniques. This section covers strategies for turning defensive situations into offensive opportunities, including creating space, reversals, sweeps, and submission counters.

### *A. Creating Space*

Creating space is the first step in transitioning from defense to offense. By creating distance between you and your opponent, you can prepare for counterattacks and offensive maneuvers.

**1. Escaping:**

  - Use escape techniques, such as shrimping or bridging, to create space between you and your opponent.

  - For example, when escaping side control, use the shrimping motion to create space and then insert your knee to recover guard or transition to another position.

**2. Framing:**

  - Use your arms and legs to frame against your opponent, maintaining distance and preparing for a counterattack.

  - Effective framing involves using your limbs to push against your opponent's hips, shoulders, or legs, creating a barrier that allows you to set up your next move.

### *B. Reversals and Sweeps*

Reversals and sweeps are techniques that use your opponent's momentum and positioning to turn the tables and gain a dominant position.

## 1. Reversals:

- Use your opponent's momentum against them to reverse the position and gain the upper hand.

- For example, when your opponent attempts a guard pass, use a bridge and roll technique to reverse their position and end up on top.

## 2. Sweeps:

- Transition from a defensive guard position to a sweep, using leverage and timing to topple your opponent.

- Common sweeps include the scissor sweep, butterfly sweep, and hip bump sweep. Each sweep involves using your legs and hips to off-balance your opponent and transition to a dominant position.

## *C. Submission Counters*

Countering submissions by transitioning into your own offensive techniques can catch your opponent off guard and quickly turn the tide of the match.

## 1. Counter Submissions:

- Transition from defending a submission to countering with your own submission attempt.

- For example, when defending an armbar, stack your opponent and transition to a choke or another armbar by using their position against them.

## 2. Flow Drills:

- Practice flow drills that incorporate transitioning from defense to offense to build muscle memory and fluidity in your movements.

- Flow drills can include sequences of escaping, creating space, and immediately transitioning to offensive techniques such as sweeps, reversals, or submissions.

Mastering the art of transitioning from defense to offense involves understanding the importance of creating space, using reversals and sweeps, and countering submissions effectively. By integrating these strategies into your training, you can develop a more dynamic and comprehensive game, allowing you to capitalize on defensive situations and turn them into opportunities for dominance and control. This approach not only improves your overall skill set but also enhances your ability to adapt and respond to various challenges on the mat.

# Chapter 12 Review: Escapes and Defense Mechanisms

Chapter 12: Escapes and Defense Mechanisms focuses on essential techniques for escaping bad positions and defending against submissions in Brazilian Jiu-Jitsu. This chapter provides you with the tools needed to turn defensive situations into offensive opportunities. Here's a summary of the key points from each section:

**- 12.1 Mount Escapes: Upa, Elbow Escape**

  - Upa (Bridge) Escape:

    - Secure one of your opponent's arms and trap their same side leg.

    - Bridge your hips explosively while pushing their trapped arm across your body to roll them over and reverse the position.

  - Elbow Escape (Hip Escape):

    - Use a shrimping motion to create space and slide your knee into the gap between your hips and the opponent's leg.

    - Continue to shrimp and bring your other leg through to recover guard or transition to another position.


**- 12.2 Side Control Escapes: Shrimping, Underhook Escape**

  - Shrimping Escape:

    - Use your legs to push your hips away from your opponent, creating space.

    - Slide your knee into the space and recover guard or transition to a safer position.

  - Underhook Escape:

    - Create an underhook with your far arm and turn onto your side.

- Combine the underhook with a shrimping motion to create space and move your hips out.

- Transition to your knees or another dominant position.

## - 12.3 Submission Defenses: Timing and Technique

- Timing:

- Recognize submission attempts early and act immediately to counter them.

- Technique:

- Maintain a strong posture and base to prevent submissions.

- Disrupt your opponent's grips and use specific counter movements to escape or alleviate pressure.

- Specific Submission Defenses:

- Defend chokes like the Rear Naked Choke by tucking your chin and controlling the attacking arm.

- Escape armbars by turning your thumb down and stacking your opponent.

- Defend leg locks by straightening your leg and pushing your opponent's grip down.

## - 12.4 Transitioning from Defense to Offense

- Creating Space:

- Use escapes and framing to create distance and prepare for counterattacks.

- Reversals and Sweeps:

- Use your opponent's momentum to reverse positions or execute sweeps to gain a dominant position.

- Submission Counters:

- Transition from defending a submission to countering with your own submission attempt.

- Practice flow drills to build fluidity in transitioning from defense to offense.

Mastering these escapes and defense mechanisms enhances a practitioner's ability to survive and thrive in challenging positions. By effectively escaping bad positions, defending against submissions, and transitioning to offensive techniques, you can improve your overall game and increase your chances of success in Brazilian Jiu-Jitsu.

# Part 5: Advanced Techniques and Tactics

Part 5 delves into advanced techniques and tactics that can significantly enhance your Brazilian Jiu-Jitsu game. By mastering these advanced submissions, transitions, and strategies, you will be able to control and submit your opponents with greater efficiency and creativity. This section covers a range of sophisticated techniques, providing you with the tools to elevate your skill set and adapt to various scenarios on the mat.

# Chapter 13: Advanced Submission Techniques

In Brazilian Jiu-Jitsu, mastering advanced submission techniques can elevate your game, making you a formidable opponent. This chapter delves into three categories of advanced submissions: chokes, joint locks, and leg locks. Each section provides detailed instructions on the application and mechanics of these advanced techniques, enabling you to apply them with precision and confidence.

## *13.1 Advanced Chokes: Bow and Arrow, Loop Choke, Ezekiel Choke*

Advanced chokes in Brazilian Jiu-Jitsu require precision, control, and a deep understanding of leverage and positioning. This section covers three highly effective chokes: the Bow and Arrow Choke, the Loop Choke, and the Ezekiel Choke.

### *A. Bow and Arrow Choke*

The Bow and Arrow Choke is a powerful gi choke that uses the opponent's lapel to create intense pressure on their neck.

**1. Initial Setup:**

- Start from the back control position.
- Secure a strong grip on the opponent's far collar with your choking hand.

## 2. Control Points:

- Use your other hand to grip the opponent's pants near the knee.

- Place your foot on their hip to create leverage and control.

## 3. Choke Execution:

- Pull the collar across the opponent's neck while simultaneously pulling their leg towards you.

- Rotate your body to the side, creating a bowing motion that tightens the choke.

- Apply continuous pressure until the opponent taps.

# *B. Loop Choke*

The Loop Choke is a versatile gi choke that can be applied from various positions, including the guard and turtle.

## 1. Initial Setup:

- Begin from a guard position with your opponent's head down.

- Secure a grip on their collar with one hand.

## 2. Choke Execution:

- Loop your gripping arm over the opponent's head and around their neck.

- Use your free hand to grab their collar or use it to create additional leverage.

- Rotate your hips out and away while pulling the collar tight, applying pressure to the neck.

- Maintain the pressure until the opponent taps.

# *C. Ezekiel Choke*

The Ezekiel Choke is a powerful choke that can be applied from both top and bottom positions, using your sleeve and forearm to create pressure.

## 1. Initial Setup:

- From top mount or side control, insert one hand inside your opposite sleeve.

- Position your forearm across the opponent's throat.

**2. Choke Execution:**

   - Apply pressure by pulling your sleeve grip towards you while pushing your forearm into the opponent's throat.

   - Ensure your body weight is applied to enhance the choke's effectiveness.

   - Continue applying pressure until the opponent taps.

Mastering these advanced chokes requires practice and a deep understanding of leverage, control, and timing. Incorporating these techniques into your arsenal will make you a more formidable opponent, capable of applying high-level submissions with precision and effectiveness.

## *13.2 Advanced Joint Locks: Omoplata, Wrist Lock*

Advanced joint locks in Brazilian Jiu-Jitsu focus on targeting specific joints to control and submit your opponent. This section covers two highly effective joint locks: the Omoplata and the Wrist Lock.

### *A. Omoplata*

The Omoplata is a shoulder lock that utilizes the legs to apply pressure and secure a submission. It is a versatile technique that can be initiated from various guard positions.

**1. Initial Setup:**

   - Start from a closed guard or open guard position.

   - Control your opponent's posture by gripping their sleeve and collar.

**2. Isolate the Arm:**

   - Use your legs to break your opponent's posture and isolate one of their arms.

   - Swing your leg over their shoulder, wrapping it around their arm.

### 3. Execution:

- Rotate your body to the side, using your legs to force the opponent's shoulder to the mat.

- Lock your legs together, securing their arm between your legs.

- Sit up and lean forward, applying pressure to the shoulder joint.

- Continue applying pressure until the opponent taps.

## *B. Wrist Lock*

The Wrist Lock is a versatile submission that targets the wrist joint, leveraging small joint manipulation to force a tap. It can be applied from various positions, including standing, guard, and top control.

### 1. Initial Setup:

- Secure a grip on your opponent's wrist from a dominant position.

- Control their arm to prevent them from escaping or countering.

### 2. Isolate the Wrist:

- Use your other hand to control the opponent's elbow or upper arm, ensuring the wrist is isolated.

- Position your thumb on the back of their hand and your fingers on the palm.

### 3. Execution:

- Apply pressure by bending the wrist towards the opponent's forearm.

- Use your body weight and leverage to increase the pressure on the wrist joint.

- Ensure the pressure is directed towards the joint for maximum effectiveness.

- Continue applying pressure until the opponent taps.

Mastering these advanced joint locks requires precision, control, and an understanding of leverage. By incorporating the Omoplata and Wrist Lock into your arsenal, you can effectively control and submit your opponents, enhancing your overall grappling game. Practice these techniques regularly to develop the sensitivity and timing needed to apply them successfully in live situations.

# 13.3 Advanced Leg Locks: Knee Bar, Calf Slicer, Heel Hook Variations

Advanced leg locks are powerful submissions in Brazilian Jiu-Jitsu that target the knee and ankle joints. These techniques require precision and control, as they can cause significant damage if not applied correctly. This section covers three advanced leg locks: the Knee Bar, Calf Slicer, and Heel Hook variations.

## *A. Knee Bar*

*Brazilian Jiu-Jitsu Knee Bar*

The Knee Bar is a powerful leg lock that hyperextends the knee joint, applying pressure to the ligaments and tendons.

**1. Initial Setup:**

  - Start from a position where you have isolated your opponent's leg, such as from the top of half guard or after a sweep.

  - Control their leg by securing their ankle and thigh.

**2. Positioning:**

  - Slide your hips near your opponent's knee joint.

  - Pinch your knees together around their thigh to trap their leg.

### 3. Execution:

- Extend your hips while pulling their leg towards you, applying pressure to the knee joint.

- Ensure that their knee is fully extended to maximize the effectiveness of the lock.

- Apply controlled pressure until the opponent taps.

## *B. Calf Slicer*

The Calf Slicer, also known as the Calf Crusher, is a compression lock that targets the calf muscle against the shin bone, causing intense pain.

### 1. Initial Setup:

- Start from a position where you can trap your opponent's leg, such as from a seated guard or during a scramble.

- Control their leg by positioning it across your shin.

### 2. Positioning:

- Trap their ankle and foot by securing it with your arms.

- Position your shin against the back of their knee.

### 3. Execution:

- Apply pressure by pulling their leg towards you while driving your shin into their calf muscle.

- Ensure that the compression is tight to maximize the pain and force a tap.

- Apply controlled pressure until the opponent taps.

## *C. Heel Hook Variations*

*Brazilian Jiu-Jitsu Heel Hook*

The Heel Hook is a highly effective but potentially dangerous submission that targets the ligaments of the knee and ankle. It involves twisting the foot to apply rotational force to the knee joint.

### 1. Initial Setup:

   - Secure control of your opponent's foot and isolate their leg from positions such as the outside Ashi Garami or the 50/50 guard.

   - Position their heel against your forearm.

### 2. Positioning:

   - Control their leg by locking your legs around it, ensuring their knee is isolated.

   - Grip their heel with your forearm and secure their foot with your other hand.

### 3. Execution:

   - Apply rotational force by twisting your body and pulling their heel towards you.

   - Ensure the pressure is directed towards the knee joint for maximum effectiveness.

- Apply controlled pressure until the opponent taps.

Mastering these advanced leg locks requires a deep understanding of the mechanics involved and a high level of control to avoid injuring your training partners. Regular practice will develop the sensitivity and timing needed to apply these submissions effectively and safely in live situations. By incorporating the Knee Bar, Calf Slicer, and Heel Hook variations into your game, you can become a more versatile and dangerous grappler.

## *Chapter 13 Review: Advanced Submission Techniques*

Chapter 13: Advanced Submission Techniques provides an in-depth look at sophisticated and highly effective submission techniques in Brazilian Jiu-Jitsu. This chapter is divided into three main sections, each focusing on a specific type of submission: chokes, joint locks, and leg locks. Here's a summary of the key points from each section:

**- 13.1 Advanced Chokes: Bow and Arrow, Loop Choke, Ezekiel Choke**

- Bow and Arrow Choke: This powerful gi choke uses the opponent's lapel to apply intense pressure on their neck. The key steps include securing a grip on the collar, controlling the pants, and using a bowing motion to tighten the choke.

- Loop Choke: A versatile and quick gi choke that can be applied from various positions. The technique involves looping the arm over the opponent's head and tightening the collar while rotating the hips away.

- Ezekiel Choke: A gi choke that can be executed from both top and bottom positions. It involves inserting one hand inside the opposite sleeve and applying pressure with the forearm across the opponent's throat.

**- 13.2 Advanced Joint Locks: Omoplata, Wrist Lock**

- Omoplata: A shoulder lock that uses the legs to apply pressure. It involves breaking the opponent's posture, isolating an arm, and rotating the body to force the shoulder to the mat.

- Wrist Lock: This versatile submission targets the wrist joint. The technique requires isolating the opponent's wrist and using leverage to bend it towards the forearm, applying pressure to the joint.

### - 13.3 Advanced Leg Locks: Knee Bar, Calf Slicer, Heel Hook Variations

- Knee Bar: A powerful leg lock that hyperextends the knee joint. The key steps include isolating the opponent's leg, positioning your hips near their knee, and applying pressure by extending your hips and pulling their leg.

- Calf Slicer: This compression lock targets the calf muscle against the shin bone, causing intense pain. It involves trapping the opponent's leg, positioning your shin against the back of their knee, and applying pressure by pulling their leg towards you.

- Heel Hook Variations: These leg locks target the ligaments of the knee and ankle, applying rotational force to the knee joint. The key steps include securing control of the opponent's foot, isolating their leg, and applying rotational pressure by twisting the body and pulling the heel.

Mastering these advanced submission techniques can significantly enhance your Brazilian Jiu-Jitsu game. By understanding the mechanics and application of these chokes, joint locks, and leg locks, you can effectively control and submit your opponents, making you a more versatile and formidable practitioner. Practice these techniques regularly to develop the sensitivity, precision, and control needed to apply them successfully in live situations.

# Chapter 14: Fluid Transitions and Flow Drills

Fluid transitions and flow drills are essential components of advanced Brazilian Jiu-Jitsu practice. They enable practitioners to move seamlessly between techniques and positions, enhancing their ability to control and submit opponents. This chapter covers strategies for linking techniques, positional transitions, and flow drills to improve coordination and reflexes.

## *14.1 Linking Techniques: Fluid Movement Strategies*

Linking techniques fluidly is essential for maintaining control, applying effective submissions, and transitioning between positions in Brazilian Jiu-Jitsu. Developing fluid movement strategies involves understanding the flow of techniques and how they connect seamlessly.

### *A. Understanding the Flow*

**1. Sequential Techniques:**

   - Recognize that many techniques naturally follow one another. For example, transitioning from an armbar attempt to a triangle choke if the opponent defends.

   - Practice chaining submissions and sweeps together to anticipate and respond to your opponent's reactions.

**2. Maintaining Pressure:**

   - Ensure constant pressure on your opponent to limit their movement and force them into positions where your next technique is effective.

   - Use your body weight and leverage to maintain control throughout transitions.

### *B. Drilling Combinations*

**1. Repetitive Drills:**

   - Practice specific combinations repeatedly to develop muscle memory and fluidity. For example, drilling the sequence of passing the guard, securing side control, and transitioning to mount.

- Focus on smooth, controlled movements rather than speed to ensure proper technique.

## 2. Partner Drills:

- Work with a partner to drill fluid transitions, starting slowly and gradually increasing speed as you become more comfortable.

- Provide resistance to each other to simulate realistic scenarios and improve timing.

## *C. Adapting to Opponent Reactions*

### 1. Reading Movements:

- Pay close attention to your opponent's reactions to anticipate their next move.

- Adjust your techniques based on their responses, ensuring you remain one step ahead.

### 2. Countering Defenses:

- Develop counters for common defenses to your techniques. For example, if your opponent defends a guard pass, transition to a different passing technique.

- Practice these counters to ensure smooth transitions and maintain control.

## *D. Examples of Linked Techniques*

### 1. Guard Pass to Submission:

- Execute a guard pass, such as the Toreando pass, and immediately transition to an armbar or choke once in side control or mount.

### 2. Sweep to Submission:

- Perform a sweep, like the scissor sweep, and transition directly to a submission such as a Kimura or guillotine choke once you have top position.

### 3. Submission Chains:

- Chain submissions together, such as transitioning from a triangle choke to an armbar if the opponent defends the initial submission.

Mastering the art of linking techniques through fluid movement strategies will significantly enhance your Brazilian Jiu-Jitsu game. By understanding the flow of techniques, drilling combinations, adapting to opponent reactions, and practicing linked techniques, you can maintain control and apply effective submissions or transitions seamlessly. This fluidity will make you a more versatile and formidable practitioner on the mat.

## *14.2 Positional Transitions: Guard to Mount, etc.*

Positional transitions are a key aspect of Brazilian Jiu-Jitsu, allowing practitioners to move smoothly between various positions to maintain control and apply effective techniques. Mastering these transitions is crucial for both offensive and defensive strategies. This section covers essential positional transitions, focusing on movement from guard to mount and other important positions.

### *A. Guard to Mount*

**1. Closed Guard to Mount:**

 - Breaking Posture: Use your legs and grips to break your opponent's posture, pulling them close to you.

 - Hip Movement: Shrimp out to create an angle, allowing you to slide your knee across your opponent's belly.

 - Leg Swing: Swing your leg over their back while maintaining control of their upper body, transitioning into the mount position.

**2. Open Guard to Mount:**

 - Control Points: Establish control points such as collar grips or underhooks.

 - Sweeping Motion: Execute a sweep, such as the flower sweep or scissor sweep, to off-balance your opponent and create an opening.

 - Mount Transition: Use the momentum of the sweep to transition into the mount position, securing your knees on either side of their torso.

## *B. Side Control to Mount*

1. Establishing Control: From side control, secure an underhook and control their far arm to limit their movement.

2. Knee on Belly: Transition to knee on belly by placing your knee on their stomach, applying pressure to keep them pinned.

3. Sliding Mount: Slide your knee across their torso while maintaining control of their upper body, moving into the mount position.

## *C. Half Guard to Mount*

1. Breaking Half Guard: From top half guard, use your free leg to pry open their half guard, creating space.

2. Underhook and Crossface: Secure an underhook and crossface to control their upper body.

3. Leg Freeing: Use your hips and pressure to free your trapped leg, sliding it over their body to transition into mount.

## *D. Back Control to Mount*

1. Controlling the Back: From back control, secure a seatbelt grip and control their hips with your legs.

2. Hip Shift: Shift your hips to one side while maintaining control of their upper body.

3. Transition to Mount: Slide your leg over their body and transition to mount while keeping control, ensuring they cannot escape.

## *E. Guard to Side Control*

1. Guard Pass: Execute a guard pass such as the knee slice pass or over-under pass to bypass your opponent's legs.

2. Establishing Side Control: Secure side control by placing your body perpendicular to theirs, controlling their hips and upper body with pressure.

## F. Mount to Back Control

1. High Mount: Move to a high mount position, controlling their arms and isolating their head.

2. Back Take Setup: Use your grips to pull them to one side, creating an angle to slide your leg under their shoulder.

3. Securing Back Control: Transition to back control by securing hooks with your legs and maintaining a seatbelt grip, ensuring control of their upper body.

Mastering positional transitions enhances your ability to maintain control and apply effective techniques in various scenarios. By practicing these transitions, you can move smoothly between positions, creating opportunities for submissions and maintaining a dominant position. This fluidity is essential for becoming a versatile and effective Brazilian Jiu-Jitsu practitioner.

# 14.3 Flow Drills: Enhancing Coordination and Reflexes

Flow drills are a vital part of Brazilian Jiu-Jitsu training, designed to enhance coordination, reflexes, and fluidity in movement. These drills involve practicing sequences of techniques in a smooth, continuous manner, helping practitioners develop muscle memory and improve their ability to transition seamlessly between positions and techniques.

## A. Benefits of Flow Drills

**1. Improved Coordination:**

   - Flow drills help synchronize your movements, improving overall coordination and control.

   - Repeating sequences of techniques reinforces the connections between different movements, making transitions more natural.

## 2. Enhanced Reflexes:

- Practicing flow drills regularly sharpens your reflexes, enabling you to react quickly and effectively to your opponent's actions.

- Developing quick reflexes is crucial for both defensive and offensive maneuvers.

## 3. Fluidity in Movement:

- Flow drills promote fluid, uninterrupted motion, reducing the risk of hesitations or pauses during transitions.

- Smooth transitions between techniques make it harder for your opponent to predict and counter your moves.

## *B. Examples of Flow Drills*

### 1. Guard Passing Sequence:

- Start in Closed Guard: Begin by breaking your opponent's closed guard using a guard break technique.

- Transition to Open Guard: Move to an open guard position, establishing grips and control.

- Execute Guard Pass: Perform a guard pass such as the Toreando pass or knee slice pass.

- Establish Side Control: Transition into side control, securing your position and maintaining pressure.

### 2. Submission Chains:

- Start in Guard: Begin in closed guard and secure grips on your opponent's sleeves and collar.

- Attempt Armbar: Transition to an armbar attempt. If the opponent defends, move to the next submission.

- Transition to Triangle Choke: If the armbar fails, transition to a triangle choke by shifting your hips and locking your legs around their neck.

- Finish with Omoplata: If the triangle choke is defended, switch to an omoplata shoulder lock by rotating your body and using your legs to control their arm.

### 3. Positional Flow Drill:

- Start in Mount: Begin in the mount position, maintaining control and applying pressure.

- Transition to Back Control: Move from mount to back control by sliding one knee behind their shoulder and securing hooks with your legs.

- Attempt Submission: Apply a choke or submission from back control. If the opponent defends, transition to another position.

- Return to Guard: If the submission attempt fails, transition back to guard, ensuring you maintain control throughout the movement.

## *C. Implementing Flow Drills in Training*

### 1. Partner Drills:

- Work with a training partner to practice flow drills, starting slowly to ensure proper technique and gradually increasing speed.

- Provide resistance to each other to simulate realistic scenarios and improve timing and adaptability.

### 2. Solo Drills:

- Practice flow drills solo to develop muscle memory and coordination. Use grappling dummies or visualize the sequences to enhance your practice.

- Focus on smooth, controlled movements, ensuring each transition is fluid and precise.

### 3. Regular Practice:

- Incorporate flow drills into your regular training routine to continually improve coordination, reflexes, and fluidity.

- Set aside dedicated time for flow drills, making them an integral part of your training regimen.

Flow drills are essential for developing the skills needed to move seamlessly between techniques and positions in Brazilian Jiu-Jitsu. By regularly practicing these drills, you can enhance your coordination, sharpen your reflexes, and achieve greater fluidity in your movements, making you a more effective and versatile practitioner on the mat.

## *Chapter 14 Review: Fluid Transitions and Flow Drills*

Chapter 14: Fluid Transitions and Flow Drills focuses on the importance of smooth, continuous movement in Brazilian Jiu-Jitsu. Mastering fluid transitions and flow drills is essential for maintaining control, applying effective techniques, and enhancing coordination and reflexes. Here's a summary of the key points from each section:

### - 14.1 Linking Techniques: Fluid Movement Strategies

- Understanding the Flow: Recognize how techniques naturally follow one another and practice chaining submissions and sweeps together. Maintain constant pressure on your opponent to limit their movement.

- Drilling Combinations: Practice specific combinations repeatedly to develop muscle memory and fluidity. Partner drills with resistance help simulate realistic scenarios and improve timing.

- Adapting to Opponent Reactions: Pay close attention to your opponent's reactions and adjust your techniques accordingly. Develop counters for common defenses to your techniques.

- Examples of Linked Techniques: Combine guard passes with submissions, sweeps with submissions, and chain submissions together to maintain control and apply effective techniques.

### - 14.2 Positional Transitions: Guard to Mount, etc.

- Guard to Mount: Break your opponent's posture, create an angle, and use your knee and leg to transition from guard to mount.

- Side Control to Mount: Secure an underhook, transition to knee on belly, and slide into mount while maintaining control.

- Half Guard to Mount: Pry open the half guard, secure an underhook and crossface, and free your trapped leg to move into mount.

- Back Control to Mount: Shift your hips and slide your leg over to transition from back control to mount.

- Guard to Side Control: Execute a guard pass and secure side control by controlling the hips and upper body.

- Mount to Back Control: Move to high mount, pull your opponent to one side, and secure back control with hooks and a seatbelt grip.

**- 14.3 Flow Drills: Enhancing Coordination and Reflexes**

- Benefits of Flow Drills: Improve coordination, enhance reflexes, and promote fluid, uninterrupted motion.

- Examples of Flow Drills: Practice guard passing sequences, submission chains, and positional flow drills to develop muscle memory and fluidity.

- Implementing Flow Drills in Training: Work with partners for resistance drills, practice solo drills for muscle memory, and incorporate regular flow drill practice into your training routine.

By mastering fluid transitions and incorporating flow drills into your training, you can significantly enhance your coordination, reflexes, and overall effectiveness in Brazilian Jiu-Jitsu. These skills enable you to move seamlessly between techniques and positions, making you a more versatile and formidable practitioner on the mat.

# Chapter 15: Competition Strategies and Tactics

Competing in Brazilian Jiu-Jitsu requires not only technical skills but also strategic thinking and mental preparedness. This chapter covers essential competition strategies and tactics, including understanding points and scoring systems, differences between gi and no-gi strategies, and preparing for tournaments through mental and physical training.

*Brazilian Jiu-Jitsu Competition*

## *15.1 Understanding Points and Scoring Systems*

Understanding the points and scoring systems in Brazilian Jiu-Jitsu (BJJ) competitions is essential for developing effective competition strategies. Knowing how points are awarded and what actions lead to advantages and penalties can help you make informed decisions during a match, ultimately improving your chances of winning.

# A. Points System

## 1. Takedowns and Throws (2 points)

- Execution: Points are awarded for successfully taking your opponent down and establishing control from a standing position.

- Examples: Double-leg takedown, single-leg takedown, hip throws (e.g., O-Goshi).

## 2. Guard Passes (3 points)

- Execution: Points are earned by passing your opponent's guard and establishing a dominant position such as side control.

- Examples: Knee slice pass, Toreando pass, over-under pass.

## 3. Sweeps (2 points)

- Execution: Points are awarded for sweeping your opponent from a guard position, transitioning from bottom to top.

- Examples: Scissor sweep, hip bump sweep, flower sweep.

## 4. Mount and Back Control (4 points)

- Mount: Points are awarded for achieving and maintaining the mount position, where both knees are on the ground and your hips are controlling the opponent.

- Back Control: Points are given for achieving back control with hooks in and controlling the opponent's upper body.

- Examples: Transitioning from side control to mount, taking the back from turtle position.

## 5. Knee on Belly (2 points)

- Execution: Points are awarded for maintaining the knee on belly position with control and pressure on the opponent's torso.

- Examples: Transitioning from side control to knee on belly and holding the position for a count.

## *B. Advantages*

### 1. Near Submissions

- Criteria: Advantages are awarded for near submission attempts that force the opponent to defend actively.

- Examples: Attempting an armbar that the opponent narrowly escapes, locking in a triangle choke that the opponent defends.

### 2. Near Points

- Criteria: Advantages are given for nearly completing points-scoring techniques, such as almost passing the guard or nearly completing a sweep.

- Examples: Almost passing the guard but being stopped at the last moment, initiating a sweep that disrupts the opponent's base.

## *C. Penalties*

### 1. Stalling

- Criteria: Penalties are given for inactivity or stalling to avoid engaging in combat.

- Examples: Holding a position without attempting to advance, repeatedly disengaging to avoid action.

### 2. Illegal Techniques

- Criteria: Points can be deducted for using prohibited techniques or actions that are not allowed in the competition, especially in lower belt divisions.

- Examples: Certain leg locks (e.g., heel hooks) in lower belt divisions, slamming an opponent to escape a submission.

Understanding these points and scoring systems allows you to strategize effectively during a match. By knowing how to earn points and avoid penalties, you can make tactical decisions that increase your chances of winning. This knowledge also helps you understand when to push for a submission, when to secure a dominant position, and how to manage the clock to your advantage.

# 15.2 Gi vs. No-Gi Strategies

Competing in gi and no-gi Brazilian Jiu-Jitsu requires different approaches and strategies due to the presence or absence of the gi (kimono). Each style has unique advantages and challenges, and understanding these can help you optimize your performance in both formats.

## *A. Gi Strategies*

### 1. Grip Fighting

- Importance: Grips are crucial in gi BJJ, as the fabric of the gi allows for strong and varied grips, which can be used to control and manipulate your opponent.

- Techniques:

   - Sleeve and Collar Grips: Secure your opponent's sleeves and collar to control their posture and movement.

   - Lapels and Belt Grips: Use lapel and belt grips to set up sweeps, guard passes, and submissions.

- Strategies:

   - Breaking Grips: Learn techniques to break your opponent's grips to prevent them from controlling you.

   - Grip Dominance: Establish and maintain dominant grips to control the pace of the match.

### 2. Choke Submissions

- Utilizing the Gi: The gi provides numerous opportunities for choke submissions that are not available in no-gi.

- Techniques:

   - Bow and Arrow Choke: Use the opponent's lapel to create a tight choke.

   - Collar Chokes: Employ various collar choke techniques, such as the cross collar choke and the loop choke.

- Strategies:

- Setting Up Chokes: Use your grips to set up and secure choke submissions effectively.

- Choke Chains: Transition between different choke attempts to keep your opponent defensive.

### 3. Control and Leverage

- Using the Gi for Control: The gi allows for better control and leverage during guard passes, sweeps, and positional control.

- Techniques:

- Spider Guard: Use sleeve grips and foot placement on the biceps to control your opponent's posture and set up sweeps.

- De La Riva Guard: Utilize the gi to secure grips and control your opponent's leg and posture.

- Strategies:

- Maintaining Control: Use your grips and the friction of the gi to maintain control and prevent escapes.

- Leveraging the Gi: Leverage the gi to create angles and apply pressure during submissions and guard passes.

## *B. No-Gi Strategies*

### 1. Speed and Agility

- Increased Mobility: The absence of the gi allows for faster movements and transitions, requiring quicker reactions.

- Techniques:

- Takedowns: Utilize wrestling-based takedowns, such as single-leg and double-leg takedowns.

- Guard Passes: Employ dynamic guard passes like the knee slice pass and the Toreando pass.

- Strategies:

- Fast Transitions: Focus on rapid transitions between positions to keep your opponent off balance.

- Explosive Movements: Use explosive movements to capitalize on openings and gain positional advantage.

## 2. Leg Locks

- Leg Lock Emphasis: No-gi competitions often place a higher emphasis on leg locks and lower body submissions.

- Techniques:

- Heel Hooks: Utilize heel hooks to target the knee and ankle joints.

- Ashigarami Entries: Enter leg entanglements like Ashi Garami to set up leg locks.

- Strategies:

- Leg Lock Setups: Develop setups for leg locks from various positions, such as guard and half guard.

- Leg Lock Defense: Learn and practice leg lock defenses to protect against common attacks.

## 3. Underhooks and Head Control

- Positional Dominance: Without the gi, underhooks and head control become critical for maintaining positional dominance.

- Techniques:

- Underhook Control: Use underhooks to control your opponent's upper body and prevent guard passes.

- Head Control: Employ head control to dominate positional exchanges and set up submissions.

- Strategies:

- Positional Awareness: Focus on maintaining and transitioning between dominant positions using underhooks and head control.

- Submission Setups: Use positional control to set up submissions like guillotines and rear-naked chokes.


Mastering the different strategies for gi and no-gi competition will make you a more versatile and adaptable BJJ practitioner. By understanding the unique aspects of each style, you can develop effective game plans and adjust your techniques to suit the specific demands of gi and no-gi matches.

# 15.3 *Preparing for Tournaments: Mental and Physical Training*

Preparation for Brazilian Jiu-Jitsu tournaments involves more than just honing your techniques. It requires comprehensive mental and physical training to ensure peak performance on competition day. This section covers essential aspects of preparing for tournaments, including conditioning, strength training, mental preparation, and nutrition.

## *A. Physical Training*

### 1. Conditioning

- Cardiovascular Endurance: Develop your cardiovascular endurance through activities like running, swimming, cycling, or interval training. This will help you maintain high energy levels throughout your matches.

- Anaerobic Conditioning: Include high-intensity interval training (HIIT) to simulate the bursts of energy required during a match. Drills such as sprints, burpees, and shuttle runs are effective.

- Mobility and Flexibility: Incorporate stretching and mobility exercises to improve your flexibility and reduce the risk of injuries. Yoga and dynamic stretching can be beneficial.

### 2. Strength Training

- Functional Strength: Focus on exercises that build functional strength relevant to BJJ. Compound movements like squats, deadlifts, bench presses, and pull-ups enhance overall strength and power.

- Core Stability: Strengthen your core with exercises like planks, Russian twists, and leg raises. A strong core is essential for maintaining balance and control during grappling.

- Grip Strength: Develop your grip strength with exercises like farmer's walks, rope climbs, and grip trainers. Strong grips are crucial for controlling your opponent in both gi and no-gi competitions.

### 3. Drilling and Sparring

- Technique Drills: Regularly drill your techniques to ensure they are sharp and ingrained in muscle memory. Focus on both your A-game techniques and common scenarios you might encounter in competition.

- Live Sparring: Engage in live sparring sessions to simulate competition intensity. Practice with different training partners to adapt to various styles and strategies.

## *B. Mental Training*

### 1. Visualization

- Mental Rehearsal: Practice visualization techniques to mentally rehearse your matches. Visualize yourself executing techniques successfully, overcoming challenges, and winning matches.

- Scenario Planning: Imagine different scenarios you might face in a match, such as being in a disadvantageous position, and visualize your responses.

### 2. Goal Setting

- Short-term Goals: Set specific, achievable goals for each training session and leading up to the tournament. Examples include mastering a particular technique or improving your conditioning.

- Long-term Goals: Define long-term goals for your competition performance, such as winning a specific tournament or achieving a certain rank.

### 3. Stress Management

- Breathing Techniques: Practice deep breathing exercises to manage stress and anxiety. Techniques like diaphragmatic breathing can help calm your mind and improve focus.

- Mindfulness and Meditation: Incorporate mindfulness practices and meditation to enhance mental clarity and reduce pre-competition nerves. Regular meditation can improve your ability to stay present and focused.

## *C. Nutrition and Hydration*

### 1. Balanced Diet

- Nutritional Needs: Maintain a balanced diet rich in proteins, carbohydrates, and healthy fats to support training and recovery. Include plenty of fruits, vegetables, lean meats, and whole grains.

- Meal Timing: Plan your meals to fuel your training sessions and ensure you have enough energy. Eat a balanced meal 2-3 hours before training and a post-workout meal rich in protein and carbs for recovery.

### 2. Hydration

- Daily Hydration: Stay well-hydrated throughout the day by drinking plenty of water. Aim for at least 8 cups (2 liters) of water daily, more if you're training intensely.

- Pre-Competition Hydration: Ensure you are properly hydrated in the days leading up to the competition. Avoid excessive caffeine and alcohol, as they can dehydrate you.

### 3. Weight Management

- Monitoring Weight: Keep track of your weight to ensure you meet the requirements for your competition division. Avoid drastic weight cuts, as they can negatively impact performance.

- Cutting Weight Safely: If you need to cut weight, do so gradually and safely under the guidance of a coach or nutritionist. Focus on maintaining energy levels and avoiding dehydration.

Mastering the physical and mental aspects of tournament preparation will give you a significant advantage on competition day. By developing your conditioning, strength, mental resilience, and nutritional habits, you can approach tournaments with confidence and perform at your best.

# *Chapter 15 Review: Competition Strategies and Tactics*

Chapter 15: Competition Strategies and Tactics covers essential aspects of preparing for Brazilian Jiu-Jitsu tournaments. It focuses on understanding points and scoring systems, developing strategies for gi and no-gi competition, and preparing mentally and physically for tournaments. Here's a summary of the key points from each section:

**- 15.1 Understanding Points and Scoring Systems**

  - Points System:

  - Takedowns and Throws (2 points): Earned by successfully taking your opponent down and establishing control.

  - Guard Passes (3 points): Awarded for passing the opponent's guard and establishing a dominant position.

  - Sweeps (2 points): Given for sweeping the opponent from a guard position to a top position.

  - Mount and Back Control (4 points): Points for achieving and maintaining mount or back control with hooks.

  - Knee on Belly (2 points): Awarded for maintaining knee on belly position with control and pressure.

  - Advantages:

  - Near Submissions: Advantages for near submission attempts that force the opponent to defend.

  - Near Points: Advantages for nearly completing points-scoring techniques.

  - Penalties:

  - Stalling: Penalties for inactivity or stalling to avoid engaging in combat.

  - Illegal Techniques: Points deductions for using prohibited techniques or actions.

**- 15.2 Gi vs. No-Gi Strategies**

- Gi Strategies:

  - Grip Fighting: Utilize the gi for strong grips to control and manipulate the opponent.

  - Choke Submissions: Use the gi to apply choke submissions like the bow and arrow choke and collar chokes.

  - Control and Leverage: Employ gi grips to enhance control and leverage during guard passes and sweeps.

- No-Gi Strategies:

  - Speed and Agility: Focus on faster movements and transitions due to the lack of grips.

  - Leg Locks: Emphasize leg locks and lower body submissions, which are more prevalent in no-gi.

  - Underhooks and Head Control: Use underhooks and head control to maintain positional dominance and execute submissions.

- 15.3 Preparing for Tournaments: Mental and Physical Training

  - Physical Training:

    - Conditioning: Develop cardiovascular and anaerobic endurance, along with mobility and flexibility.

    - Strength Training: Build functional strength, core stability, and grip strength through compound movements and specific exercises.

    - Drilling and Sparring: Regularly drill techniques and engage in live sparring to simulate competition intensity.

  - Mental Training:

    - Visualization: Practice mental rehearsal and scenario planning to prepare for matches.

    - Goal Setting: Set short-term and long-term goals for training and competition performance.

    - Stress Management: Use breathing techniques, mindfulness, and meditation to manage stress and anxiety.

  - Nutrition and Hydration:

- Balanced Diet: Maintain a diet rich in proteins, carbohydrates, and healthy fats to support training and recovery.

- Hydration: Stay well-hydrated daily and ensure proper hydration leading up to the competition.

- Weight Management: Monitor weight and cut weight safely under the guidance of a coach or nutritionist.

By mastering these competition strategies and tactics, you can enhance your performance in Brazilian Jiu-Jitsu tournaments. Understanding the points and scoring systems, adapting your strategies for gi and no-gi, and preparing both mentally and physically are crucial for achieving success in competition. Incorporate these elements into your training regimen to approach tournaments with confidence and a well-rounded skill set.

# Part 6: Training, Conditioning, and Development

Part 6 focuses on enhancing your Brazilian Jiu-Jitsu skills through effective training methods, conditioning exercises, and continuous development. This section emphasizes the importance of a structured training regimen to build strength, improve technique, and apply learned skills in real-time scenarios.

# Chapter 16: Effective Training Methods

Training in Brazilian Jiu-Jitsu involves a combination of solo drills, partner drills, and live sparring to develop a well-rounded skill set. This chapter covers these three essential training methods.

## *16.1 Solo Drills: Building Strength and Coordination*

Solo drills are crucial for building the foundational strength, coordination, and muscle memory needed for effective Brazilian Jiu-Jitsu practice. These exercises can be performed alone and are designed to improve physical attributes and technique.

### *A. Bodyweight Exercises*

**1. Push-Ups**

   - Benefits: Develop upper body strength and endurance, essential for controlling opponents and performing techniques.

   - Variations:

     - Standard Push-Ups: Basic push-up position with hands shoulder-width apart.

     - Diamond Push-Ups: Hands close together under the chest to target triceps.

     - Wide-Arm Push-Ups: Hands placed wider than shoulder-width to engage the chest more.

## 2. Pull-Ups

- Benefits: Build upper body and grip strength, crucial for maintaining grips and executing techniques.

- Variations:

  - Standard Pull-Ups: Palms facing away, hands shoulder-width apart.

  - Chin-Ups: Palms facing towards you, targeting the biceps more.

  - Wide-Grip Pull-Ups: Hands wider than shoulder-width to increase back engagement.

## 3. Squats and Lunges

- Benefits: Enhance lower body strength and stability, improving balance and power in movements.

- Variations:

  - Bodyweight Squats: Basic squat movement with no added weight.

  - Jump Squats: Add a jump at the top of the squat for explosive power.

  - Walking Lunges: Step forward into a lunge, alternating legs as you move forward.

  - Split Squats: Static lunge position, lowering and raising the body without moving the feet.

## *B. Movement Drills*

## 1. Shrimping

- Benefits: Essential for escaping bottom positions and creating space.

- Technique:

  - Lie on your back, one foot planted on the ground.

  - Push off the planted foot, moving your hips away and creating space.

  - Repeat on both sides, focusing on smooth, controlled movements.

## 2. Bridging

- Benefits: Develops core strength and explosive power for escapes and reversals.

- Technique:

   - Lie on your back with knees bent and feet flat on the ground.

   - Lift your hips towards the ceiling, pushing off your shoulders.

   - Rotate onto one shoulder to create a bridge, then return to the starting position.

   - Practice bridging to both sides to develop symmetry and strength.

## 3. Technical Stand-Up

*Brazilian Jiu-Jitsu Technical Stand-Up*

  - Benefits: Teaches how to safely stand up from the ground while maintaining balance and protecting yourself.

  - Technique:

   - From a seated position, plant one hand on the ground behind you.

   - Use your opposite foot to push off the ground while keeping the other leg extended for balance.

   - Stand up while maintaining a defensive posture, ready to engage.

## C. Shadow Grappling

### 1. Visualization

- Benefits: Improves mental rehearsal and technique flow without a partner.
- Technique:
  - Visualize grappling scenarios and move through techniques in the air.
  - Practice transitions, guard passes, and submission setups with imagined resistance.
  - Focus on smooth, controlled movements and proper form.

### 2. Flow Drills

- Benefits: Combines different movements into a continuous sequence, enhancing coordination and fluidity.
- Technique:
  - Create sequences of movements, such as transitioning from guard to mount, then to back control.
  - Practice these sequences repeatedly, focusing on maintaining a continuous flow.
  - Incorporate different techniques and transitions to develop versatility.

Mastering these solo drills will build the foundational strength, coordination, and muscle memory needed for effective Brazilian Jiu-Jitsu practice. By regularly incorporating bodyweight exercises, movement drills, and shadow grappling into your training routine, you can enhance your physical attributes and technique, preparing you for more advanced drills and sparring sessions with partners.

# 16.2 Partner Drills: Technique and Resistance Training

Partner drills are essential for applying techniques with resistance and understanding timing, leverage, and body mechanics. Training with a partner allows you to practice and refine your skills in a realistic context, preparing you for live sparring and competition.

## A. Technique Drills

### 1. Repetitive Drilling

- Purpose: Develop muscle memory and precision in executing techniques.

- Examples:

  - Armbar from Guard: Repeatedly practice the armbar from the guard position, focusing on proper setup, hip movement, and finishing mechanics.

  - Triangle Choke Setup: Drill the triangle choke, ensuring correct leg positioning and grip control.

  - Guard Passes: Practice passes like the knee slice pass or Toreando pass to build efficiency and control.

### 2. Positional Drills

- Purpose: Improve specific positional skills, escapes, and transitions.

- Examples:

  - Escaping Side Control: Practice techniques such as shrimping and bridging to escape from side control.

  - Maintaining Mount: Work on maintaining the mount position, applying pressure, and transitioning to submissions.

  - Sweeping from Half Guard: Drill sweeps from the half guard, focusing on timing and leverage.

## B. Resistance Training

### 1. Controlled Resistance

- Purpose: Simulate realistic scenarios with a partner providing controlled resistance to enhance timing and adaptability.

- Examples:

  - Guard Passing with Resistance: Have your partner provide realistic resistance as you attempt to pass their guard. Focus on maintaining control and adjusting techniques based on their reactions.

- Submission Defense and Counter: Your partner attempts a submission, and you practice defending and countering with controlled resistance.

- Positional Control Drills: Maintain positions like side control or mount while your partner attempts to escape, providing resistance to test your control and pressure.

## 2. Flow Rolling

- Purpose: Engage in light rolling with an emphasis on fluidity, technique, and continuous movement rather than strength and aggression.

- Examples:

- Dynamic Transitions: Move between positions and techniques smoothly, focusing on maintaining a flow without pausing.

- Technique Application: Apply techniques learned during repetitive and positional drills in a flowing, less intense sparring context.

- Partner Feedback: Communicate with your partner to provide feedback and adjust intensity, ensuring a productive flow rolling session.

## *C. Implementation Tips*

### 1. Consistency and Focus

- Schedule regular partner drilling sessions to ensure consistent practice and improvement.

- Set specific goals for each session, such as mastering a particular technique or improving a specific positional skill.

### 2. Communication and Safety

- Communicate with your partner about the level of resistance and intensity to maintain a safe and productive training environment.

- Ensure both partners are comfortable with the drills and adjust as needed to prevent injury.

### 3. Variation and Adaptability

- Incorporate a variety of drills to address different aspects of your game, such as submissions, escapes, and positional control.

- Be adaptable and open to feedback, using each session to identify areas for improvement and refine your techniques.

Mastering partner drills through consistent practice and focused training will significantly enhance your Brazilian Jiu-Jitsu skills. By working with a partner to drill techniques and resistance training, you can develop the timing, leverage, and adaptability needed for effective application in live sparring and competition.

# *16.3 Sparring (Rolling): Applying Techniques in Real Time*

Sparring, or rolling, is the practical application of techniques in a live setting. It simulates real competition and helps develop timing, adaptability, and resilience. This section covers various types of sparring and strategies to maximize your training sessions.

## *A. Types of Sparring*

**1. Positional Sparring**

- Purpose: Focus on specific positions to improve escapes, maintenance, and transitions.

- Examples:

- Side Control: Start in side control and practice escaping, maintaining, or transitioning to mount or back control.

- Mount: Begin in the mount position and work on maintaining control, applying submissions, or escaping to guard.

- Back Control: Start with back control and practice retaining the position, transitioning to submissions, or escaping to a neutral position.

**2. Full Sparring**

- Purpose: Engage in full rounds of rolling to simulate real matches, applying techniques and strategies learned during drills.

- Examples:

- Starting from Standing: Begin each round from a standing position to practice takedowns, throws, and guard pulls.

- Starting from Guard: Begin in guard to focus on passing, sweeping, and submission attempts.

- Open Sparring: Allow for a free-flowing sparring session where partners can move through various positions and techniques.

## *B. Sparring Strategies*

### 1. Goal-Oriented Rolling

- Purpose: Set specific goals for each sparring session to focus on particular aspects of your game.

- Examples:

- Guard Passing: Concentrate on successfully passing your partner's guard using different techniques.

- Submission Focus: Aim to set up and execute a particular submission, such as an armbar or triangle choke.

- Defensive Strategies: Focus on improving your defensive skills, such as escaping bad positions or defending against submissions.

### 2. Technical Rolling

- Purpose: Prioritize technique and control over strength and speed to refine your skills.

- Examples:

- Slow Rolling: Engage in slower-paced sparring to focus on precise technique execution and fluid transitions.

- Controlled Movements: Maintain control and deliberate movements, avoiding the use of excessive force.

### 3. Intensity Management

- Purpose: Vary the intensity of sparring sessions to balance learning and physical conditioning.

- Examples:

- Light Sparring: Focus on technical improvement and flow without excessive physical exertion.

- Moderate Sparring: Increase intensity to simulate more realistic match conditions, maintaining a balance between technique and physicality.

- Hard Sparring: Engage in high-intensity sparring to prepare for the physical demands of competition, ensuring safety and control.

## *C. Implementation Tips*

### 1. Preparation and Warm-Up

- Ensure proper warm-up before sparring sessions to prevent injuries and improve performance.

- Incorporate dynamic stretches and mobility exercises to prepare your body for the physical demands of sparring.

### 2. Safety and Respect

- Maintain a focus on safety and mutual respect during sparring sessions.

- Communicate with your partner about intensity levels and any potential injuries or limitations.

### 3. Reflection and Analysis

- After each sparring session, reflect on your performance and identify areas for improvement.

- Consider keeping a training journal to track progress and set goals for future sessions.

Mastering sparring through consistent practice and focused training will significantly enhance your Brazilian Jiu-Jitsu skills. By engaging in various types of sparring and employing strategic approaches, you can develop the timing, adaptability, and resilience needed for effective application in live scenarios and competition.

# *Chapter 16 Review: Effective Training Methods*

Chapter 16: Effective Training Methods covers the essential components of Brazilian Jiu-Jitsu training, emphasizing the importance of a structured regimen to build strength, improve technique, and apply learned skills in real-time scenarios. Here's a summary of the key points from each section:

### - 16.1 Solo Drills: Building Strength and Coordination

- Bodyweight Exercises: Develop upper and lower body strength with exercises like push-ups, pull-ups, squats, and lunges. Variations help target different muscle groups and enhance overall strength.

- Movement Drills: Improve core strength, mobility, and technique with shrimping, bridging, and technical stand-up exercises. These drills are essential for escaping positions and maintaining balance.

- Shadow Grappling: Enhance coordination and muscle memory through visualization and flow drills. Practicing transitions and techniques in the air helps develop fluidity and precision.

### - 16.2 Partner Drills: Technique and Resistance Training

- Technique Drills: Practice specific techniques repeatedly to build muscle memory and precision. Examples include armbar from guard, triangle choke setups, and various guard passes.

- Positional Drills: Focus on specific positions and transitions, such as escaping side control, maintaining mount, and sweeping from half guard. These drills improve positional skills and adaptability.

- Resistance Training: Apply techniques with controlled resistance to simulate realistic scenarios. Engage in flow rolling to practice continuous movement and technique application with a partner providing resistance.

### - 16.3 Sparring (Rolling): Applying Techniques in Real Time

- Types of Sparring:

- Positional Sparring: Start in specific positions to practice escapes, maintenance, and transitions.

- Full Sparring: Engage in full rounds of rolling to simulate real matches, starting from standing or guard positions.

- Sparring Strategies:

- Goal-Oriented Rolling: Set specific goals for each session, such as focusing on guard passes or submission setups.

- Technical Rolling: Prioritize technique and control over strength and speed to refine skills.

- Intensity Management: Vary sparring intensity to balance learning and conditioning, incorporating light, moderate, and hard sparring sessions.


By mastering these training methods, you can develop a well-rounded skill set, improve physical conditioning, and effectively apply techniques in real-time scenarios. This comprehensive approach to training will enhance your overall performance in Brazilian Jiu-Jitsu and prepare you for competition and live sparring situations.

# Chapter 17: Physical Conditioning for BJJ

Physical conditioning is a critical aspect of Brazilian Jiu-Jitsu, enhancing your strength, flexibility, mobility, and cardiovascular endurance. This chapter covers the key components of physical conditioning, providing exercises and strategies to optimize your performance on the mat.

## *17.1 Strength Training: Building Functional Strength*

Strength training is essential for developing the power and stability needed in Brazilian Jiu-Jitsu. Functional strength focuses on movements that mimic the demands of BJJ, improving overall performance and reducing the risk of injury.

### *A. Core Exercises*

#### 1. Compound Movements

  - Squats:

   - Benefits: Strengthen the legs, hips, and core, essential for maintaining base and performing takedowns.

   - Technique: Stand with feet shoulder-width apart, lower your hips as if sitting back in a chair, keep your chest up, and return to standing. Ensure your knees do not extend beyond your toes.

  - Deadlifts:

   - Benefits: Build posterior chain strength, including the back, glutes, and hamstrings.

   - Technique: Stand with feet hip-width apart, bend at the hips and knees to grasp the bar, keep your back straight, and lift by extending your hips and knees. Keep the bar close to your body throughout the movement.

#### 2. Upper Body Exercises

  - Pull-Ups:

   - Benefits: Develop upper body and grip strength, crucial for maintaining grips and performing techniques.

- Technique: Hang from a bar with palms facing away, hands shoulder-width apart. Pull your body up until your chin is above the bar, then lower back down with control.

   - Bench Press:

   - Benefits: Strengthen the chest, shoulders, and triceps, enhancing pushing movements.

   - Technique: Lie on a bench, grasp the bar with hands slightly wider than shoulder-width, lower the bar to your chest, and press back up. Keep your feet flat on the floor and your lower back in contact with the bench.

### 3. Core Stability

   - Planks:

   - Benefits: Strengthen the core, improving stability and balance.

   - Technique: Hold a push-up position with your body in a straight line from head to heels, engaging your core. Hold this position for as long as possible while maintaining proper form.

   - Russian Twists:

   - Benefits: Enhance rotational strength and core stability.

   - Technique: Sit on the ground with knees bent, lean back slightly, and twist your torso from side to side while holding a weight. Keep your feet elevated for an added challenge.

## *B. Accessory Exercises*

### 1. Farmers Walks

   - Benefits: Build grip strength, core stability, and overall conditioning.

   - Technique: Hold a heavy weight in each hand, keep your posture upright, and walk a set distance. Focus on maintaining a strong grip and steady pace.

### 2. Kettlebell Swings

   - Benefits: Develop explosive power and hip drive, important for many BJJ movements.

- Technique: Stand with feet shoulder-width apart, hold a kettlebell with both hands, and swing it between your legs. Drive your hips forward to lift the kettlebell to shoulder height, then control its return.

### 3. Turkish Get-Ups

- Benefits: Improve full-body strength, coordination, and mobility.

- Technique: Lie on your back holding a weight in one hand. Perform a series of movements to stand up, keeping the weight overhead, then reverse the movements to return to the starting position. Focus on control and stability throughout the exercise.

## *C. Program Structure*

### 1. Frequency

- Training Days: Aim for 2-3 strength training sessions per week, allowing for adequate recovery between sessions.

- Balance: Combine strength training with your regular BJJ practice to ensure a well-rounded conditioning program.

### 2. Progressive Overload

- Increasing Intensity: Gradually increase the weight, sets, or repetitions to continuously challenge your muscles.

- Tracking Progress: Keep a training log to monitor your improvements and adjust your program as needed.

### 3. Rest and Recovery

- Rest Intervals: Allow 1-2 minutes of rest between sets to ensure proper recovery and maintain performance.

- Recovery Practices: Incorporate stretching, foam rolling, and adequate sleep to support muscle recovery and prevent injuries.

By integrating these strength training exercises into your routine, you can build the functional strength necessary for effective performance in Brazilian Jiu-Jitsu. Focus on compound movements, core stability, and accessory exercises to develop a balanced and powerful physique that enhances your grappling abilities.

## 17.2 Flexibility and Mobility: Essential Exercises

Flexibility and mobility are vital for preventing injuries, improving technique execution, and maintaining an optimal range of motion. Incorporating these exercises into your routine will enhance your BJJ performance.

### *A. Dynamic Stretching*

**1. Leg Swings**

- Benefits: Improve hip mobility and flexibility.

- Technique: Stand on one leg, swing the other leg forward and backward, then side to side.

**2. Arm Circles**

- Benefits: Enhance shoulder mobility and flexibility.

- Technique: Extend your arms to the sides and make circular motions, gradually increasing the circle size.

### *B. Static Stretching*

**1. Hamstring Stretch**

- Benefits: Increase hamstring flexibility, essential for guard work and transitions.

- Technique: Sit on the ground with one leg extended and the other bent, reach towards your toes, and hold the stretch.

**2. Hip Flexor Stretch**

- Benefits: Improve hip flexibility and mobility, aiding in guard retention and transitions.

- Technique: Kneel on one knee, push your hips forward, and hold the stretch.

## C. Mobility Drills

### 1. Hip Openers

- Benefits: Enhance hip mobility for improved guard work and submissions.

- Technique: Perform exercises like the butterfly stretch and deep squat holds to open the hips.

### 2. Shoulder Dislocations

- Benefits: Improve shoulder mobility, crucial for escaping submissions and maintaining grips.

- Technique: Use a resistance band or broomstick, hold it with a wide grip, and rotate it over your head and back.

## D. Implementation Tips

### 1. Consistency

- Daily Practice: Incorporate flexibility and mobility exercises into your daily routine to ensure consistent improvement.

- Warm-Up and Cool-Down: Include dynamic stretching in your warm-up and static stretching in your cool-down to enhance performance and recovery.

### 2. Progressive Approach

- Gradual Increase: Gradually increase the intensity and duration of your stretches to avoid injury and ensure steady progress.

- Listen to Your Body: Pay attention to your body's signals and avoid pushing too hard, especially when starting a new exercise.

### 3. Variety

- Mix It Up: Use a variety of exercises to target different muscle groups and maintain overall flexibility and mobility.

- Balanced Routine: Ensure your routine includes stretches and drills for both the upper and lower body to maintain balanced flexibility.

By incorporating these flexibility and mobility exercises into your training regimen, you can improve your overall performance in Brazilian Jiu-Jitsu.

Regular practice will enhance your range of motion, reduce the risk of injury, and enable you to execute techniques more effectively.

## 17.3 Cardiovascular Conditioning: Enhancing Endurance

Cardiovascular conditioning is essential for maintaining high energy levels during training and competition. Incorporating various forms of cardio to build endurance will improve overall performance in Brazilian Jiu-Jitsu.

### A. High-Intensity Interval Training (HIIT)

**1. Sprints**

- Benefits: Improve anaerobic capacity and explosive power.

- Technique: Perform short bursts of sprints (20-30 seconds) followed by rest periods (30-60 seconds).

- Example: Sprint for 30 seconds, rest for 60 seconds, and repeat for 8-10 rounds.

**2. Circuit Training**

- Benefits: Enhance cardiovascular fitness and muscular endurance.

- Technique: Create circuits of various exercises (e.g., burpees, jumping jacks, push-ups) performed in quick succession with minimal rest.

- Example: Perform 30 seconds of burpees, 30 seconds of push-ups, 30 seconds of jumping jacks, and rest for 60 seconds. Repeat for 5-7 rounds.

### B. Steady-State Cardio

**1. Running**

- Benefits: Build cardiovascular endurance and improve overall fitness.

- Technique: Maintain a steady pace for 20-40 minutes, adjusting intensity based on fitness level.

- Example: Run at a moderate pace for 30 minutes, gradually increasing distance or speed over time.

## 2. Cycling

- Benefits: Low-impact cardio exercise that builds leg strength and endurance.

- Technique: Cycle at a moderate pace for 30-45 minutes, incorporating intervals for added intensity.

- Example: Cycle steadily for 30 minutes, with 1-minute sprints every 5 minutes.

## *C. Sport-Specific Drills*

### 1. Grappling Drills

- Benefits: Mimic the cardiovascular demands of a BJJ match.

- Technique: Perform drills like guard passing, positional sparring, and flow rolling with minimal rest.

- Example: Guard pass drills for 3 minutes, rest for 1 minute, and repeat for 5 rounds.

### 2. Bag Work

- Benefits: Improve cardiovascular endurance and striking power.

- Technique: Practice striking combinations on a heavy bag, incorporating footwork and head movement.

- Example: Perform 3-minute rounds of continuous striking on a heavy bag with 1-minute rest periods. Repeat for 5-8 rounds.

## *D. Implementation Tips*

### 1. Consistency

- Regular Sessions: Schedule regular cardio sessions throughout the week to ensure consistent improvement.

- Variety: Incorporate a mix of HIIT, steady-state cardio, and sport-specific drills to keep your routine engaging and well-rounded.

## 2. Intensity Management

- Balanced Intensity: Alternate between high-intensity and moderate-intensity workouts to balance effort and recovery.

- Recovery: Allow adequate recovery time between intense cardio sessions to prevent overtraining and injuries.

## 3. Monitoring Progress

- Tracking Performance: Keep a log of your cardio workouts, noting duration, intensity, and any improvements.

- Adjustments: Gradually increase the intensity, duration, or complexity of your cardio workouts as your endurance improves.

By incorporating these cardiovascular conditioning exercises into your training routine, you can significantly enhance your endurance, improve overall fitness, and maintain high energy levels during Brazilian Jiu-Jitsu training and competitions. Regular cardio training will enable you to perform techniques more effectively and sustain a high level of performance throughout your matches.

# *Chapter 17 Review: Physical Conditioning for BJJ*

Chapter 17: Physical Conditioning for BJJ covers the essential aspects of building the strength, flexibility, mobility, and cardiovascular endurance necessary for Brazilian Jiu-Jitsu. Here's a summary of the key points from each section:

- **17.1 Strength Training: Building Functional Strength**
  - Core Exercises:
    - Compound Movements: Strengthen the legs, hips, and core with exercises like squats and deadlifts. Upper body strength is enhanced with pull-ups and bench presses.
    - Core Stability: Develop stability and balance through planks and Russian twists.
  - Accessory Exercises:

- Farmers Walks: Improve grip strength, core stability, and overall conditioning.
  - Kettlebell Swings: Build explosive power and hip drive.
  - Turkish Get-Ups: Enhance full-body strength, coordination, and mobility.
- Program Structure:
  - Frequency: Aim for 2-3 strength training sessions per week, balanced with BJJ practice.
  - Progressive Overload: Gradually increase weight, sets, or repetitions to continuously challenge muscles.
  - Rest and Recovery: Allow 1-2 minutes of rest between sets and incorporate recovery practices like stretching and foam rolling.

- **17.2 Flexibility and Mobility: Essential Exercises**
  - Dynamic Stretching:
    - Leg Swings: Improve hip mobility and flexibility.
    - Arm Circles: Enhance shoulder mobility and flexibility.
  - Static Stretching:
    - Hamstring Stretch: Increase hamstring flexibility for guard work and transitions.
    - Hip Flexor Stretch: Improve hip flexibility and mobility.
  - Mobility Drills:
    - Hip Openers: Enhance hip mobility for improved guard work and submissions.
    - Shoulder Dislocations: Improve shoulder mobility for escaping submissions and maintaining grips.
  - Implementation Tips:
    - Consistency: Incorporate flexibility and mobility exercises daily, and include dynamic stretching in warm-ups and static stretching in cool-downs.
    - Progressive Approach: Gradually increase intensity and duration of stretches.

- Variety: Use a mix of exercises to target different muscle groups and maintain balanced flexibility.

## - 17.3 Cardiovascular Conditioning: Enhancing Endurance

- High-Intensity Interval Training (HIIT):

- Sprints: Improve anaerobic capacity and explosive power with short bursts of sprints followed by rest periods.

- Circuit Training: Enhance cardiovascular fitness and muscular endurance with circuits of various exercises performed in quick succession.

- Steady-State Cardio:

- Running: Build cardiovascular endurance with moderate pace runs.

- Cycling: Low-impact cardio exercise that builds leg strength and endurance.

- Sport-Specific Drills:

- Grappling Drills: Mimic the cardiovascular demands of a BJJ match with guard passing, positional sparring, and flow rolling.

- Bag Work: Improve cardiovascular endurance and striking power with heavy bag striking combinations.

- Implementation Tips:

- Consistency: Schedule regular cardio sessions and incorporate a mix of HIIT, steady-state cardio, and sport-specific drills.

- Intensity Management: Alternate between high-intensity and moderate-intensity workouts, allowing for recovery.

- Monitoring Progress: Keep a log of cardio workouts, noting duration, intensity, and improvements, and adjust as needed.

By integrating these physical conditioning components into your training routine, you can enhance your overall performance, reduce the risk of injury, and improve your endurance and strength on the mat. This comprehensive approach to physical conditioning will prepare you for the demands of Brazilian Jiu-Jitsu training and competition.

# Chapter 18: Mental Preparation and Focus

Mental preparation is as crucial as physical conditioning in Brazilian Jiu-Jitsu. Developing the right mindset, setting clear goals, visualizing success, and managing stress can significantly impact your performance on the mat. This chapter delves into the essential aspects of mental preparation, including goal setting, visualization techniques, and strategies for managing competition anxiety, providing a comprehensive guide to cultivating mental resilience and focus.

*Brazilian Jiu-Jitsu Mindset*

## *18.1 Goal Setting: Short-term and Long-term*

Setting clear, achievable goals is fundamental to improving in Brazilian Jiu-Jitsu. Goals provide direction, motivation, and a measure of progress. By establishing both short-term and long-term goals, practitioners can maintain focus, track their development, and stay motivated throughout their BJJ journey.

## *A. Short-term Goals*

### 1. Daily and Weekly Objectives

- Purpose: Focus on immediate improvements and tasks.

- Examples:

  - Mastering a specific technique, such as a sweep or submission.

  - Improving a particular aspect of your game, like guard retention or passing.

  - Drilling a new move consistently over a week to ensure proficiency.

### 2. Training Session Goals

- Purpose: Maximize the effectiveness of each training session.

- Examples:

  - Successfully execute a new move during live rolling.

  - Maintain positional control for a set amount of time.

  - Sparring with a focus on applying specific techniques learned in class.

## *B. Long-term Goals*

### 1. Belt Promotion

- Purpose: Provide a clear milestone and motivation for continuous improvement.

- Examples:

  - Achieving the next belt rank within a specific timeframe.

  - Meeting the technical and competition requirements for promotion.

  - Attending seminars and additional classes to broaden knowledge and skillset.

### 2. Competition Achievements

- Purpose: Set targets for success in tournaments and competitions.

- Examples:

  - Winning a local or regional BJJ tournament.

  - Qualifying for national or international competitions.

- Consistently placing in the top three in your division.

### 3. Skill Mastery

- Purpose: Focus on long-term development and deepening your understanding of BJJ.

- Examples:

  - Mastering advanced techniques or positions, such as the De La Riva guard or advanced leg locks.

  - Becoming proficient in both gi and no-gi grappling.

  - Teaching and mentoring lower belts to solidify your understanding and contribute to the BJJ community.

By clearly defining short-term and long-term goals, practitioners can create a structured path for improvement, stay motivated, and achieve continuous progress in their Brazilian Jiu-Jitsu journey.

## *18.2 Visualization and Mental Rehearsal*

Visualization and mental rehearsal are powerful tools that can significantly enhance your Brazilian Jiu-Jitsu performance. By mentally simulating techniques, scenarios, and successful outcomes, you can improve your focus, confidence, and execution during actual training and competition.

## *A. Visualization Techniques*

### 1. Detailed Imagery

- Purpose: Create a vivid mental picture of executing techniques and movements correctly.

- Technique:

  - Close your eyes and visualize yourself performing a specific BJJ technique.

  - Imagine every detail, from the grips and movements to the reaction of your opponent.

- Focus on the feel of the mat, the pressure applied, and the sequence of steps involved.

## 2. Scenario Planning

- Purpose: Prepare for various scenarios you might encounter during a match.
- Technique:
- Visualize different match situations, such as escaping a bad position, executing a sweep, or applying a submission.
- Imagine how you would react to your opponent's movements and strategize your responses.
- Practice visualizing both offensive and defensive scenarios to be well-prepared for any situation.

## *B. Mental Rehearsal*

### 1. Pre-Competition Routine

- Purpose: Establish a consistent mental routine before competitions to enhance focus and reduce anxiety.
- Technique:
- Mentally rehearse your pre-competition routine, including warming up, entering the competition area, and visualizing a successful match.
- Focus on positive outcomes and reaffirm your confidence in your abilities.
- Use this routine consistently to build familiarity and reduce nerves before competitions.

### 2. Post-Training Reflection

- Purpose: Reinforce learning and identify areas for improvement.
- Technique:
- After each training session, take a few minutes to mentally review what you practiced.
- Visualize the techniques you worked on and how you can refine them.
- Reflect on any mistakes or challenges and imagine how you will overcome them in future sessions.

## *C. Benefits of Visualization and Mental Rehearsal*

### 1. Improved Performance

- Explanation: By visualizing techniques and scenarios, you can enhance your muscle memory and execution, leading to better performance during training and competitions.

- Example: A competitor who regularly visualizes executing a triangle choke will likely perform it more smoothly and confidently during a match.

### 2. Enhanced Focus and Confidence

- Explanation: Visualization helps sharpen your focus and build confidence by mentally rehearsing successful outcomes.

- Example: A practitioner who visualizes successfully escaping from side control will approach the situation with more confidence and composure during actual sparring.

### 3. Stress Reduction

- Explanation: Mental rehearsal can reduce pre-competition anxiety by creating a sense of familiarity and preparedness.

- Example: A competitor who mentally rehearses their match routine will feel more relaxed and focused when it's time to compete.

By incorporating visualization and mental rehearsal into your training routine, you can significantly enhance your Brazilian Jiu-Jitsu performance. These techniques help you prepare mentally for various scenarios, build confidence, and improve your focus, ultimately leading to better execution and success on the mat.

## *18.3 Managing Stress and Competition Anxiety*

Managing stress and competition anxiety is crucial for optimal performance in Brazilian Jiu-Jitsu. Effective stress management techniques can help you stay calm, focused, and composed during training and competitions, allowing you to perform at your best.

## *A. Breathing Techniques*

### 1. Diaphragmatic Breathing

 - Purpose: Calm the mind and body by engaging the diaphragm.

 - Technique:

   - Sit or lie down in a comfortable position.

   - Place one hand on your chest and the other on your abdomen.

   - Inhale deeply through your nose, allowing your abdomen to rise while keeping your chest relatively still.

   - Exhale slowly through your mouth, feeling your abdomen fall.

   - Repeat for several minutes, focusing on the rhythm of your breath.

### 2. Box Breathing

 - Purpose: Regulate breathing and reduce stress.

 - Technique:

   - Inhale deeply through your nose for a count of four.

   - Hold your breath for a count of four.

   - Exhale slowly through your mouth for a count of four.

   - Hold your breath again for a count of four.

   - Repeat the cycle several times.

## *B. Mindfulness and Meditation*

### 1. Mindfulness Meditation

 - Purpose: Increase awareness and reduce anxiety by focusing on the present moment.

 - Technique:

   - Find a quiet, comfortable place to sit.

   - Close your eyes and take a few deep breaths.

   - Focus on your breath, noticing the sensation of each inhale and exhale.

- When your mind wanders, gently bring your focus back to your breath.

- Practice for 5-10 minutes daily.

## 2. Body Scan Meditation

- Purpose: Reduce tension and increase relaxation by scanning the body for areas of stress.

- Technique:

  - Lie down in a comfortable position.

  - Close your eyes and take a few deep breaths.

  - Starting from your toes, mentally scan your body, noticing any areas of tension or discomfort.

  - As you identify each area, consciously relax those muscles and let go of the tension.

  - Continue scanning up through your entire body.

# *C. Mental Strategies*

## 1. Positive Self-Talk

- Purpose: Build confidence and reduce negative thoughts.

- Technique:

  - Replace negative thoughts with positive affirmations.

  - Examples: "I am prepared and capable," "I can handle any situation that arises," "I have trained hard for this moment."

  - Repeat these affirmations regularly, especially before and during competitions.

## 2. Pre-Competition Routine

- Purpose: Establish a consistent routine to reduce anxiety and increase focus.

- Technique:

  - Develop a pre-competition routine that includes warming up, mental rehearsal, and relaxation techniques.

- Stick to this routine for every competition to create a sense of familiarity and control.

- Examples: Listening to calming music, performing specific warm-up exercises, and visualizing success.

## *D. Professional Support*

### 1. Coaching and Mentorship

- Purpose: Gain guidance and support from experienced coaches or mentors.

- Technique:

- Regularly discuss your progress, goals, and challenges with your coach or mentor.

- Seek their advice on stress management techniques and competition strategies.

- Use their feedback to refine your approach and build confidence.

### 2. Therapy or Counseling

- Purpose: Address deeper issues of anxiety and stress with professional help.

- Technique:

- Consider seeking therapy or counseling if stress and anxiety significantly impact your performance and well-being.

- Work with a mental health professional to develop personalized strategies for managing stress and anxiety.

By incorporating these stress management techniques into your training routine, you can effectively manage competition anxiety and enhance your performance in Brazilian Jiu-Jitsu. Staying calm, focused, and composed will enable you to perform at your best and achieve your goals on the mat.

# *Chapter 18 Review: Mental Preparation and Focus*

Chapter 18: Mental Preparation and Focus emphasizes the importance of developing the right mindset, setting clear goals, visualizing success, and managing stress to enhance performance in Brazilian Jiu-Jitsu. Here's a summary of the key points from each section:

## - 18.1 Goal Setting: Short-term and Long-term

  - Short-term Goals:

    - Daily and Weekly Objectives: Focus on immediate improvements and tasks, such as mastering a specific technique or improving an aspect of your game.

    - Training Session Goals: Maximize the effectiveness of each training session by setting goals like successfully executing a new move during live rolling or maintaining positional control.

  - Long-term Goals:

    - Belt Promotion: Set milestones for achieving the next belt rank and meeting technical and competition requirements.

    - Competition Achievements: Establish targets for success in tournaments and competitions, such as winning a local or regional BJJ tournament.

    - Skill Mastery: Focus on long-term development and deepening your understanding of BJJ, like mastering advanced techniques or becoming proficient in both gi and no-gi grappling.

## - 18.2 Visualization and Mental Rehearsal

  - Visualization Techniques:

    - Detailed Imagery: Create a vivid mental picture of executing techniques correctly, focusing on every detail.

    - Scenario Planning: Prepare for various match scenarios, imagining how you would react and strategize your responses.

  - Mental Rehearsal:

    - Pre-Competition Routine: Establish a consistent mental routine before competitions to enhance focus and reduce anxiety.

    - Post-Training Reflection: Mentally review what you practiced after each session, visualizing techniques and identifying areas for improvement.

  - Benefits:

- Improved Performance: Enhance muscle memory and execution through visualization.

- Enhanced Focus and Confidence: Sharpen focus and build confidence by mentally rehearsing successful outcomes.

- Stress Reduction: Reduce pre-competition anxiety by creating a sense of familiarity and preparedness.

- **18.3 Managing Stress and Competition Anxiety**

  - Breathing Techniques:

  - Diaphragmatic Breathing: Calm the mind and body by engaging the diaphragm.

  - Box Breathing: Regulate breathing and reduce stress with a structured breathing pattern.

  - Mindfulness and Meditation:

  - Mindfulness Meditation: Increase awareness and reduce anxiety by focusing on the present moment.

  - Body Scan Meditation: Reduce tension and increase relaxation by mentally scanning the body for areas of stress.

  - Mental Strategies:

  - Positive Self-Talk: Build confidence and reduce negative thoughts with affirmations.

  - Pre-Competition Routine: Establish a consistent routine to reduce anxiety and increase focus.

  - Professional Support:

  - Coaching and Mentorship: Gain guidance and support from experienced coaches or mentors.

  - Therapy or Counseling: Address deeper issues of anxiety and stress with professional help if needed.

By integrating these mental preparation techniques into your training routine, you can significantly enhance your Brazilian Jiu-Jitsu performance. Setting clear goals, practicing visualization, and managing stress effectively will help you stay focused, confident, and composed, enabling you to achieve success on the mat.

# Part 7: Practical Applications and Self-Defense

Part 7 focuses on the real-world applications of Brazilian Jiu-Jitsu techniques for self-defense. This section highlights how BJJ can be effectively utilized to protect oneself in various scenarios outside the gym or competition. The techniques covered are designed to address common attacks, defend against strikes, and escape holds and grabs, providing practical skills for real-life situations.

# Chapter 19: Real-World Self-Defense Applications

Brazilian Jiu-Jitsu is not only a competitive sport but also a highly effective self-defense system. This chapter explores how BJJ techniques can be applied to protect oneself in real-world situations. By understanding and practicing these techniques, practitioners can gain confidence and preparedness for various self-defense scenarios.

## *19.1 Techniques for Common Attacks*

Understanding and effectively responding to common attacks is crucial for self-defense in real-world situations. Brazilian Jiu-Jitsu offers practical techniques to defend against these common attacks, allowing you to protect yourself and neutralize threats effectively.

### *A. Headlock Defense*

**1. Standing Headlock Defense**

   - Purpose: Escape from a standing headlock, a common street attack.

   - Technique:

      - Step 1: Turn your chin towards the attacker's body to create space and protect your airway.

- Step 2: Use your hands to push against the attacker's hip and shoulder to create leverage.

- Step 3: Step behind the attacker and apply a takedown, transitioning to a dominant position such as side control.

## 2. Ground Headlock Defense

- Purpose: Escape from a headlock when taken to the ground.

- Technique:

    - Step 1: Turn your chin towards the attacker's body to relieve pressure.

    - Step 2: Use your hands to frame against the attacker's face or hip.

- Step 3: Bridge your hips up and towards the attacker, then roll them over, ending up in a top position.

## *B. Bear Hug Escape*

### 1. Front Bear Hug (Over the Arms)

- Purpose: Escape from a bear hug where the attacker's arms are over your arms.

- Technique:

    - Step 1: Lower your center of gravity by bending your knees.

    - Step 2: Push against the attacker's hips with your hands to create space.

- Step 3: Use your hips to bump the attacker backwards, creating an opportunity to escape or counter-attack.

### 2. Rear Bear Hug (Under the Arms)

- Purpose: Escape from a bear hug where the attacker's arms are under your arms.

- Technique:

    - Step 1: Drop your weight and widen your stance to prevent being lifted.

    - Step 2: Use your hands to pry the attacker's fingers apart.

- Step 3: Turn towards the attacker while using your elbows to break free and create distance.

## C. Choke Defense

### 1. Standing Rear Choke Defense

- Purpose: Defend against a choke applied from behind while standing.
- Technique:
  - Step 1: Tuck your chin and grab the attacker's arm with both hands.
  - Step 2: Pull down on the arm while stepping back to create space.
  - Step 3: Use a hip throw or trip to take the attacker down, transitioning to a dominant position.

### 2. Front Choke Defense

- Purpose: Defend against a two-handed choke from the front.
- Technique:
  - Step 1: Tuck your chin and raise your shoulders to protect your neck.
  - Step 2: Use both hands to strike the attacker's arms in a downward motion, breaking their grip.
  - Step 3: Step to the side and apply a counter-attack or create distance to escape.

Mastering these techniques for common attacks enhances your ability to protect yourself in real-world scenarios. Regular practice and situational awareness are key to effectively applying these self-defense techniques when needed.

## *19.2 Defending Against Strikes*

Defending against strikes is a critical component of self-defense. Brazilian Jiu-Jitsu offers effective strategies to close the distance, neutralize the attacker's striking advantage, and take control of the situation. Here are some key techniques for defending against strikes:

## *A. Cover and Clinch*

### 1. Covering Up

  - Purpose: Protect vital areas such as the head and torso from strikes.

  - Technique:

  - Step 1: Raise your arms to cover your head, keeping your elbows close to your body.

  - Step 2: Use your forearms to absorb and deflect incoming strikes.

  - Step 3: Keep your chin tucked and move towards the attacker to close the distance.

### 2. Entering the Clinch

  - Purpose: Neutralize the attacker's striking by closing the distance and controlling their arms.

  - Technique:

  - Step 1: Move forward quickly while maintaining your guard to protect against strikes.

  - Step 2: Secure underhooks or overhooks to control the attacker's arms.

  - Step 3: Pull the attacker close to limit their ability to strike and prepare for a takedown or control position.

## *B. Takedown Defense*

### 1. Sprawling

  - Purpose: Prevent the attacker from taking you down by defending against single or double-leg takedown attempts.

  - Technique:

  - Step 1: As the attacker shoots for your legs, push your hips down and back.

  - Step 2: Drop your weight onto the attacker's back, driving your legs back to a sprawl position.

  - Step 3: Maintain control by placing your hands on the attacker's shoulders or head, and work to transition to a dominant position.

## 2. Framing and Footwork

- Purpose: Use frames and footwork to maintain distance and prevent takedowns.

- Technique:

  - Step 1: Use your hands to frame against the attacker's shoulders or head, creating space.

  - Step 2: Use lateral footwork to move side-to-side, making it harder for the attacker to grab your legs.

  - Step 3: Counter with strikes or transition to a clinch if the attacker persists.

## *C. Ground Defense*

### 1. Guard Position

- Purpose: Control the attacker and limit their ability to strike effectively while on the ground.

- Technique:

  - Step 1: Pull the attacker into your guard by wrapping your legs around their waist.

  - Step 2: Control their posture by grabbing their collar (in gi) or head and arms (in no-gi).

  - Step 3: Use your legs and hips to keep the attacker off-balance and prevent powerful strikes.

### 2. Sweep and Escape

- Purpose: Reverse the position or create space to stand up and escape.

- Technique:

  - Step 1: Use sweeps such as the scissor sweep or hip bump to reverse the attacker's position.

  - Step 2: If sweeping isn't possible, use techniques like shrimping to create space.

  - Step 3: Perform a technical stand-up to safely get back to your feet while maintaining your guard.

### 3. Submission Defense

- Purpose: Defend against submission attempts while on the ground.

- Technique:

- Step 1: Recognize and anticipate common submissions, such as arm bars, triangle chokes, and guillotines.

- Step 2: Use proper posture, hand positioning, and technique to defend and escape these submissions.

- Step 3: Counter-attack or create space to stand up and disengage.

Mastering these techniques for defending against strikes will significantly enhance your ability to protect yourself in real-world scenarios. Regular practice, combined with an understanding of how to control distance and neutralize an attacker's striking advantage, will improve your overall self-defense capabilities.

## 19.3 Escaping Holds and Grabs

Escaping holds and grabs is a critical aspect of self-defense in Brazilian Jiu-Jitsu. These techniques enable you to break free from an attacker's grip and regain control of the situation. Here are key methods for escaping common holds and grabs:

## A. Wrist Grab Escape

### 1. Same-Side Wrist Grab

- Purpose: Break free from an attacker's grip on your wrist.

- Technique:

- Step 1: Rotate your wrist towards the attacker's thumb, the weakest part of their grip.

- Step 2: Pull your wrist out forcefully while stepping back to create distance.

- Step 3: Follow up with strikes or create further distance to ensure your safety.

### 2. Cross-Side Wrist Grab

- Purpose: Escape when the attacker grabs your wrist with their opposite hand.
- Technique:
  - Step 1: Use your free hand to grasp your trapped hand's fist or forearm.
  - Step 2: Rotate and pull your wrist towards the attacker's thumb while stepping back.
  - Step 3: Follow up with a counter-attack or disengage to a safe distance.

## *B. Bear Hug Escape*

### 1. Front Bear Hug (Over the Arms)

- Purpose: Free yourself when the attacker's arms are over yours.
- Technique:
  - Step 1: Lower your center of gravity by bending your knees.
  - Step 2: Use your hands to push against the attacker's hips to create space.
  - Step 3: Apply knee strikes to the groin or use an upward elbow strike to the face to break the grip.

### 2. Rear Bear Hug (Under the Arms)

- Purpose: Escape from a bear hug from behind where the attacker's arms are under yours.
- Technique:
  - Step 1: Drop your weight and widen your stance to prevent being lifted.
  - Step 2: Use your hands to pry the attacker's fingers apart.
  - Step 3: Step to the side while turning towards the attacker, using your hips and shoulders to break free.

## *C. Choke Hold Escape*

### 1. Standing Rear Choke

- Purpose: Escape from a choke applied from behind while standing.

- Technique:

　- Step 1: Tuck your chin and turn your head towards the crook of the attacker's elbow to protect your airway.

　- Step 2: Use both hands to grab the attacker's choking arm and pull down to relieve pressure.

　- Step 3: Step to the side and use your hips to throw the attacker off balance, transitioning to a dominant position or escaping.

## 2. Front Choke

- Purpose: Break free from a two-handed choke from the front.

- Technique:

　- Step 1: Tuck your chin and raise your shoulders to protect your neck.

　- Step 2: Use both hands to strike the attacker's arms in a downward motion to break the grip.

　- Step 3: Step to the side and counter-attack or create distance to escape.

## *D. Full Nelson Escape*

### 1. Breaking the Full Nelson

- Purpose: Escape from a full nelson hold.

- Technique:

　- Step 1: Tuck your chin to protect your neck and prevent the attacker from applying full pressure.

　- Step 2: Use your hands to grab the attacker's fingers and peel them away from your neck.

　- Step 3: Lower your center of gravity, turn towards the attacker, and break their grip while creating space.

### 2. Creating Distance

- Purpose: Ensure a safe escape from the full nelson.

- Technique:

- Step 1: After breaking the grip, use your body weight to lean forward, pulling the attacker off balance.

- Step 2: Turn towards the attacker while using your elbows to create further distance.

- Step 3: Escape or counter-attack as needed to ensure your safety.

Mastering these techniques for escaping holds and grabs enhances your ability to protect yourself in real-world scenarios. Regular practice and situational awareness are key to effectively applying these self-defense techniques when needed.

## Chapter 19 Review: Real-World Self-Defense Applications

Chapter 19: Real-World Self-Defense Applications focuses on practical techniques for protecting oneself in real-world situations. This chapter emphasizes the application of Brazilian Jiu-Jitsu techniques to common self-defense scenarios, including defending against common attacks, strikes, and escaping holds and grabs. Here's a summary of the key points:

- 19.1 Techniques for Common Attacks

  - Headlock Defense: Protect your airway, create space, and apply a takedown to transition to a dominant position.

  - Bear Hug Escape: Use leverage and strikes to break free from front and rear bear hugs.

  - Choke Defense: Defend against standing and ground chokes by creating space, applying throws, and securing dominant positions.

- 19.2 Defending Against Strikes

  - Cover and Clinch: Protect vital areas by covering up, then close the distance to neutralize the attacker's striking advantage by clinching.

- Takedown Defense: Maintain a strong base, use sprawls, frames, and footwork to prevent takedowns.

- Ground Defense: Utilize the guard to control the attacker's posture, execute sweeps, and perform technical stand-ups to return to your feet.

**- 19.3 Escaping Holds and Grabs**

- Wrist Grab Escape: Rotate and pull your wrist towards the attacker's thumb to break free from same-side and cross-side wrist grabs.

- Bear Hug Escape: Lower your center of gravity, push against the attacker's hips, and use strikes to escape from over-the-arms and under-the-arms bear hugs.

- Choke Hold Escape: Protect your airway, use leverage to relieve pressure, and apply throws or strikes to escape standing and front chokes.

- Full Nelson Escape: Tuck your chin, peel the attacker's fingers away, and turn towards the attacker to break their grip and create distance.

By practicing these real-world self-defense techniques, you can increase your confidence and preparedness for various self-defense scenarios. These skills will enable you to protect yourself effectively and ensure your safety in real-life situations. Regular training and situational awareness are key to successfully applying these techniques when needed.

# Chapter 20: BJJ for Law Enforcement and Military

Brazilian Jiu-Jitsu offers valuable techniques and strategies for law enforcement and military personnel, focusing on control, restraint, and non-lethal force applications. This chapter explores how BJJ can be tailored to meet the specific needs of these professionals, ensuring effective and safe outcomes in high-stress situations.

## *20.1 Control and Restraint Techniques*

Control and restraint techniques are essential for law enforcement and military personnel to safely and effectively subdue and manage suspects or opponents. Brazilian Jiu-Jitsu provides practical methods to achieve this, emphasizing leverage, position, and technique over brute strength.

### *A. Positional Control*

**1. Mount Position**

   - Purpose: Secure a dominant position to control the suspect.

   - Technique:

   - Step 1: Transition to the mount by placing your knees on either side of the suspect's torso.

   - Step 2: Maintain a low center of gravity and use your hips to apply pressure.

   - Step 3: Use your hands to control the suspect's wrists or head to prevent escapes and strikes.

**2. Side Control**

   - Purpose: Maintain control over a grounded suspect.

   - Technique:

   - Step 1: Position yourself perpendicular to the suspect with your weight distributed evenly.

   - Step 2: Use your arms to control the suspect's head and hips.

- Step 3: Apply pressure with your chest and hips to immobilize the suspect and prevent movement.

## 3. Back Control

- Purpose: Control a suspect from behind, providing a secure position to manage their movements.

- Technique:

- Step 1: Secure hooks with your legs by wrapping them around the suspect's waist.

- Step 2: Use your arms to control the suspect's shoulders or neck, applying a seatbelt grip or body lock.

- Step 3: Maintain chest-to-back contact to prevent the suspect from escaping or turning into you.

## *B. Restraint Techniques*

### 1. Kimura Control

- Purpose: Control the suspect's arm and prevent resistance.

- Technique:

- Step 1: Secure the suspect's wrist with one hand and loop your other arm over their elbow.

- Step 2: Lock your hands together and use your body to apply leverage.

- Step 3: Rotate the suspect's arm behind their back, maintaining control to prevent escapes.

### 2. Arm Triangle Control

- Purpose: Subdue a suspect using a head and arm control technique.

- Technique:

- Step 1: Wrap one arm around the suspect's neck and the other around their arm.

- Step 2: Lock your hands together and apply pressure with your shoulder against the neck.

- Step 3: Use your body weight to maintain control and prevent resistance.

### 3. Rear Naked Choke (Control Variation)

- Purpose: Control a suspect without applying full choking pressure.

- Technique:

  - Step 1: Position yourself behind the suspect and wrap one arm around their neck.

  - Step 2: Instead of locking the choke, place your hand on the back of the suspect's head to control their posture.

  - Step 3: Use your other arm to secure the suspect's arm, limiting their ability to resist.

### 4. Wrist Lock

- Purpose: Control and subdue a suspect with minimal force.

- Technique:

  - Step 1: Secure the suspect's hand with both of yours.

  - Step 2: Apply pressure to the wrist by bending it towards the forearm.

  - Step 3: Use controlled force to maintain compliance without causing injury.

## *C. Implementation Tips*

### 1. Leverage Over Strength

- Focus: Use leverage and body mechanics to control the suspect rather than relying on brute strength.

- Example: Apply techniques that utilize your whole body to create force, ensuring effectiveness regardless of size or strength differences.

### 2. Maintaining Safety

- Priority: Always prioritize the safety of both the officer and the suspect.

- Example: Use control and restraint techniques that minimize the risk of injury and allow for quick adjustments if the situation changes.

### 3. Communication

- Technique: Communicate clearly with the suspect to de-escalate the situation.

- Example: Use verbal commands in conjunction with physical control techniques to encourage compliance and reduce resistance.

Mastering these control and restraint techniques enables law enforcement and military personnel to effectively manage high-stress situations, ensuring the safety and compliance of suspects while minimizing the risk of injury. Regular training and practice are essential for maintaining proficiency and readiness.

## *20.2 Non-Lethal Force Application*

Non-lethal force is crucial for law enforcement and military personnel to manage situations effectively without causing unnecessary harm. Brazilian Jiu-Jitsu provides a range of techniques that allow for the controlled application of force to subdue suspects safely.

### *A. Joint Locks*

**1. Wrist Lock**

- Purpose: Control and subdue a suspect with minimal force.
- Technique:
    - Step 1: Secure the suspect's hand with both of yours.
    - Step 2: Apply pressure to the wrist by bending it towards the forearm.
    - Step 3: Use controlled force to maintain compliance without causing injury.

**2. Arm Bar**

- Purpose: Subdue a suspect by controlling their arm.
- Technique:
    - Step 1: Secure the suspect's arm and position your body perpendicular to theirs.
    - Step 2: Place their elbow over your hip or thigh and apply pressure to the arm.

- Step 3: Control the suspect by maintaining leverage on the arm, preventing resistance.

### 3. Kimura Lock

- Purpose: Control the suspect's arm and prevent resistance.

- Technique:

- Step 1: Secure the suspect's wrist with one hand and loop your other arm over their elbow.

- Step 2: Lock your hands together and use your body to apply leverage.

- Step 3: Rotate the suspect's arm behind their back, maintaining control to prevent escapes.

## *B. Control Holds*

### 1. Rear Naked Choke (Control Variation)

- Purpose: Subdue a suspect without causing lasting harm.

- Technique:

- Step 1: Position yourself behind the suspect and wrap one arm around their neck.

- Step 2: Lock the choke by placing your other arm behind their head and clasping your hands together.

- Step 3: Apply controlled pressure to induce compliance without cutting off the air supply.

### 2. Standing Guillotine

- Purpose: Control a suspect from a standing position.

- Technique:

- Step 1: Wrap one arm around the suspect's neck from the front.

- Step 2: Lock your hands together and apply pressure by lifting the suspect's head upwards.

- Step 3: Maintain control and leverage to prevent the suspect from resisting.

### 3. Arm Triangle Control

- Purpose: Subdue a suspect using head and arm control.

- Technique:

   - Step 1: Wrap one arm around the suspect's neck and the other around their arm.

   - Step 2: Lock your hands together and apply pressure with your shoulder against the neck.

   - Step 3: Use your body weight to maintain control and prevent resistance.

## *C. Implementation Tips*

### 1. Proportionality

- Focus: Use force proportional to the threat level to ensure safety and compliance.

- Example: Apply more force only when necessary to control an aggressive or resistant suspect, and reduce force once compliance is achieved.

### 2. De-escalation

- Technique: Combine physical techniques with verbal commands to encourage de-escalation.

- Example: While applying a control hold, communicate clearly with the suspect to instruct them to comply and reassure them to reduce panic and resistance.

### 3. Monitoring and Adjustment

- Technique: Continuously monitor the suspect's condition and adjust the applied force as needed.

- Example: Ensure that holds and locks do not cause unnecessary pain or injury, and be ready to release or adjust the technique if the suspect becomes compliant or if the situation changes.

Mastering non-lethal force application techniques enables law enforcement and military personnel to effectively manage suspects while minimizing harm.

Regular training and practice in these techniques, combined with a focus on proportionality and de-escalation, ensure that these professionals can handle a wide range of situations safely and effectively.

## *20.3 Specialized Training Considerations*

Specialized training considerations ensure that law enforcement and military personnel can effectively integrate Brazilian Jiu-Jitsu techniques into their operations. This section covers scenario-based training, stress inoculation, legal and ethical considerations, and the importance of continuous learning.

### *A. Scenario-Based Training*

**1. Realistic Scenarios**

- Purpose: Prepare for real-life encounters by simulating realistic situations.

- Technique:

  - Step 1: Create training scenarios that mimic potential situations, such as arresting a suspect or defending against an ambush.

  - Step 2: Practice BJJ techniques within these scenarios to develop practical skills.

  - Step 3: Evaluate and adjust strategies based on performance and outcomes.

- Example: Simulate a traffic stop where the suspect becomes aggressive, requiring the use of control and restraint techniques.

**2. Stress Inoculation**

- Purpose: Build resilience and maintain performance under stress.

- Technique:

  - Step 1: Incorporate stress-inducing elements into training, such as loud noises, multiple attackers, or time constraints.

  - Step 2: Practice techniques and decision-making under these stressful conditions.

  - Step 3: Gradually increase stress levels to enhance adaptability and composure in real situations.

- Example: Train with high-intensity drills that simulate the chaotic environment of a real confrontation, including unexpected variables and high stakes.

## *B. Legal and Ethical Considerations*

### 1. Use of Force Policies

- Purpose: Ensure compliance with legal and organizational standards.

- Technique:

- Step 1: Understand and adhere to the use of force policies specific to your agency or organization.

- Step 2: Incorporate these policies into BJJ training to ensure techniques are applied appropriately.

- Step 3: Regularly review and update training to align with changes in policies and laws.

- Example: Train officers to apply control holds and restraint techniques within the bounds of what is legally permissible, emphasizing the use of minimal force necessary to achieve compliance.

### 2. Ethical Training

- Purpose: Promote the responsible and ethical application of BJJ techniques.

- Technique:

- Step 1: Emphasize the importance of proportionality and necessity when using force.

- Step 2: Foster a culture of respect and accountability in training and operations.

- Step 3: Encourage continuous learning and ethical decision-making in all aspects of law enforcement and military duties.

- Example: Incorporate discussions and case studies on the ethical implications of using force, encouraging personnel to reflect on their actions and decisions.

## C. Continuous Learning and Improvement

### 1. Regular Training and Drills

- Purpose: Maintain and enhance skills through consistent practice.

- Technique:

- Step 1: Schedule regular training sessions to practice BJJ techniques and integrate them with other defensive tactics.

- Step 2: Use a variety of drills to address different aspects of control, restraint, and non-lethal force.

- Step 3: Evaluate performance and provide feedback to ensure continuous improvement.

- Example: Incorporate monthly BJJ refresher courses and quarterly scenario-based training sessions to keep skills sharp and up-to-date.

### 2. Feedback and Adaptation

- Purpose: Adapt training methods based on feedback and real-world experiences.

- Technique:

- Step 1: Collect feedback from personnel about the effectiveness of BJJ techniques in the field.

- Step 2: Analyze incidents where BJJ techniques were used to identify strengths and areas for improvement.

- Step 3: Adjust training programs based on this analysis to address any gaps or weaknesses.

- Example: After an incident review, modify training to emphasize better situational awareness or specific escape techniques that were challenging in the field.

By incorporating these specialized training considerations, law enforcement and military personnel can effectively integrate Brazilian Jiu-Jitsu techniques into their operations. Scenario-based training, stress inoculation, and adherence to legal and ethical standards are crucial for ensuring that these professionals are prepared to handle real-world situations safely and effectively. Continuous learning and improvement are essential for maintaining a high level of proficiency and readiness.

# Chapter 20 Review: BJJ for Law Enforcement and Military

Chapter 20: BJJ for Law Enforcement and Military focuses on the application of Brazilian Jiu-Jitsu techniques tailored to the specific needs of law enforcement and military personnel. This chapter highlights the importance of control and restraint techniques, non-lethal force application, and specialized training considerations to ensure effective and safe outcomes in high-stress situations. Here's a summary of the key points:

### - 20.1 Control and Restraint Techniques

- Positional Control:

  - Mount Position: Secure a dominant position by placing knees on either side of the suspect's torso, applying hip pressure, and controlling the suspect's wrists or head.

  - Side Control: Maintain control over a grounded suspect by positioning yourself perpendicular, using arms to control the head and hips, and applying chest and hip pressure to immobilize the suspect.

  - Back Control: Control a suspect from behind by securing hooks with your legs, using your arms to control the suspect's shoulders or neck, and maintaining chest-to-back contact.

- Restraint Techniques:

  - Kimura Control: Secure the suspect's wrist and elbow, lock hands together, and rotate the suspect's arm behind their back to maintain control.

  - Arm Triangle Control: Wrap one arm around the suspect's neck and the other around their arm, lock hands together, and apply shoulder pressure to subdue the suspect.

  - Rear Naked Choke (Control Variation): Position behind the suspect, wrap one arm around their neck, and place your hand on the back of their head to control posture without applying full choking pressure.

- Wrist Lock: Secure the suspect's hand, apply pressure to the wrist by bending it towards the forearm, and use controlled force to maintain compliance.

## - 20.2 Non-Lethal Force Application

- Joint Locks:

  - Wrist Lock: Control and subdue a suspect with minimal force by securing the hand and applying pressure to the wrist.

  - Arm Bar: Subdue a suspect by controlling their arm, placing their elbow over your hip or thigh, and applying pressure.

  - Kimura Lock: Control the suspect's arm by securing the wrist, locking hands together, and rotating the arm behind the back.

- Control Holds:

  - Rear Naked Choke (Control Variation): Subdue a suspect without causing lasting harm by wrapping an arm around the neck and applying controlled pressure.

  - Standing Guillotine: Control a suspect from a standing position by wrapping an arm around the neck and lifting the head upwards.

  - Arm Triangle Control: Subdue a suspect using head and arm control by wrapping an arm around the neck and the other around the arm, locking hands together, and applying shoulder pressure.

- Implementation Tips:

  - Proportionality: Use force proportional to the threat level to ensure safety and compliance.

  - De-escalation: Combine physical techniques with verbal commands to encourage de-escalation.

  - Monitoring and Adjustment: Continuously monitor the suspect's condition and adjust the applied force as needed.

## - 20.3 Specialized Training Considerations

- Scenario-Based Training:

- Realistic Scenarios: Prepare for real-life encounters by simulating realistic situations and practicing BJJ techniques within these scenarios.

- Stress Inoculation: Build resilience by incorporating stress-inducing elements into training and practicing techniques under these conditions.

- Legal and Ethical Considerations:

- Use of Force Policies: Ensure compliance with legal and organizational standards by understanding and adhering to use of force policies.

- Ethical Training: Promote responsible and ethical application of BJJ techniques by emphasizing proportionality, necessity, and continuous learning.

- Continuous Learning and Improvement:

- Regular Training and Drills: Maintain and enhance skills through consistent practice, using a variety of drills to address different aspects of control and restraint.

- Feedback and Adaptation: Adapt training methods based on feedback and real-world experiences, continuously improving performance and readiness.

By integrating these techniques and strategies, law enforcement and military personnel can effectively utilize Brazilian Jiu-Jitsu to manage high-stress situations, ensure compliance, and maintain the safety of both officers and suspects. Regular training, adherence to legal and ethical standards, and a focus on continuous improvement are crucial for the responsible application of these skills.

# Chapter 21: Empowering Women Through BJJ

Brazilian Jiu-Jitsu is an empowering martial art for women, offering effective self-defense techniques and building confidence and awareness. This chapter explores how BJJ can help women protect themselves, enhance their confidence, and navigate real-world scenarios safely.

## *21.1 Building Confidence and Awareness*

Building confidence and awareness through Brazilian Jiu-Jitsu (BJJ) is crucial for women's empowerment. Training in BJJ helps women develop a sense of self-assurance and situational awareness, which are essential for personal safety.

### *A. Physical Confidence*

**1. Skill Development**

   - Purpose: Gain confidence through mastering BJJ techniques.

   - Technique:

      - Step 1: Consistently practice and refine techniques during training sessions.

      - Step 2: Participate in sparring sessions to test and improve skills in a controlled environment.

      - Step 3: Set and achieve personal goals, such as learning new moves or improving existing ones, to track progress and build confidence.

**2. Strength and Fitness**

   - Purpose: Improve physical fitness, which enhances overall confidence and self-image.

   - Technique:

      - Step 1: Engage in regular strength training and conditioning exercises to build physical strength.

      - Step 2: Incorporate flexibility and mobility drills to enhance physical capabilities and prevent injuries.

- Step 3: Monitor fitness improvements and celebrate milestones, such as increased endurance or muscle tone, to reinforce confidence.

## *B. Mental Confidence*

### 1. Mindset Training

- Purpose: Develop a resilient and positive mindset essential for personal and physical challenges.

- Technique:

- Step 1: Practice visualization and positive self-talk to reinforce confidence and mental strength.

- Step 2: Reflect on training experiences to identify strengths and areas for improvement, focusing on growth rather than setbacks.

- Step 3: Surround yourself with supportive training partners and mentors who encourage and challenge you to improve.

### 2. Situational Awareness

- Purpose: Enhance awareness of surroundings to prevent potential threats and respond effectively if necessary.

- Technique:

- Step 1: Learn to recognize and assess potential risks in various environments, both familiar and unfamiliar.

- Step 2: Practice maintaining awareness during training and daily activities, such as walking to your car or navigating crowded spaces.

- Step 3: Develop strategies for avoiding dangerous situations and staying alert, such as trusting your instincts and knowing escape routes.

By focusing on both physical and mental aspects of confidence and awareness, women can enhance their ability to protect themselves and navigate the world with greater assurance and security. Regular BJJ training provides the tools and mindset needed to build and maintain this confidence, empowering women in all aspects of their lives.

# 21.2 Techniques for Women's Self-Defense

Brazilian Jiu-Jitsu provides practical and effective self-defense techniques tailored to women's needs. These techniques focus on leveraging body mechanics and strategy to overcome larger and stronger opponents, empowering women to protect themselves in various situations.

## *A. Common Self-Defense Techniques*

### 1. Escape from Mount

- Purpose: Free yourself from being pinned to the ground.

- Technique:

- Step 1: Bridge your hips forcefully to create space and disrupt the attacker's balance.

- Step 2: Trap one of the attacker's arms and the same side leg to limit their movement.

- Step 3: Roll the attacker over by bridging and turning towards the trapped side, ending up on top.

### 2. Guard Position

- Purpose: Control the attacker from the bottom position and set up for submissions or sweeps.

- Technique:

- Step 1: Wrap your legs around the attacker's waist to secure the guard.

- Step 2: Control the attacker's posture by gripping their collar (if in a gi) or head and wrists (if no-gi).

- Step 3: Use your legs and hips to keep the attacker off-balance and set up sweeps, submissions, or strikes.

### 3. Defending Against Chokes

- Purpose: Prevent and escape choke attempts.

- Technique:

- Step 1: Tuck your chin and protect your neck with your hands to prevent the choke.

- Step 2: Use your hips and legs to create space and disrupt the attacker's grip.

- Step 3: Apply a counter technique, such as a hip escape or arm trap, to break free from the choke.

## *B. Specialized Techniques for Common Scenarios*

### 1. Defending Against Hair Grabs

- Purpose: Prevent control through hair grabs and create an opportunity to escape or counter-attack.

- Technique:

- Step 1: Secure the attacker's hand holding your hair to prevent movement.

- Step 2: Use your free hand to strike or push the attacker away, targeting vulnerable areas like the eyes or throat.

- Step 3: Apply a leverage-based escape technique, such as a wrist lock or arm bar, to break free and create distance.

### 2. Countering Wrist Grabs

- Purpose: Break free from an attacker's grip on your wrist and regain control.

- Technique:

- Step 1: Rotate your wrist towards the attacker's thumb, the weakest part of their grip, to weaken the hold.

- Step 2: Pull your wrist out forcefully while stepping back to create space.

- Step 3: Follow up with strikes or escape to a safe distance, ensuring you're out of immediate danger.

### 3. Escaping Bear Hugs

- Purpose: Break free from an attacker's bear hug and regain control.

- Technique:

- Step 1: Lower your center of gravity by bending your knees to stabilize your base.

- Step 2: Use your hands to create space by pushing against the attacker's hips or pulling their hands apart.

- Step 3: Use your elbows to strike the attacker's face or ribs, or step to the side and apply a leverage-based escape technique.

By mastering these self-defense techniques, women can effectively protect themselves in a variety of situations. Regular practice of these techniques builds muscle memory, making it easier to react quickly and efficiently in real-world scenarios.

## *21.3 Real-World Scenarios and Prevention*

Understanding real-world scenarios where Brazilian Jiu-Jitsu (BJJ) techniques can be applied is crucial for practical self-defense and situational awareness. This section explores common scenarios and offers strategies for prevention and effective response.

### *A. Street Altercations*

**Scenario:**

- You are approached by an aggressive individual on the street who attempts to engage in a physical confrontation.

**Prevention:**

- Maintain situational awareness and avoid isolated areas.

- Use verbal de-escalation techniques to defuse the situation.

- Keep a safe distance and adopt a non-threatening but ready stance.

**Response:**

- Use BJJ techniques to control the aggressor without escalating violence.

- Apply holds and submissions to neutralize the threat if physical engagement is unavoidable.

- Ensure a quick escape route is available once the aggressor is subdued.

## *B. Public Transport Incidents*

### Scenario:

- A woman is harassed or physically threatened while using public transportation.

### Prevention:

- Choose well-lit and populated areas of the transport system.

- Remain alert and aware of your surroundings and other passengers.

- Position yourself near the driver or conductor if you feel unsafe.

### Response:

- Utilize standing grappling techniques to maintain balance while controlling the aggressor.

- Use knee strikes or elbow strikes in conjunction with BJJ holds to create space and deter the attacker.

- If seated, use the leverage from the seated position to apply joint locks or control holds effectively.


## *C. Domestic Violence Situations*

### Scenario:

- A woman faces physical aggression from a partner or family member in a domestic setting.

### Prevention:

- Establish a safe space and clear escape routes within the home.

- Keep communication devices accessible to contact authorities quickly.

- Reach out to support networks or organizations that provide assistance for domestic violence victims.

### Response:

- Use close-quarter control techniques like clinches and sweeps to subdue the aggressor.

- Apply chokes or submission holds to neutralize the threat without causing permanent harm.

- Prioritize escaping the environment and seeking help once the aggressor is controlled.

## D. Workplace Violence

**Scenario:**

- A woman is physically threatened or harassed by a colleague or client in the workplace.

**Prevention:**

- Maintain professionalism and avoid situations that may escalate into physical confrontations.

- Report any inappropriate behavior to human resources or a superior immediately.

- Develop a workplace safety plan, including knowing the layout and escape routes.

**Response:**

- Use BJJ techniques to maintain control over the aggressor without causing severe injury.

- Apply wrist locks, arm drags, or standing chokes to neutralize the threat.

- Focus on escaping the situation and seeking help from coworkers or security personnel.

## E. Anti-Bullying Defense for Youth

**Scenario:**

- A child or teenager is being bullied physically at school or in a social setting.

**Prevention:**

- Educate children on the importance of non-violent conflict resolution.

- Encourage open communication about bullying incidents.

- Ensure schools have anti-bullying policies and support systems in place.

**Response:**

- Teach children basic BJJ techniques to protect themselves without escalating violence.

- Emphasize the use of control and escape techniques over striking.

- Instruct them to seek help from authorities or trusted adults immediately.

## F. Women's Self-Defense

**Scenario:**

- A woman is targeted by an assailant in a public or private setting.

**Prevention:**

- Promote awareness and self-defense education for women.

- Encourage women to trust their instincts and avoid risky situations.

- Equip them with tools such as personal alarms and self-defense training.

**Response:**

- Use BJJ techniques focused on leverage and technique to overcome size and strength disadvantages.

- Employ wrist locks, arm bars, and chokeholds to incapacitate the assailant.

- Prioritize escape and contacting authorities over prolonged engagement.

By understanding these real-world scenarios and applying BJJ techniques effectively, practitioners can enhance their personal safety and the safety of those around them. Prevention strategies combined with practical response skills create a comprehensive approach to self-defense.

# Chapter 21 Review: Empowering Women Through BJJ

Chapter 21 focuses on empowering women through Brazilian Jiu-Jitsu (BJJ) by building confidence, enhancing awareness, and providing practical self-defense techniques. It also explores real-world scenarios and prevention strategies to bolster personal safety and resilience.

## 21.1 Building Confidence and Awareness

- BJJ instills confidence in women by teaching them effective self-defense techniques that can be applied in various situations.

- Awareness is heightened through situational training and mindfulness practices, helping women stay alert and prepared.

- Regular practice leads to improved physical fitness, mental resilience, and a strong sense of self-assurance.

## 21.2 Techniques for Women's Self-Defense

- Emphasis on leverage and technique enables women to neutralize larger and stronger opponents effectively.

- Practical moves include wrist locks, arm bars, and chokeholds tailored for real-life scenarios, ensuring applicability.

- Training incorporates scenario-based drills to simulate common threats women might face, enhancing readiness and response.

## 21.3 Real-World Scenarios and Prevention

- Street Altercations: Techniques to control aggressors and create escape opportunities, prioritizing safety and de-escalation.

- Public Transport Incidents: Strategies for maintaining balance and using grappling techniques in confined spaces, ensuring effective self-defense in crowded environments.

- Domestic Violence Situations: Close-quarter control techniques to neutralize threats without causing harm, focusing on protection and safe exit strategies.

- Workplace Violence: Professional and controlled responses to physical threats in the workplace, promoting a safe and respectful environment.

- Anti-Bullying Defense for Youth: Teaching children non-violent conflict resolution and self-protection techniques, fostering confidence and security in young practitioners.

- Women's Self-Defense: Promoting awareness, trusting instincts, and using BJJ techniques to overcome size and strength disadvantages, empowering women to protect themselves effectively.

By mastering the techniques and strategies discussed in this chapter, women can significantly enhance their self-defense capabilities and overall confidence. This empowerment through BJJ not only improves physical preparedness but also builds mental resilience, enabling women to navigate various situations with assurance and strength.

# Chapter 22: The Culture and Community of BJJ

Brazilian Jiu-Jitsu (BJJ) is more than a martial art; it's a way of life that encompasses a rich culture and a vibrant community. Understanding the traditions, the belt system, and the importance of community involvement is essential for anyone practicing BJJ. This chapter delves into the core aspects that define the BJJ lifestyle, emphasizing the significance of etiquette, progression, and community building.

## 22.1 Dojo Etiquette and Traditions

Dojo etiquette and traditions form the backbone of the Brazilian Jiu-Jitsu (BJJ) training environment. They create a respectful, disciplined, and safe space for all practitioners, fostering a culture of mutual respect and continuous learning.

### A. Respect and Discipline

**1. Bowing:**

 - Practitioners bow upon entering and leaving the mat, signifying humility and reverence for the training space and those within it.

**2. Addressing Instructors:**

 - Using appropriate titles (e.g., Professor, Sensei) for instructors and higher belts shows respect for their experience and dedication.

**3. Training Partner Respect:**

 - Treating training partners with respect, acknowledging their contributions to one's learning process.

### B. Cleanliness

**1. Personal Hygiene:**

 - Practitioners must maintain a clean gi (uniform) and ensure they are free from any infections or skin conditions.

- Fingernails and toenails should be trimmed to prevent injuries.

### 2. Dojo Cleanliness:

- The dojo should be kept clean and orderly.

- Mats should be disinfected regularly to prevent the spread of bacteria and viruses.

## *C. Punctuality*

### 1. Arriving on Time:

- Arriving on time for classes and events demonstrates respect and commitment.

- Late arrivals can disrupt the flow of training and show a lack of regard for the instructor's time.

### 2. Joining Late:

- If late, practitioners should wait at the edge of the mat until given permission to join the class.

## *D. Hierarchy*

### 1. Structured Learning Environment:

- The dojo operates on a hierarchical structure, from black belts to white belts, fostering a disciplined and structured learning environment.

### 2. Respecting Higher Belts:

- Practitioners should follow the lead of higher belts during training and respect their guidance and corrections.

## *E. Rituals*

### 1. Lining Up by Rank:

- Dojos often have unique rituals, such as lining up by rank, which enhances the sense of belonging and continuity within the BJJ community.

## 2. Formal Greetings:

- Bowing to the mat, instructors, and training partners before and after sparring sessions symbolizes mutual respect and readiness to learn.

## 3. Practice Traditions:

- Specific ways of practicing techniques that are unique to each dojo.

## *F. Communication*

### 1. Informing Partners:

- Practitioners should inform their partners of any injuries or limitations before training.

### 2. Using Safety Signals:

- Using phrases like "tap" when submitting ensures safety and prevents injuries.

## *G. Safety*

### 1. Controlled Training:

- Practitioners should always train with control and be mindful of their partner's well-being.

### 2. Executing Techniques:

- Techniques should be executed with precision and care, avoiding unnecessary force or aggression.

Adhering to dojo etiquette and traditions not only cultivates a respectful and disciplined environment but also enhances the overall training experience. These practices build a strong foundation of trust and camaraderie among practitioners, contributing to their growth both on and off the mat.

## 22.2 The Belt System: Progress and Milestones

The belt system in Brazilian Jiu-Jitsu (BJJ) represents a practitioner's journey, progress, and milestones achieved through dedication, perseverance, and continuous learning. Understanding this system is crucial for appreciating the structure and goals within BJJ training.

## A. Ranking Structure

### 1. Belt Colors:

- The BJJ belt system consists of a series of colored belts representing different levels of expertise.

- Progression typically follows this order: white, blue, purple, brown, and black belts.

### 2. Youth Belts:

- For children, the belt colors include additional stages like yellow, orange, and green before transitioning to the adult belt system.

## B. Criteria for Advancement

### 1. Technical Proficiency:

- Mastery of specific techniques and concepts is required for each belt level.

- Practitioners must demonstrate a deep understanding and application of these techniques during training and sparring.

### 2. Time and Experience:

- Time spent training is a significant factor in belt promotion.

- Consistent attendance and active participation in classes and seminars are essential.

### 3. Competition Performance:

- Success in competitions can influence belt advancement, showcasing a practitioner's skill level under pressure.

### 4. Community Contribution:

- Contributions to the BJJ community, such as helping lower belts, teaching, or assisting with dojo activities, are also considered.

## *C. Milestones*

### 1. Earning a New Belt:

- Achieving a new belt is a significant milestone celebrated within the dojo.

- Belt promotions are often accompanied by a formal ceremony recognizing the practitioner's hard work and dedication.

### 2. Stripes:

- In addition to colored belts, practitioners can earn stripes as intermediate markers of progress.

- Stripes provide motivation and recognition of improvement between belt promotions.

### 3. Black Belt and Beyond:

- Earning a black belt in BJJ is a prestigious accomplishment, often taking a decade or more of consistent training.

- Even after achieving a black belt, practitioners continue to advance through degrees of black belt, reflecting ongoing learning and contribution to the art.

## *D. The Journey of Continuous Growth*

### 1. Learning Never Stops:

- BJJ emphasizes that earning a black belt is not the end but rather a new beginning in the journey of martial arts mastery.

- Continuous learning, refinement of techniques, and personal development are integral parts of the BJJ philosophy.

### 2. Role Models and Mentors:

- Higher belts serve as role models and mentors, guiding lower belts through their journey.

- This mentorship fosters a supportive and encouraging environment within the dojo.

## *E. Cultural Significance*

### 1. Tradition and Respect:
  - The belt system embodies the tradition and respect that are central to BJJ.
  - It symbolizes the values of perseverance, humility, and respect for the art and fellow practitioners.

### 2. Community and Belonging:
  - Belts create a sense of community and belonging, connecting practitioners through shared goals and achievements.
  - The belt system reinforces the idea that every practitioner, regardless of rank, is part of a larger BJJ family.

Understanding the belt system in BJJ provides insight into the structured path of growth and achievement that practitioners follow. It highlights the importance of dedication, technical proficiency, and community involvement, making the journey through the belts a deeply enriching experience.

# *22.3 Building and Participating in the BJJ Community*

The Brazilian Jiu-Jitsu (BJJ) community is a vital aspect of the martial art, offering practitioners a sense of belonging, support, and camaraderie. Building and participating in this community enriches the training experience and fosters personal and collective growth.

## *A. Fostering Connections*

### 1. Training Partners:
  - BJJ practitioners often form strong bonds with their training partners through shared experiences on the mat.

- These relationships create a supportive and encouraging environment, essential for growth and improvement.

## 2. Mentorship:

- Higher belts and instructors serve as mentors, guiding and supporting lower belts in their journey.

- Mentorship helps cultivate a sense of responsibility and community among practitioners.

## *B. Seminars and Workshops*

### 1. Learning Opportunities:

- Participating in seminars and workshops with high-level instructors provides exposure to diverse techniques and philosophies.

- These events offer valuable learning experiences that enhance one's BJJ skills and knowledge.

### 2. Networking:

- Seminars and workshops are excellent opportunities to meet practitioners from other dojos and regions.

- Building a network of BJJ connections can lead to lifelong friendships and training opportunities.

## *C. Competitions*

### 1. Testing Skills:

- Engaging in competitions helps practitioners test their skills and gain valuable experience.

- Competitions range from local tournaments to international events, catering to all skill levels.

### 2. Building Resilience:

- Competing fosters resilience, mental toughness, and the ability to perform under pressure.

- The experience of competition can significantly enhance a practitioner's growth and confidence.

### 3. Community Spirit:

- Competitions bring together practitioners from various backgrounds, promoting a sense of unity and shared purpose within the BJJ community.

## *D. Supporting Events*

### 1. Belt Promotions:

- Attending belt promotion ceremonies to support fellow practitioners strengthens community ties.

- Celebrating others' achievements fosters a positive and encouraging atmosphere within the dojo.

### 2. Tournaments and Charity Events:

- Supporting and participating in tournaments and charity events helps promote the growth of BJJ and contributes to the broader community.

- These events often raise awareness and funds for important causes, demonstrating the positive impact of the BJJ community.

## *E. Online Communities*

### 1. Knowledge Sharing:

- Joining online forums, social media groups, and virtual training sessions allows practitioners to share knowledge and seek advice.

- Online communities provide a platform for discussing techniques, training tips, and BJJ-related topics.

### 2. Global Connections:

- The internet enables practitioners to connect with the global BJJ community, expanding their network and learning opportunities.

- Engaging with practitioners from different cultures and backgrounds enriches one's understanding of BJJ.

## F. Contribution to the Community

### 1. Volunteering:

- Volunteering at events, helping organize competitions, or assisting with dojo activities contributes to the community's growth and success.

- Active involvement fosters a sense of ownership and pride in the BJJ community.

### 2. Teaching and Mentoring:

- Experienced practitioners can give back by teaching and mentoring newer students.

- Sharing knowledge and skills helps perpetuate the art of BJJ and supports the development of the next generation of practitioners.


Building and participating in the BJJ community is integral to the martial art's culture and philosophy. By fostering connections, engaging in learning opportunities, supporting events, and contributing to the community, practitioners can fully embrace the BJJ lifestyle. This active involvement not only enhances personal growth but also strengthens the collective spirit and resilience of the BJJ community.

# Chapter 22 Review: The Culture and Community of BJJ

Chapter 22 delves into the rich culture and vibrant community that define Brazilian Jiu-Jitsu (BJJ). This chapter highlights the importance of dojo etiquette, the belt system, and active participation in the BJJ community, emphasizing how these elements contribute to personal growth and a deeper connection to the martial art.

### 22.1 Dojo Etiquette and Traditions

- Respect and Discipline: BJJ emphasizes respect for instructors, training partners, and the dojo, with practices such as bowing and using appropriate titles.

- Cleanliness: Maintaining personal hygiene and a clean gi, along with keeping the dojo clean, is crucial for a healthy training environment.

- Punctuality: Arriving on time for classes shows respect and commitment, while late arrivals should wait for permission to join the class.

- Hierarchy: The dojo operates on a hierarchical structure, respecting higher belts fosters a disciplined learning environment.

- Rituals: Unique dojo rituals, such as lining up by rank and formal greetings, enhance the sense of belonging and continuity within the BJJ community.

- Communication: Clear and respectful communication, including informing partners of any injuries, ensures safety and builds trust.

- Safety: Training with control and executing techniques with precision prevents injuries and promotes a safe training atmosphere.

## 22.2 The Belt System: Progress and Milestones

- Ranking Structure: The belt system in BJJ includes a progression through white, blue, purple, brown, and black belts, with additional youth belts.

- Criteria for Advancement: Promotion criteria include technical proficiency, time spent training, competition performance, and community contributions.

- Milestones: Achieving new belts and earning stripes are significant milestones celebrated within the dojo.

- Black Belt and Beyond: Earning a black belt is a prestigious accomplishment, with ongoing advancement through degrees of black belt reflecting continuous learning.

- The Journey of Continuous Growth: BJJ emphasizes lifelong learning, with higher belts serving as role models and mentors.

- Cultural Significance: The belt system embodies tradition, respect, and a sense of community and belonging within the BJJ family.

## 22.3 Building and Participating in the BJJ Community

- Fostering Connections: Strong bonds with training partners and mentorship from higher belts create a supportive environment.

- Seminars and Workshops: Participating in events with high-level instructors enhances learning and provides networking opportunities.

- Competitions: Engaging in competitions tests skills, builds resilience, and fosters community spirit.

- Supporting Events: Attending belt promotions, tournaments, and charity events strengthens community ties and promotes BJJ.

- Online Communities: Joining online forums and social media groups facilitates knowledge sharing and global connections.

- Contribution to the Community: Volunteering, teaching, and mentoring contribute to the growth and success of the BJJ community.

By embracing dojo etiquette, understanding the belt system, and actively participating in the BJJ community, practitioners can fully immerse themselves in the Brazilian Jiu-Jitsu lifestyle. This holistic approach not only enhances skills on the mat but also cultivates a supportive network and a deeper appreciation for the art, fostering personal and collective growth.

# Chapter 23: Nutrition and Diet for Practitioners

Proper nutrition and diet play a crucial role in the performance, recovery, and overall health of Brazilian Jiu-Jitsu (BJJ) practitioners. This chapter explores the nutritional needs for training and recovery, strategies for weight management and competition preparation, and the importance of hydration and supplementation.

## *23.1 Nutritional Needs for Training and Recovery*

Proper nutrition is fundamental to the performance and recovery of Brazilian Jiu-Jitsu (BJJ) practitioners. This section delves into the essential nutritional requirements that support training intensity, aid in muscle recovery, and promote overall health.

### *A. Macronutrients*

**1. Proteins**

  - Importance: Essential for muscle repair and growth, proteins help rebuild tissues broken down during intense training sessions.

  - Sources:

    - Animal-based: Lean meats (chicken, turkey), fish, eggs, and dairy products.

    - Plant-based: Legumes (beans, lentils), tofu, tempeh, and plant-based protein powders.

  - Daily Intake: Aim for 1.2 to 2.0 grams of protein per kilogram of body weight, depending on training intensity.

**2. Carbohydrates**

  - Importance: The primary energy source for high-intensity training, carbohydrates fuel workouts and aid in glycogen replenishment post-exercise.

  - Sources:

    - Complex carbs: Whole grains (brown rice, quinoa, oats), vegetables, and fruits.

- Simple carbs: Use sparingly, but can be beneficial immediately post-training for quick energy.

- Daily Intake: Carbohydrates should make up about 45-65% of total daily caloric intake.

## 3. Fats

- Importance: Fats are vital for hormone production, joint lubrication, and overall health. They also provide a secondary energy source.

- Sources:

  - Healthy fats: Avocados, nuts, seeds, olive oil, and fatty fish (salmon, mackerel).

- Daily Intake: Fats should constitute about 20-35% of total daily calories, focusing on unsaturated fats.

## *B. Micronutrients*

### 1. Vitamins

- Importance: Crucial for energy production, immune function, and bone health.

- Key Vitamins:

  - Vitamin A: Supports immune function and vision. Found in carrots, sweet potatoes, and leafy greens.

  - Vitamin C: Essential for tissue repair and immune health. Found in citrus fruits, strawberries, and bell peppers.

  - Vitamin D: Important for bone health and muscle function. Obtained from sunlight exposure and fortified foods.

### 2. Minerals

- Importance: Important for muscle contraction, nerve function, and fluid balance.

- Key Minerals:

- Calcium: Necessary for bone health and muscle function. Found in dairy products, leafy greens, and fortified plant milks.

- Magnesium: Aids in muscle relaxation and recovery. Found in nuts, seeds, and whole grains.

- Iron: Vital for oxygen transport in the blood. Found in red meat, beans, and spinach.

## *C. Timing and Meal Composition*

### 1. Pre-Training Nutrition

- Timing: Eat a balanced meal 2-3 hours before training.
- Composition:
  - Carbohydrates for sustained energy.
  - Moderate protein to support muscle function.
  - Limited fats to avoid sluggishness.
- Example: Grilled chicken with quinoa and steamed vegetables.

### 2. Post-Training Nutrition

- Timing: Consume a recovery meal or snack within 30-60 minutes post-training.
- Composition:
  - Protein to support muscle repair.
  - Carbohydrates to replenish glycogen stores.
- Example: A smoothie with protein powder, banana, and spinach, or Greek yogurt with berries and honey.

### 3. Intra-Training Nutrition

- When Needed: For long or intense training sessions, consuming small amounts of carbohydrates can help maintain energy levels.
- Options: Sports drinks, bananas, or energy gels.

## D. Hydration

### 1. Daily Hydration:

- Importance: Essential for maintaining performance, preventing dehydration, and aiding in recovery.

- Recommendation: Drink at least 8-10 glasses of water per day, adjusting for activity level and climate.

### 2. During Training:

- Importance: Prevents dehydration and maintains energy levels.

- Recommendation: Sip water regularly during training sessions. Consider electrolyte drinks for intense or prolonged training.


By focusing on these nutritional needs, BJJ practitioners can enhance their training performance, speed up recovery, and maintain overall health. Proper nutrition tailored to the demands of BJJ ensures that practitioners are physically prepared and resilient, both on and off the mat.

# 23.2 Weight Management and Competition Prep

Effective weight management and competition preparation are critical aspects of Brazilian Jiu-Jitsu (BJJ) that help practitioners maintain optimal performance, meet weight class requirements, and prepare both mentally and physically for competitions. This section outlines strategies for managing weight and preparing for competition.

## A. Dietary Strategies

### 1. Caloric Intake

- Importance: Adjusting caloric intake based on training intensity and goals (e.g., weight loss, maintenance, or gain) is essential for achieving desired weight and performance levels.

- Implementation:

  - Use a food diary or app to track daily caloric intake and macronutrient ratios.

- Ensure a balance of proteins, carbohydrates, and fats to support training and recovery.

## 2. Portion Control

- Importance: Practicing portion control helps avoid overeating and maintains a healthy weight.

- Implementation:

  - Use smaller plates to help manage portion sizes.

  - Measure portions to ensure appropriate serving sizes, focusing on nutrient-dense foods.

## *B. Weight Cutting*

### 1. Gradual Approach

- Importance: Gradual weight cutting helps avoid drastic measures that can negatively impact performance and health.

- Implementation:

  - Start weight cutting several weeks before the competition date.

  - Gradually reduce caloric intake and increase training intensity to lose weight safely.

### 2. Hydration Management

- Importance: Proper hydration management is crucial to avoid dehydration and maintain performance during weight cutting.

- Implementation:

  - Monitor fluid intake and adjust accordingly to maintain hydration while cutting weight.

  - Use methods such as water loading and controlled fluid restriction closer to the weigh-in date.

## *C. Competition Day Nutrition*

### 1. Pre-Competition Meal

  - Importance: A proper pre-competition meal provides the necessary energy and nutrients for optimal performance.

  - Timing: Consume this meal 3-4 hours before competing.

  - Composition:

    - Easily Digestible Carbohydrates: Provide quick and sustained energy.

    - Moderate Protein: Supports muscle function without causing digestive discomfort.

  - Example: Oatmeal with berries and a boiled egg.

### 2. During Competition

  - Importance: Maintaining energy and hydration levels during competition is crucial for peak performance.

  - Implementation:

    - Stay hydrated by sipping water or electrolyte drinks between matches.

    - Consume small amounts of easily digestible carbohydrates to sustain energy levels.

  - Options: Sports drinks, bananas, or energy gels.

By following these dietary strategies, weight cutting techniques, and competition day nutrition guidelines, BJJ practitioners can effectively manage their weight and prepare for competitions. Proper preparation ensures that practitioners are physically and mentally ready to perform at their best, meet weight class requirements, and achieve their competition goals.

## *23.3 Hydration and Supplementation*

Proper hydration and appropriate supplementation are essential for Brazilian Jiu-Jitsu (BJJ) practitioners to maintain peak performance, support recovery, and ensure overall health. This section outlines the importance of hydration and the role of various supplements in a BJJ athlete's diet.

## *A. Hydration*

### 1. Daily Hydration

- Importance: Staying hydrated is crucial for maintaining physical performance, cognitive function, and overall health.

- Recommendations:

  - Drink at least 8-10 glasses of water per day.

  - Adjust fluid intake based on activity level, climate, and individual needs.

- Tips:

  - Carry a water bottle throughout the day to encourage regular drinking.

  - Monitor urine color as a simple gauge of hydration; pale yellow is ideal.

### 2. During Training

- Importance: Maintaining hydration during training sessions helps prevent dehydration, cramps, and heat-related illnesses.

- Recommendations:

  - Sip water regularly during training sessions.

  - For sessions lasting longer than an hour or in hot climates, consider electrolyte drinks to replenish lost minerals.

- Tips:

  - Take small, frequent sips rather than large gulps to maintain hydration without discomfort.

  - Use electrolyte tablets or powders to enhance water with necessary minerals like sodium and potassium.

## *B. Supplementation*

### 1. Protein Supplements

- Importance: Protein supplements can help meet daily protein requirements, support muscle repair, and enhance recovery.

- Types:

- Whey Protein: Fast-digesting, ideal post-training.

- Casein Protein: Slow-digesting, good for sustained release, such as before sleep.

- Plant-Based Proteins: Options like pea, hemp, and rice protein for those avoiding dairy.

- Usage:

- Consume a protein shake within 30 minutes post-training for optimal recovery.

- Incorporate protein supplements into meals or snacks to meet daily protein targets.

## 2. Creatine

- Importance: Creatine enhances performance, strength, and muscle mass by increasing energy availability in muscles.

- Recommended Dosage: Typically 3-5 grams per day.

- Usage:

- Take creatine consistently, either mixed with water or in a protein shake.

- Loading phase (20 grams per day for 5-7 days) can be followed by a maintenance dose.

## 3. Multivitamins

- Importance: Multivitamins ensure adequate intake of essential vitamins and minerals, filling potential nutritional gaps.

- Choosing a Multivitamin:

- Select a high-quality multivitamin tailored to active individuals.

- Ensure it contains key nutrients such as vitamins A, C, D, E, and B-complex, along with minerals like zinc and magnesium.

- Usage:

- Take as directed, usually with a meal to enhance absorption.

## 4. Omega-3 Fatty Acids

- Importance: Omega-3s support heart health, reduce inflammation, and aid in recovery.

- Sources:

  - Fish Oil Supplements: Rich in EPA and DHA, beneficial omega-3 fatty acids.

  - Plant-Based Alternatives: Flaxseed oil, chia seeds, and walnuts for ALA, a precursor to EPA and DHA.

  - Recommended Dosage: 1-3 grams of combined EPA and DHA per day.

  - Usage:

  - Take with meals to enhance absorption and reduce the likelihood of digestive discomfort.

By focusing on proper hydration and smart supplementation, BJJ practitioners can optimize their training, support recovery, and maintain overall health. These strategies ensure that athletes are well-prepared to perform at their best and sustain their training regimen effectively.

# *Chapter 23 Review: Nutrition and Diet for Practitioners*

Chapter 23 delves into the critical aspects of nutrition and diet for Brazilian Jiu-Jitsu (BJJ) practitioners. It emphasizes the importance of proper nutrition, weight management, and hydration to enhance performance, recovery, and overall health.

### 23.1 Nutritional Needs for Training and Recovery

- Macronutrients:

  - Proteins: Essential for muscle repair and growth, sourced from lean meats, fish, eggs, dairy, legumes, and plant-based protein powders.

  - Carbohydrates: The primary energy source for training, obtained from whole grains, vegetables, fruits, and, sparingly, simple carbs.

  - Fats: Vital for hormone production and overall health, focusing on healthy fats from avocados, nuts, seeds, and olive oil.

- Micronutrients:

  - Vitamins: Crucial for energy production, immune function, and bone health, sourced from a variety of fruits and vegetables.

  - Minerals: Important for muscle contraction, nerve function, and fluid balance, sourced from dairy products, leafy greens, nuts, seeds, and lean meats.

- Timing and Meal Composition:

  - Pre-Training Nutrition: Balanced meals with carbohydrates and proteins consumed 2-3 hours before training.

  - Post-Training Nutrition: Protein and carbohydrates consumed within 30-60 minutes post-training to support recovery.

  - Intra-Training Nutrition: Small amounts of carbohydrates during long or intense sessions to maintain energy levels.

## 23.2 Weight Management and Competition Prep

- Dietary Strategies:

  - Caloric Intake: Adjust caloric intake based on training intensity and goals, using food diaries or apps to track intake.

  - Portion Control: Practice portion control to avoid overeating, using smaller plates and measuring portions.

- Weight Cutting:

  - Gradual Approach: Begin weight cutting several weeks before competition to avoid drastic measures, reducing calories and increasing training intensity gradually.

  - Hydration Management: Monitor fluid intake to avoid dehydration, using methods like water loading and controlled fluid restriction closer to weigh-in.

- Competition Day Nutrition:

  - Pre-Competition Meal: Easily digestible carbohydrates and moderate protein consumed 3-4 hours before competing.

  - During Competition: Maintain energy and hydration levels with small amounts of easily digestible carbs and regular sips of water or electrolyte drinks.

## 23.3 Hydration and Supplementation

- Hydration:

  - Daily Hydration: Aim for 8-10 glasses of water per day, adjusting for activity level and climate.

  - During Training: Sip water regularly and consider electrolyte drinks for intense or prolonged training sessions.

- Supplementation:

  - Protein Supplements: Help meet daily protein requirements, support muscle repair, and enhance recovery.

  - Creatine: Enhances performance, strength, and muscle mass, with a recommended dosage of 3-5 grams per day.

  - Multivitamins: Ensure adequate intake of essential vitamins and minerals, filling potential nutritional gaps.

  - Omega-3 Fatty Acids: Support heart health, reduce inflammation, and aid in recovery, sourced from fish oil supplements and plant-based alternatives.


By focusing on proper nutrition, weight management, hydration, and smart supplementation, BJJ practitioners can optimize their performance and recovery, ensuring they are at their best both on and off the mat. This holistic approach to diet and supplementation supports overall health and enhances training outcomes, preparing practitioners for competition success and sustained practice.

# Chapter 24: Injury Prevention and Recovery

Injury prevention and effective recovery strategies are crucial for Brazilian Jiu-Jitsu (BJJ) practitioners to maintain peak performance and long-term participation in the sport. This chapter explores common injuries in BJJ, preventive measures, rehabilitation strategies, and tips for maintaining longevity in practice.

## 24.1 Common Injuries in BJJ and Their Prevention

Understanding common injuries in Brazilian Jiu-Jitsu (BJJ) and how to prevent them is crucial for maintaining a healthy and sustainable practice. This section outlines typical injuries, their causes, and effective prevention strategies to minimize the risk of injury.

### *A. Common Injuries*

**1. Joint Injuries**

  - Shoulder Dislocations:

    - Cause: Often result from submissions like Kimuras and armbars.

    - Prevention: Strengthen shoulder muscles and practice proper technique to avoid excessive force.

  - Knee Injuries:

    - Cause: Frequently occur from positions like the guard and during takedowns.

    - Prevention: Strengthen leg muscles, practice safe takedown techniques, and use proper alignment.

  - Elbow Sprains:

    - Cause: Typically happen due to arm locks and other joint manipulation techniques.

    - Prevention: Warm up thoroughly and ensure controlled application of techniques.

## 2. Muscle Strains

- Hamstring Strains:
  - Cause: Result from explosive movements and guard play.
  - Prevention: Incorporate dynamic stretching and strengthen hamstrings.
- Back Strains:
  - Cause: Can occur due to poor lifting technique or overuse.
  - Prevention: Maintain proper posture during training and strengthen core muscles.

## 3. Skin Injuries

- Mat Burns:
  - Cause: Caused by friction against the mats.
  - Prevention: Wear rash guards and ensure mats are clean and smooth.
- Infections:
  - Cause: Result from contact with bacteria or fungi on the mats.
  - Prevention: Maintain personal hygiene, clean mats regularly, and use antifungal soap.

## *B. Prevention Strategies*

### 1. Proper Warm-Up

- Importance: A thorough warm-up increases blood flow to muscles, enhancing flexibility and reducing injury risk.
- Examples:
  - Dynamic stretching
  - Light jogging
  - Sport-specific drills

### 2. Technique Mastery

- Importance: Proper technique execution reduces the risk of injury.
- Examples:

- Learning to fall correctly (breakfalls)

- Practicing controlled movements

- Receiving proper instruction and feedback

**3. Strength and Conditioning**

- Importance: A strong body supports joints and muscles, reducing injury likelihood.

- Examples:

  - Incorporating strength training exercises

  - Flexibility exercises such as yoga or Pilates

  - Cardiovascular conditioning like running or cycling

**4. Hygiene**

- Importance: Maintaining personal and mat hygiene prevents skin infections.

- Examples:

  - Showering immediately after practice

  - Cleaning mats regularly with disinfectant

  - Using antifungal soap

By understanding and implementing these prevention strategies, BJJ practitioners can significantly reduce the risk of common injuries. This proactive approach not only ensures a safer training environment but also promotes longevity and enjoyment in the practice of Brazilian Jiu-Jitsu.

## *24.2 Effective Rehabilitation Strategies*

Rehabilitation is a critical aspect of recovery for Brazilian Jiu-Jitsu (BJJ) practitioners. Effective strategies ensure a safe and efficient return to training, minimizing the risk of re-injury and promoting overall health.

# *A. Immediate Response*

## 1. RICE Method

- Rest:

   - Importance: Avoid putting weight or strain on the injured area to prevent further damage.

   - Application: Take a break from training and any activities that might exacerbate the injury.

- Ice:

   - Importance: Apply ice packs to reduce swelling and numb pain.

   - Application: Use ice for 20 minutes every hour during the first 48 hours post-injury.

- Compression:

   - Importance: Use bandages or wraps to minimize swelling and support the injured area.

   - Application: Wrap the injured area snugly but not too tight to avoid restricting blood flow.

- Elevation:

   - Importance: Keep the injured limb raised above heart level to reduce swelling.

   - Application: Use pillows to elevate the injured area, especially while resting or sleeping.

# *B. Professional Care*

## 1. Seeking Medical Attention

   - Importance: Professional diagnosis ensures proper treatment and prevents further injury.

   - Application: Visit a sports medicine specialist or physiotherapist for a thorough assessment.

## 2. Physical Therapy

- Importance: Customized rehabilitation programs aid recovery and restore function.

- Application: Engage in exercises prescribed by a physical therapist to strengthen the injured area and improve flexibility.

## *C. Rehabilitation Exercises*

### 1. Strengthening Exercises

- Importance: Rebuild muscle strength and stability around the injured area.
- Examples:
  - Resistance band exercises
  - Weight lifting with controlled movements
  - Bodyweight exercises like squats and lunges

### 2. Flexibility Exercises

- Importance: Restoring flexibility reduces stiffness and improves movement.
- Examples:
  - Gentle stretching routines
  - Yoga poses that focus on the injured area
  - Mobility drills

### 3. Gradual Return to Training

- Importance: Slowly reintroducing training reduces the risk of re-injury.
- Examples:
  - Begin with light drills and controlled sparring
  - Gradually increase intensity and duration of training sessions
  - Monitor pain and adjust activities as needed

By implementing these effective rehabilitation strategies, BJJ practitioners can ensure a safe and efficient recovery process. These steps help minimize the risk of re-injury, promote healing, and support a successful return to training.

## 24.3 Maintaining Longevity in BJJ Practice

Maintaining longevity in Brazilian Jiu-Jitsu (BJJ) practice involves adopting strategies that promote physical health, mental well-being, and sustainable training habits. This section outlines key practices to ensure a long and fulfilling BJJ journey.

### A. Consistent Conditioning

**1. Regular Exercise**

   - Importance: Maintaining overall fitness supports sustained practice and reduces injury risk.

   - Examples:

     - Combining BJJ training with strength training, cardiovascular exercises, and flexibility workouts.

     - Regularly incorporating activities like running, cycling, weight lifting, and yoga into your routine.

**2. Balanced Diet**

   - Importance: Proper nutrition fuels performance, aids in recovery, and supports overall health.

   - Examples:

     - Consuming a balanced diet rich in proteins, carbohydrates, fats, vitamins, and minerals.

     - Eating whole foods like lean meats, fruits, vegetables, whole grains, and healthy fats.

## *B. Listening to Your Body*

### 1. Recognizing Signs of Overtraining

- Importance: Avoiding burnout and injury by recognizing fatigue and pain.

- Examples:

  - Paying attention to signs like persistent soreness, decreased performance, and lack of motivation.

  - Taking rest days and adjusting training intensity based on physical feedback.

### 2. Incorporating Rest

- Importance: Rest is essential for muscle recovery and mental rejuvenation.

- Examples:

  - Scheduling regular rest days to allow the body to heal.

  - Ensuring adequate sleep and incorporating relaxation techniques like meditation and deep breathing.

## *C. Mental Health*

### 1. Stress Management

- Importance: Mental well-being is crucial for overall health and performance.

- Examples:

  - Practicing mindfulness and meditation to reduce stress and improve focus.

  - Engaging in activities that promote relaxation and mental clarity, such as reading or spending time in nature.

### 2. Goal Setting

- Importance: Setting realistic goals keeps practitioners motivated and focused.

- Examples:

  - Establishing short-term goals like mastering a specific technique or improving conditioning.

  - Creating long-term goals such as earning a new belt or competing in tournaments.

By adopting these practices, BJJ practitioners can maintain longevity in their training, ensuring a healthy and sustainable approach to the sport. Consistent conditioning, listening to the body, and prioritizing mental health are essential components of a long and successful BJJ journey.

## Chapter 24 Review: Injury Prevention and Recovery

Chapter 24 focuses on the crucial aspects of injury prevention and effective recovery strategies for Brazilian Jiu-Jitsu (BJJ) practitioners. It emphasizes understanding common injuries, implementing preventive measures, and adopting rehabilitation strategies to maintain longevity in practice.

**24.1 Common Injuries in BJJ and Their Prevention**

- Joint Injuries:

  - Shoulder Dislocations: Caused by submissions like Kimuras and armbars; prevention includes strengthening shoulder muscles and practicing proper technique.

  - Knee Injuries: Result from positions like the guard and during takedowns; prevention involves strengthening leg muscles and using proper alignment.

  - Elbow Sprains: Occur due to arm locks and other joint manipulations; prevention includes thorough warm-ups and controlled technique application.

- Muscle Strains:

  - Hamstring Strains: Caused by explosive movements and guard play; prevention includes dynamic stretching and strengthening hamstrings.

  - Back Strains: Result from poor lifting technique or overuse; prevention involves maintaining proper posture and strengthening core muscles.

- Skin Injuries:

  - Mat Burns: Caused by friction against the mats; prevention includes wearing rash guards and ensuring clean mats.

  - Infections: Result from contact with bacteria or fungi on the mats; prevention involves maintaining personal hygiene and cleaning mats regularly.

## 24.2 Effective Rehabilitation Strategies

- Immediate Response:

  - RICE Method: Rest, Ice, Compression, and Elevation to manage acute injuries and reduce swelling.

- Professional Care:

  - Seeking Medical Attention: Ensures proper diagnosis and treatment to prevent further injury.

  - Physical Therapy: Customized rehabilitation programs aid recovery and restore function.

- Rehabilitation Exercises:

  - Strengthening Exercises: Rebuild muscle strength and stability around the injured area.

  - Flexibility Exercises: Restoring flexibility reduces stiffness and improves movement.

  - Gradual Return to Training: Slowly reintroducing training reduces the risk of re-injury.

## 24.3 Maintaining Longevity in BJJ Practice

- Consistent Conditioning:

  - Regular Exercise: Combining BJJ training with strength, cardio, and flexibility workouts supports sustained practice.

  - Balanced Diet: Proper nutrition fuels performance and aids in recovery.

- Listening to Your Body:

  - Recognizing Signs of Overtraining: Avoiding burnout and injury by recognizing fatigue and pain.

  - Incorporating Rest: Rest is essential for muscle recovery and mental rejuvenation.

- Mental Health:

- Stress Management: Mental well-being is crucial for overall health and performance.

 - Goal Setting: Setting realistic goals keeps practitioners motivated and focused.

By understanding and implementing these injury prevention and recovery strategies, BJJ practitioners can enhance their training longevity, reduce downtime due to injuries, and maintain optimal performance. Adopting a holistic approach to physical and mental health ensures a sustainable and rewarding BJJ practice.

# Part 9: The Future of Brazilian Jiu-Jitsu

As Brazilian Jiu-Jitsu (BJJ) continues to grow globally, its evolution is marked by modern innovations, the incorporation of techniques from other martial arts, and the influence of emerging technologies. Practitioners and enthusiasts alike are constantly seeking new ways to enhance their skills and adapt to the ever-changing landscape of BJJ. This part explores the ongoing development of BJJ, highlighting the modern innovations, the impact of Mixed Martial Arts (MMA), and future trends in training and competition. Understanding these factors is crucial for practitioners who aim to stay at the forefront of the sport and contribute to its dynamic future.

# Chapter 25: The Continuing Evolution of BJJ

Brazilian Jiu-Jitsu (BJJ) continues to evolve, driven by the creativity and innovation of its practitioners. This chapter delves into the modern innovations and techniques that have emerged, the significant impact of Mixed Martial Arts (MMA) on BJJ, and the future trends that will shape the sport. By exploring these aspects, we can gain insight into how BJJ will continue to develop and remain relevant in the years to come.

## *25.1 Modern Innovations and Techniques*

The landscape of Brazilian Jiu-Jitsu (BJJ) is continuously evolving with the introduction of new techniques and innovative strategies. Practitioners are always exploring and integrating novel approaches to enhance their skills and effectiveness on the mat.

### *A. New Techniques and Strategies*

**1. Guard Variations**

- Modern Guards:
  - Examples: Berimbolo, Worm Guard, and Lapel Guard.

- Importance: These innovative guard positions provide practitioners with new ways to control and submit opponents, showcasing the creativity within BJJ.

- Development: Practitioners continuously experiment and adapt, leading to new guard variations that enhance the effectiveness of traditional positions.

## 2. Submission Advancements

- Leg Locks:

   - Examples: Heel hooks, knee bars, and toe holds.

   - Importance: Leg locks, once considered taboo, have gained acceptance and become integral to modern BJJ, offering powerful submission options.

- Choke Variations:

   - Examples: Ezekiel choke, loop choke, and Darce choke.

   - Importance: New choke variations provide practitioners with additional ways to secure submissions, adding depth to their arsenal.

## *B. Technology in Training*

### 1. Digital Learning Platforms

- Online Instruction:

   - Importance: Access to high-quality instruction from renowned practitioners worldwide has become more accessible.

   - Examples: Subscription-based platforms, YouTube tutorials, and virtual seminars.

   - Benefits: Allows practitioners to learn at their own pace, revisit techniques as needed, and gain insights from top-level instructors regardless of geographical location.

### 2. Performance Tracking

- Wearable Technology:

   - Examples: Fitness trackers, heart rate monitors, and motion sensors.

   - Importance: These tools help practitioners monitor their physical condition, optimize training routines, and track their progress over time.

- Data Analysis:

- Examples: Software applications that analyze performance metrics.

- Benefits: Provides insights into areas for improvement, helping practitioners refine their techniques and strategies based on empirical data.

Modern innovations and techniques in BJJ not only enhance the skills of individual practitioners but also contribute to the overall advancement of the sport. As these new approaches are integrated into training and competition, they push the boundaries of what is possible in Brazilian Jiu-Jitsu.

## *25.2 The Impact of Mixed Martial Arts (MMA)*

The rise of Mixed Martial Arts (MMA) has significantly influenced Brazilian Jiu-Jitsu (BJJ), shaping its techniques, training methods, and competition strategies. This section explores how MMA has integrated and transformed BJJ.

### *A. Integration of Techniques*

#### 1. Cross-Training

- Importance: BJJ practitioners often cross-train in other martial arts like wrestling, judo, and striking disciplines to enhance their overall skill set.

- Benefits: Cross-training improves adaptability in various combat situations, making BJJ practitioners more versatile and well-rounded fighters.

#### 2. Technique Adaptation

- Ground and Pound:

  - Importance: Incorporating striking from dominant positions in BJJ.

  - Examples: Effective use of elbows and punches from mount or guard.

- Defensive Tactics:

  - Importance: Adapting BJJ techniques to defend against strikes.

  - Examples: Improved guard retention, use of frames to create distance, and strategic positioning to avoid damage.

## B. *MMA Influence on BJJ Competitions*

### 1. Rule Changes

  - Evolution:

  - Examples: Introduction of no-gi divisions, changes in point systems, and time limits.

  - Importance: Keeps competitions dynamic and aligned with real-world combat scenarios.

  - Impact: Encourages the development of techniques that are effective in both sport and self-defense contexts, enhancing the practicality of BJJ.

### 2. Athleticism and Conditioning

  - Importance: Increased focus on physical conditioning and athleticism to meet the demands of MMA.

  - Examples: Strength training, cardio conditioning, and flexibility work.

  - Benefits: Produces well-rounded athletes who excel in both BJJ and MMA, improving overall performance and endurance.

## C. *Cultural and Perceptual Changes*

### 1. Mainstream Exposure

  - Visibility:

  - Examples: High-profile MMA fights featuring BJJ practitioners, media coverage, and documentaries.

  - Importance: Increased visibility has popularized BJJ and attracted new practitioners.

  - Impact: BJJ's effectiveness in real combat situations showcased through MMA has enhanced its reputation and credibility.

### 2. Evolution of Training Camps

  - Development:

  - Examples: Creation of specialized training camps that integrate BJJ with other martial arts.

- Importance: These camps provide comprehensive training environments that foster the growth of multi-disciplinary fighters.

- Impact: Promotes a holistic approach to martial arts training, where BJJ is seen as a foundational element within a broader combat skill set.

The influence of MMA on BJJ has led to significant changes in how practitioners train, compete, and perceive the martial art. By integrating techniques from other disciplines, adapting to new competition rules, and emphasizing athleticism, BJJ continues to evolve and thrive in the modern combat sports landscape. This synergy between MMA and BJJ ensures that practitioners remain versatile, effective, and prepared for various combat scenarios.

## *25.3 Future Trends in BJJ Training and Competition*

As Brazilian Jiu-Jitsu (BJJ) continues to evolve, several emerging trends in training and competition are shaping the future of the sport. These trends highlight the integration of technology, accessibility, and innovative training methods that aim to enhance the overall experience and effectiveness of BJJ practice.

### *A. Hybrid Training Models*

#### 1. Combination of Online and In-Person Training

- Importance: Blending digital learning with traditional dojo training provides flexibility and access to a broader range of instruction.

- Benefits:

- Practitioners can learn from world-class instructors through online platforms while continuing to receive hands-on guidance in their local dojos.

- Online resources allow for revisiting techniques and concepts at one's own pace, reinforcing in-person training.

#### 2. Virtual Reality (VR) Training

- Emergence: VR technology is starting to make its way into BJJ training, offering immersive training experiences.

- Examples:
    - VR simulations for practicing techniques and scenarios.
    - Virtual sparring partners for solo training sessions.
  - Potential: Enhances learning by providing realistic, interactive environments where practitioners can practice safely and repeatedly.

## *B. Increased Accessibility*

### 1. Global Expansion

  - Importance: BJJ is spreading to more countries, increasing its global reach and cultural exchange.
  - Examples:
    - Establishment of new academies worldwide.
    - International competitions that draw participants from diverse backgrounds.
  - Impact: Promotes cultural exchange and broadens the BJJ community, making the art more inclusive and widespread.

### 2. Adaptive BJJ Programs

  - Importance: Developing programs tailored to individuals with disabilities or special needs to make BJJ accessible to everyone.
  - Examples:
    - Adaptive classes that modify techniques for practitioners with physical limitations.
    - Inclusive programs that emphasize the therapeutic benefits of BJJ.
  - Impact: Ensures that BJJ is an inclusive sport, providing benefits to a wider audience.

## *C. Advanced Training Methods*

### 1. Data-Driven Training

  - Performance Analytics:

- Examples: Use of software to track progress, analyze techniques, and monitor physical conditioning.

  - Importance: Helps practitioners and coaches make informed decisions to optimize training plans.

  - Biofeedback:

  - Examples: Devices that monitor heart rate, muscle activity, and recovery.

  - Benefits: Provides real-time data to adjust training intensity and prevent injuries.

## 2. Holistic Training Approaches

  - Mind-Body Integration:

  - Examples: Incorporating mindfulness, meditation, and mental conditioning into regular training.

  - Importance: Enhances focus, reduces stress, and improves overall mental resilience.

  - Cross-Disciplinary Training:

  - Examples: Integrating elements of yoga, Pilates, and functional fitness into BJJ routines.

  - Benefits: Improves flexibility, core strength, and functional movement, contributing to better performance on the mat.

## *D. Competition Evolution*

## 1. Unified Rule Sets

  - Development: Efforts are being made to standardize competition rules across different organizations.

  - Importance: Creates a more cohesive competitive environment and simplifies the rules for participants and audiences.

  - Impact: Ensures fair play and consistency in how competitions are judged and conducted.

## 2. Innovative Competition Formats

  - Examples:

- Submission-only tournaments.

  - Team-based competitions.

  - Round-robin formats to ensure more matches per participant.

  - Importance: These new formats keep the competitive scene exciting and engaging for both participants and spectators.

  - Impact: Encourages strategic diversity and showcases different aspects of BJJ skills.

By embracing these future trends, BJJ practitioners and enthusiasts can look forward to a dynamic and inclusive evolution of the sport. The integration of technology, increased accessibility, advanced training methods, and innovative competition formats will continue to enhance the practice and appreciation of Brazilian Jiu-Jitsu globally.

## *Chapter 25 Review: The Continuing Evolution of BJJ*

Chapter 25 explores the ongoing development and future trends in Brazilian Jiu-Jitsu (BJJ), highlighting modern innovations, the impact of Mixed Martial Arts (MMA), and emerging trends in training and competition. This chapter provides insights into how BJJ is evolving and what practitioners can expect in the future.

### 25.1 Modern Innovations and Techniques

- New Techniques and Strategies:

  - Guard Variations: Modern guards like Berimbolo, Worm Guard, and Lapel Guard offer new ways to control and submit opponents, showcasing BJJ's creativity.

  - Submission Advancements: Leg locks (heel hooks, knee bars, toe holds) and choke variations (Ezekiel choke, loop choke, Darce choke) add depth to practitioners' arsenals.

- Technology in Training:

- Digital Learning Platforms: Access to high-quality instruction from renowned practitioners worldwide via subscription-based platforms, YouTube tutorials, and virtual seminars.

- Performance Tracking: Wearable technology (fitness trackers, heart rate monitors, motion sensors) and software applications that analyze performance metrics provide insights into areas for improvement and track progress over time.

## 25.2 The Impact of Mixed Martial Arts (MMA)

- Integration of Techniques:

  - Cross-Training: BJJ practitioners enhance their overall skill set by cross-training in wrestling, judo, and striking disciplines.

  - Technique Adaptation: Incorporating ground and pound (effective use of elbows and punches from mount or guard) and defensive tactics (improved guard retention, use of frames to create distance) into BJJ.

- MMA Influence on BJJ Competitions:

  - Rule Changes: Introduction of no-gi divisions, changes in point systems, and time limits keep competitions dynamic and aligned with real-world combat scenarios.

  - Athleticism and Conditioning: Increased focus on strength training, cardio conditioning, and flexibility work produces well-rounded athletes who excel in both BJJ and MMA.

- Cultural and Perceptual Changes:

  - Mainstream Exposure: High-profile MMA fights featuring BJJ practitioners and media coverage have popularized BJJ and attracted new practitioners.

  - Evolution of Training Camps: Creation of specialized training camps that integrate BJJ with other martial arts promotes a holistic approach to martial arts training.

## 25.3 Future Trends in BJJ Training and Competition

- Hybrid Training Models:

- Combination of Online and In-Person Training: Blending digital learning with traditional dojo training provides flexibility and access to a broader range of instruction.

- Virtual Reality (VR) Training: VR technology offers immersive training experiences, enhancing learning by providing realistic, interactive environments.

- Increased Accessibility:

- Global Expansion: Establishment of new academies worldwide and international competitions promote cultural exchange and broaden the BJJ community.

- Adaptive BJJ Programs: Developing programs tailored to individuals with disabilities or special needs makes BJJ accessible to everyone.

- Advanced Training Methods:

- Data-Driven Training: Use of software to track progress, analyze techniques, and monitor physical conditioning helps practitioners and coaches optimize training plans.

- Holistic Training Approaches: Incorporating mindfulness, meditation, and cross-disciplinary training (yoga, Pilates, functional fitness) improves flexibility, core strength, and mental resilience.

- Competition Evolution:

- Unified Rule Sets: Efforts to standardize competition rules create a more cohesive competitive environment.

- Innovative Competition Formats: Submission-only tournaments, team-based competitions, and round-robin formats keep the competitive scene exciting and engaging for participants and spectators.

By understanding and embracing these modern innovations, MMA influences, and future trends, BJJ practitioners can stay at the forefront of the sport. These developments ensure that BJJ continues to evolve, offering new opportunities for growth, learning, and excellence in both training and competition.

# Chapter 26: BJJ in Popular Culture

Brazilian Jiu-Jitsu (BJJ) has significantly permeated popular culture, influencing various forms of media and entertainment. This chapter explores the representation of BJJ in movies and media, shares stories of famous BJJ practitioners, and examines its influence in video games and literature.

## *26.1 Representation in Movies and Media*

Brazilian Jiu-Jitsu (BJJ) has made significant inroads into movies and media, enhancing its visibility and popularity worldwide. This section explores how BJJ is represented in various forms of visual media and the impact of this representation on the martial art's growth and public perception.

### *A. Movies*

#### 1. Action Films

   - Integration of BJJ:

     - Examples: "John Wick" series, "Warrior," "Never Back Down."

     - Importance: These movies showcase realistic fight scenes that incorporate BJJ techniques, helping to popularize the martial art.

   - Impact:

     - BJJ's representation in action films has brought attention to its effectiveness in combat and self-defense, attracting new practitioners.

     - The depiction of BJJ in high-stakes, action-packed scenarios elevates the martial art's profile and appeal.

#### 2. Documentaries

   - Educational Content:

     - Examples: "Choke," "Roll: Jiu-Jitsu in SoCal," "Jiu-Jitsu vs. The World."

     - Importance: Documentaries provide in-depth looks at BJJ's history, philosophy, and impact on practitioners' lives.

   - Impact:

- These films educate viewers about BJJ's culture and benefits, promoting a deeper understanding and appreciation of the art.

- Documentaries often highlight personal stories and struggles, making BJJ relatable and inspiring to a wider audience.

## *B. Television Shows*

### 1. Reality TV

- Exposure:

  - Examples: "The Ultimate Fighter," "Fight Quest," "Human Weapon."

  - Importance: Reality shows featuring BJJ expose a broad audience to the training, discipline, and challenges of practicing the martial art.

  - Impact:

  - The visibility of BJJ on television has helped demystify the sport and inspire viewers to take up training.

  - Reality TV shows often depict the transformative power of BJJ, showcasing personal growth and resilience.

### 2. Fictional Series

- BJJ in Storylines:

  - Examples: "Kingdom," "Banshee."

  - Importance: Incorporating BJJ into fictional narratives adds authenticity to fight scenes and introduces the art to new audiences.

  - Impact:

  - BJJ's inclusion in popular TV series enhances its cultural relevance and visibility.

  - These portrayals can spark interest and curiosity, leading viewers to explore BJJ further.

The representation of BJJ in movies and media plays a crucial role in its global expansion and acceptance. By featuring BJJ in various contexts, from action films to educational documentaries and reality TV shows, the martial art gains widespread recognition and appreciation. This visibility not only attracts new practitioners but also fosters a deeper understanding of BJJ's techniques, philosophy, and benefits.

## *26.2 Stories of Famous BJJ Practitioners*

The stories of famous Brazilian Jiu-Jitsu (BJJ) practitioners serve as powerful inspirations for both current and aspiring martial artists. These individuals have significantly contributed to the art through their achievements, innovations, and personal journeys. This section highlights the stories of some of the most influential figures in BJJ.

### *A. Pioneers and Legends*

### 1. Helio Gracie

   - Contribution: Helio Gracie, one of the founders of BJJ, is renowned for refining and popularizing the art. Despite his small stature and health challenges, he adapted traditional Japanese Jujutsu techniques to create a more effective system for smaller, weaker practitioners.

   - Legacy: Helio's innovations and teaching methods have shaped modern BJJ, and his legacy continues through his family and students. His emphasis on leverage and technique over strength is a cornerstone of BJJ philosophy.

### 2. Carlos Gracie

   - Contribution: Carlos Gracie, the older brother of Helio Gracie, is credited with bringing Japanese Jujutsu to Brazil and adapting it to what would become Brazilian Jiu-Jitsu. He founded the first Gracie Jiu-Jitsu Academy in Rio de Janeiro.

   - Legacy: Carlos's establishment of the academy and development of training methods laid the groundwork for the Gracie family's dominance in BJJ. His teachings and philosophy are integral to the history of BJJ.

### 3. Rickson Gracie

   - Achievements: Rickson Gracie, Helio's son, is considered one of the greatest BJJ practitioners of all time. He holds an undefeated record in professional fights and has multiple world championships to his name.

- Impact: Rickson's success in competitions and his philosophical approach to BJJ have inspired countless practitioners worldwide. His teachings on breathing, mindset, and the holistic aspects of BJJ continue to influence the art profoundly.

## 4. Royce Gracie

- Achievements: Royce Gracie gained international fame for his victories in the early UFC tournaments, showcasing the effectiveness of BJJ against larger and stronger opponents.

- Impact: Royce's success in the UFC played a crucial role in popularizing BJJ worldwide and demonstrated the practicality of the art in real combat situations.

## 5. Rolls Gracie

- Achievements: Rolls Gracie is considered one of the most innovative members of the Gracie family. He integrated techniques from wrestling, judo, and sambo into BJJ, greatly expanding the art's repertoire.

- Impact: Rolls's open-minded approach to incorporating techniques from other martial arts has influenced modern BJJ's adaptability and continuous evolution.

## *B. Modern Icons*

### 1. Marcelo Garcia

- Achievements: Marcelo Garcia is renowned for his success in both gi and no-gi competitions, with multiple ADCC (Abu Dhabi Combat Club) and World Championship titles. Known for his technical proficiency and innovative techniques, Marcelo has become a benchmark in the BJJ community.

- Contribution: Marcelo's development of the X-Guard and his exceptional submission skills have significantly influenced modern BJJ practice. His instructional materials and academies continue to produce top-level practitioners.

### 2. Roger Gracie

- Achievements: Roger Gracie is one of the most successful BJJ competitors of all time, with multiple world championships in both gi and no-gi competitions. He is known for his impeccable technique and dominance in competition.

- Contribution: Roger's clean, fundamental approach to BJJ and his success in high-level competitions have set a high standard for practitioners worldwide. His techniques and strategies are widely studied and emulated.

### 3. Andre Galvao

- Achievements: Andre Galvao is a multi-time world champion and ADCC champion. He is also the founder of the Atos Jiu-Jitsu Academy, which has produced numerous top-level competitors.

- Contribution: Andre's aggressive and dynamic style has influenced many practitioners. His success as both a competitor and coach has helped elevate the overall level of competition in BJJ.

### 4. Mackenzie Dern

- Achievements: Mackenzie Dern has achieved remarkable success in both BJJ and MMA, with numerous world championships and a rising career in the UFC. She is one of the few women to transition successfully from elite BJJ competition to professional MMA.

- Impact: Mackenzie serves as a role model for women in BJJ, demonstrating the art's applicability in professional MMA. Her success has inspired many women to pursue BJJ and highlights the growing presence of female athletes in the sport.

## *C. Inspirational Figures*

### 1. Eddie Bravo

- Achievements: Eddie Bravo is known for his innovative approach to no-gi BJJ, particularly with his development of the 10th Planet Jiu-Jitsu system. He gained fame after defeating Royler Gracie in the ADCC, which was a monumental victory at the time.

- Contribution: Eddie's 10th Planet system, which focuses on no-gi techniques and flexibility, has expanded the scope of BJJ. His techniques, such as the Rubber Guard, have become integral parts of no-gi grappling.

### 2. BJ Penn

- Achievements: BJ Penn is a legendary figure in both BJJ and MMA, being one of the few to hold titles in multiple weight classes in the UFC. He earned his BJJ black belt in just three years, an extraordinary accomplishment.

- Impact: BJ's success in MMA has brought significant attention to BJJ, showcasing its effectiveness in real combat situations. His journey from BJJ to becoming a UFC champion serves as an inspiration to many martial artists.

**3. Renzo Gracie**

  - Achievements: Renzo Gracie has been successful in both BJJ and MMA, competing in organizations like Pride FC and the UFC. He is known for his charismatic personality and technical expertise.

  - Contribution: Renzo has been a major ambassador for BJJ, spreading its popularity worldwide through his academies and involvement in MMA. His teaching and mentorship have influenced many top practitioners.

**4. Kron Gracie**

  - Achievements: Kron Gracie, the son of Rickson Gracie, has achieved success in both BJJ and MMA. He is known for his aggressive style and submission prowess.

  - Impact: Kron continues the Gracie legacy in both BJJ and MMA, inspiring a new generation of practitioners with his competitive spirit and dedication.

The stories of these famous BJJ practitioners highlight the diversity and richness of the martial art. Their achievements and contributions have not only advanced BJJ but also inspired countless individuals to pursue and excel in this discipline. Through their legacies, BJJ continues to grow and evolve, reaching new heights and touching lives around the world.

## *26.3 Influence in Video Games and Literature*

Brazilian Jiu-Jitsu (BJJ) has significantly influenced popular culture, extending its reach into video games and literature. This section explores how BJJ is represented in these media, highlighting its impact on audiences and its role in promoting the martial art.

## *A. Video Games*

### 1. Fighting Games

- Representation:

  - Examples: "EA Sports UFC" series, "Tekken," "Street Fighter."

  - Importance: These games feature characters who use BJJ techniques, introducing the martial art to gamers.

  - Impact:

  - The inclusion of BJJ in popular fighting games has raised awareness and interest in the martial art among a younger audience.

  - Players can learn about BJJ techniques and strategies through interactive gameplay, fostering a deeper appreciation for the sport.

### 2. Simulation Games

- Training Simulators:

  - Examples: VR and simulation games that allow players to practice BJJ techniques.

  - Importance: These games provide an interactive and engaging way to learn and refine BJJ skills.

  - Impact:

  - The gamification of BJJ training can supplement traditional practice and attract tech-savvy individuals to the sport.

  - VR simulations offer a safe environment for repetitive practice of complex techniques, enhancing learning efficiency.

## *B. Literature*

### 1. Instructional Books

- Educational Value:

  - Examples: "Jiu-Jitsu University" by Saulo Ribeiro, "Mastering Jujitsu" by Renzo Gracie and John Danaher.

- Importance: These books offer detailed techniques, philosophies, and training methods for practitioners of all levels.

- Impact:

- Instructional books serve as valuable resources for BJJ students, complementing their hands-on training.

- Readers can revisit techniques and concepts at their own pace, reinforcing their understanding and skills.

## 2. Biographies and Memoirs

- Personal Stories:

- Examples: "Breathe: A Life in Flow" by Rickson Gracie, "The Cauliflower Chronicles" by Marshal D. Carper.

- Importance: Biographies and memoirs provide insights into the lives and journeys of notable BJJ practitioners.

- Impact:

- These personal stories inspire and motivate readers, offering a deeper connection to the BJJ community and its values.

- The struggles and triumphs of famous practitioners highlight the transformative power of BJJ, encouraging readers to pursue their own martial arts journeys.

## 3. Fictional Works

- Incorporation of BJJ:

- Examples: Novels and graphic novels that feature BJJ practitioners or techniques as part of their storyline.

- Importance: Fictional works can introduce BJJ to a wider audience by weaving the martial art into compelling narratives.

- Impact:

- Characters and plots involving BJJ can spark interest and curiosity, leading readers to explore the martial art further.

- Fictional representations of BJJ showcase its practical applications and philosophical aspects, broadening its appeal.

The influence of BJJ in video games and literature has significantly contributed to its popularity and acceptance in mainstream culture. By appearing in various forms of media, BJJ reaches diverse audiences, educating and inspiring them to engage with the martial art. This widespread representation ensures that BJJ continues to grow and evolve, leaving a lasting impact on popular culture and the martial arts community.

## Chapter 26 Review: BJJ in Popular Culture

Chapter 26 explores the widespread influence of Brazilian Jiu-Jitsu (BJJ) in popular culture, highlighting its representation in movies and media, the stories of famous practitioners, and its impact on video games and literature. This chapter demonstrates how BJJ has permeated various forms of entertainment and media, increasing its visibility and popularity worldwide.

### 26.1 Representation in Movies and Media

- *Movies:*

  - Action Films: BJJ techniques are prominently featured in movies like the "John Wick" series, "Warrior," and "Never Back Down," showcasing its effectiveness in combat and self-defense.

  - Documentaries: Films like "Choke," "Roll: Jiu-Jitsu in SoCal," and "Jiu-Jitsu vs. The World" provide in-depth looks at BJJ's history, philosophy, and impact on practitioners, educating viewers and promoting a deeper understanding of the art.

- *Television Shows:*

  - Reality TV: Shows like "The Ultimate Fighter," "Fight Quest," and "Human Weapon" expose a broad audience to BJJ training, discipline, and challenges, inspiring viewers to take up the martial art.

  - Fictional Series: TV series like "Kingdom" and "Banshee" incorporate BJJ into their storylines, adding authenticity to fight scenes and introducing the art to new audiences.

### 26.2 Stories of Famous BJJ Practitioners

- *Pioneers and Legends:*

- Helio Gracie: Co-founder of BJJ, known for adapting traditional Japanese Jujutsu techniques and emphasizing leverage and technique over strength.

- Carlos Gracie: Brought Japanese Jujutsu to Brazil and founded the first Gracie Jiu-Jitsu Academy, laying the groundwork for the Gracie family's dominance in BJJ.

- Rickson Gracie: Considered one of the greatest BJJ practitioners, known for his undefeated record and philosophical approach to BJJ.

- Royce Gracie: Gained international fame for his victories in early UFC tournaments, demonstrating BJJ's effectiveness against larger and stronger opponents.

- Rolls Gracie: Integrated techniques from wrestling, judo, and sambo into BJJ, influencing modern BJJ's adaptability and continuous evolution.

- *Modern Icons:*

- Marcelo Garcia: Renowned for his success in both gi and no-gi competitions, known for developing the X-Guard and his exceptional submission skills.

- Roger Gracie: One of the most successful BJJ competitors, known for his impeccable technique and dominance in high-level competitions.

- Andre Galvao: Multi-time world champion and ADCC champion, founder of the Atos Jiu-Jitsu Academy, which has produced numerous top-level competitors.

- Mackenzie Dern: Achieved remarkable success in both BJJ and MMA, serving as a role model for women in BJJ.

- *Inspirational Figures:*

- Eddie Bravo: Known for his innovative approach to no-gi BJJ and the development of the 10th Planet Jiu-Jitsu system.

- BJ Penn: Legendary figure in both BJJ and MMA, one of the few to hold titles in multiple weight classes in the UFC.

- Renzo Gracie: Successful in both BJJ and MMA, known for his charismatic personality and technical expertise.

- Kron Gracie: Achieved success in both BJJ and MMA, continuing the Gracie legacy with his aggressive style and submission prowess.

## 26.3 Influence in Video Games and Literature

- *Video Games:*

  - Fighting Games: Games like the "EA Sports UFC" series, "Tekken," and "Street Fighter" feature characters using BJJ techniques, raising awareness and interest among gamers.

  - Simulation Games: VR and simulation games offer interactive ways to practice BJJ techniques, supplementing traditional training and attracting tech-savvy individuals.

- *Literature:*

  - Instructional Books: Titles like "Jiu-Jitsu University" by Saulo Ribeiro and "Mastering Jujitsu" by Renzo Gracie and John Danaher provide detailed techniques and training methods, serving as valuable resources for practitioners.

  - Biographies and Memoirs: Books like "Breathe: A Life in Flow" by Rickson Gracie and "The Cauliflower Chronicles" by Marshal D. Carper offer insights into the lives of notable BJJ practitioners, inspiring readers with personal stories of struggle and triumph.

  - Fictional Works: Novels and graphic novels featuring BJJ practitioners introduce the martial art to a wider audience through compelling narratives, sparking interest and curiosity.


Chapter 26 highlights how BJJ has permeated various forms of entertainment and media, increasing its visibility and popularity. The representation of BJJ in movies, television shows, video games, and literature not only attracts new practitioners but also fosters a deeper understanding and appreciation of the martial art. This widespread influence ensures that BJJ continues to grow and evolve, leaving a lasting impact on popular culture and the martial arts community.

# Part 10: Resources and References

Part 10 provides essential resources and references for Brazilian Jiu-Jitsu (BJJ) practitioners. This section includes a comprehensive glossary of BJJ terms, recommended reading and viewing materials, and information on key BJJ organizations and competitions. These resources are designed to enhance understanding, deepen knowledge, and support continuous learning in BJJ.

# Chapter 27: Glossary of BJJ Terms from A to Z

A comprehensive glossary of Brazilian Jiu-Jitsu (BJJ) terms is essential for both beginners and advanced practitioners to understand and communicate effectively about the techniques, positions, and concepts of the martial art. This chapter provides an alphabetical list of key BJJ terms, along with their definitions and explanations.

## A

- Armbar: A submission technique that hyperextends the opponent's elbow joint by locking their arm and applying pressure.

- Americana: A shoulder lock where the opponent's arm is bent at a 90-degree angle, and pressure is applied to the shoulder joint.

## B

- Berimbolo: A modern guard technique used to take the opponent's back or sweep them, involving a rolling motion.

- Bridge: A fundamental movement used to create space and escape from bottom positions by lifting the hips off the ground.

## C

- Closed Guard: A guard position where the practitioner wraps their legs around the opponent's waist and controls their posture.

- Cross Collar Choke: A choke using the opponent's collar, typically applied from the guard or mount position.

## D

- De La Riva Guard: A guard position where one leg is wrapped around the outside of the opponent's leg, and the other leg controls their far hip.

- Double Leg Takedown: A takedown technique where the practitioner grabs both of the opponent's legs and drives forward to bring them to the ground.

## E

- Escape: A technique used to move from a disadvantageous position to a neutral or advantageous one.

- Ezekiel Choke: A choke performed using the sleeve of the gi to apply pressure to the opponent's neck.

## F

- Full Mount: A dominant position where the practitioner sits on the opponent's torso with their knees on the ground.

## G

- Guard: A fundamental position where the practitioner uses their legs to control the opponent from the bottom.

- Guillotine Choke: A front headlock choke that applies pressure to the opponent's neck.

## H

- Half Guard: A guard position where one of the opponent's legs is trapped between the practitioner's legs.

- Hip Escape (Shrimping): A fundamental movement used to create space and escape from bottom positions by moving the hips away from the opponent.

## I

- Inside Control: A position where the practitioner has control of the opponent's arms from the inside, typically used for passing the guard.

## J

- Joint Lock: A submission technique that applies pressure to the opponent's joints to cause pain or damage.

# K

- Kimura: A shoulder lock where the opponent's arm is bent behind their back, and pressure is applied to the shoulder joint.

# L

- Leg Lock: A category of submission techniques targeting the opponent's legs and ankles.

# M

- Mount: A dominant position where the practitioner sits on the opponent's torso, controlling their movement.

# N

- North-South Position: A control position where the practitioner is on top of the opponent, with their head facing the opponent's feet.

# O

- Omoplata: A shoulder lock submission using the legs to apply pressure to the opponent's shoulder joint.

# P

- Pass Guard: A technique used to move from the opponent's guard to a more dominant position, such as side control or mount.

# Q

- Quarter Guard: A variation of the half guard where the practitioner traps only the opponent's ankle.

# R

- Rear Naked Choke (RNC): A choke applied from the back control position, using the arms to squeeze the opponent's neck.

# S

- Side Control: A dominant position where the practitioner lies across the opponent's torso, controlling their upper body.

- Sweep: A technique used to reverse positions, moving from the bottom to the top.

## T

- Takedown: A technique used to bring the opponent from a standing position to the ground.

- Triangle Choke: A choke performed by trapping the opponent's neck and one arm between the practitioner's legs.

## U

- Underhook: A grip where the practitioner's arm is positioned under the opponent's arm, typically used for control and positional advancements.

## V

- Von Flue Choke: A choke that capitalizes on the opponent's failed guillotine attempt, applying pressure to the neck with the shoulder.

## W

- Wrist Lock: A submission technique that applies pressure to the opponent's wrist joint.

## X

- X-Guard: A guard position where the practitioner uses their legs to control the opponent's legs, typically used for sweeps and transitions.

## Y

- Yoko-Sankaku: A variation of the triangle choke performed from a side position.

## Z

- Z-Guard: A guard variation where one leg is placed across the opponent's torso, providing control and creating opportunities for sweeps and submissions.


This glossary provides a foundation for understanding the key terms and concepts in BJJ, helping practitioners communicate more effectively and deepen their knowledge of the art.

# Chapter 28: Recommended Reading and Viewing

Expanding your knowledge and understanding of Brazilian Jiu-Jitsu (BJJ) through additional resources is essential for continuous learning and improvement. This chapter provides a curated list of recommended books, documentaries, and online content that offer valuable insights into the techniques, history, and philosophy of BJJ.

## *A. Recommended Reading*

### *1. Instructional Books*

- "Jiu-Jitsu University" by Saulo Ribeiro

   - Overview: A comprehensive guide covering fundamental techniques and principles for practitioners of all levels, emphasizing progression through the belt system.

   - Key Features: Detailed explanations, step-by-step photos, and insights from a world champion.

- "Mastering Jujitsu" by Renzo Gracie and John Danaher

   - Overview: A deep dive into the principles and strategies that make BJJ effective, co-authored by one of the most respected figures in the sport and a renowned coach.

   - Key Features: Conceptual approach to learning, historical context, and advanced techniques.

- "The Gracie Diet" by Rorion Gracie

   - Overview: An exploration of the dietary principles that have supported the Gracie family's success in BJJ and overall health.

   - Key Features: Nutritional advice, meal plans, and the philosophy behind the Gracie diet.

## *2. Biographies and Memoirs*

### - "Breathe: A Life in Flow" by Rickson Gracie

- Overview: The autobiography of Rickson Gracie, offering a personal look at his life, philosophy, and the development of BJJ.

- Key Features: Personal anecdotes, insights into the Gracie family, and reflections on the martial art.

### - "The Cauliflower Chronicles" by Marshal D. Carper

- Overview: A memoir that chronicles the author's journey to Hawaii to train in BJJ, blending personal stories with insights into the culture and practice of the sport.

- Key Features: Engaging narrative, cultural exploration, and training experiences.

### - "Becoming the Natural: My Life In and Out of the Cage" by Randy Couture

- Overview: The autobiography of MMA legend Randy Couture, detailing his journey in wrestling, BJJ, and mixed martial arts.

- Key Features: Inspirational story, training insights, and competitive experiences.

## *3. Historical and Analytical Books*

### - "Brazilian Jiu-Jitsu: Theory and Technique" by Renzo & Royler Gracie

- Overview: A foundational text that covers the essential techniques and theories of BJJ, authored by prominent members of the Gracie family.

- Key Features: Historical context, detailed techniques, and philosophical insights.

### - "Opening Closed Guard: The Origins of Jiu-Jitsu in Brazil" by Robert Drysdale

- Overview: An exploration of the origins and development of BJJ, challenging common myths and providing a well-researched history of the art.

- Key Features: Historical analysis, interviews, and in-depth research.

# B. Recommended Viewing

## 1. Documentaries

### - "Choke"

- Overview: A documentary that follows Rickson Gracie as he prepares for and competes in the 1995 Vale Tudo Japan tournament, showcasing his training and philosophy.

- Key Features: Behind-the-scenes footage, competitive insights, and personal interviews.

### - "Roll: Jiu-Jitsu in SoCal"

- Overview: A documentary that explores the vibrant BJJ community in Southern California, featuring interviews with practitioners and instructors.

- Key Features: Cultural exploration, personal stories, and community insights.

### - "Jiu-Jitsu vs. The World"

- Overview: A film that examines the global impact of BJJ, highlighting its growth and the personal journeys of practitioners around the world.

- Key Features: International perspectives, diverse experiences, and inspirational stories.

## 2. Online Resources

### - YouTube Channels

#### - "Gracie Breakdown"

- Overview: A channel by Rener and Ryron Gracie that breaks down BJJ techniques and self-defense principles, often using real-life scenarios and fight footage.

- Key Features: Technique analysis, self-defense tips, and instructional videos.

- *"BJJ Fanatics"*

- Overview: A popular channel featuring instructional content from various top-level BJJ practitioners and coaches.

- Key Features: Technique tutorials, interviews, and training tips.

### - Online Courses

- *"Gracie University"*

- Overview: An online learning platform offering structured BJJ courses for all levels, created by the Gracie family.

- Key Features: Step-by-step lessons, comprehensive curriculum, and progress tracking.

- *"MG in Action" by Marcelo Garcia*

- Overview: An online library of techniques and training sessions from Marcelo Garcia, one of the most successful BJJ competitors.

- Key Features: Detailed technique videos, sparring footage, and instructional content.

## *3. Podcasts*

### - "The Grappling Central Podcast"

- Overview: A podcast featuring interviews with prominent figures in the BJJ community, discussing techniques, training, and the culture of BJJ.

- Key Features: In-depth interviews, expert insights, and community stories.

### - "BJJ Mental Models"

- Overview: A podcast that explores the conceptual and strategic aspects of BJJ, helping practitioners think critically about their training.

- Key Features: Conceptual discussions, strategic advice, and practical applications.

By exploring these recommended readings and viewings, BJJ practitioners can deepen their understanding of the art, gain new insights, and continuously improve their skills. These resources provide a wealth of knowledge from some of the most respected figures in the BJJ community, supporting a well-rounded and informed approach to training.

# Chapter 29: BJJ Organizations and Competitions

Brazilian Jiu-Jitsu (BJJ) has grown into a global sport, with numerous organizations and competitions that govern and promote the practice of BJJ around the world. This chapter provides an overview of the major BJJ organizations, their roles, and the most prestigious competitions in the sport.

## A. Major BJJ Organizations

### 1. International Brazilian Jiu-Jitsu Federation (IBJJF)

   - Overview: The IBJJF is the largest and most influential organization in BJJ, responsible for organizing some of the most prestigious tournaments globally.

   - Roles and Responsibilities:

   - Establishing and maintaining the official rules and regulations for BJJ competitions.

   - Organizing major tournaments such as the World Jiu-Jitsu Championship (Mundials), Pan Jiu-Jitsu Championship, and European Open Jiu-Jitsu Championship.

   - Providing a ranking system for competitors and academies.

   - Impact: The IBJJF sets the standard for competitive BJJ, ensuring consistency and fairness in tournaments worldwide.

### 2. United Arab Emirates Jiu-Jitsu Federation (UAEJJF)

   - Overview: The UAEJJF is a major organization based in the United Arab Emirates, known for hosting high-profile events with significant prize money.

   - Roles and Responsibilities:

   - Organizing the Abu Dhabi World Professional Jiu-Jitsu Championship (ADWPJJC), one of the most prestigious events in the BJJ calendar.

   - Promoting BJJ in the Middle East and supporting the development of the sport at the grassroots level.

- Impact: The UAEJJF has elevated the profile of BJJ by offering substantial financial incentives and attracting top competitors from around the world.

### 3. North American Grappling Association (NAGA)

- Overview: NAGA is a prominent organization that hosts grappling and BJJ tournaments across North America.

- Roles and Responsibilities:

- Organizing a wide range of events for both gi and no-gi competitors at various skill levels.

- Promoting BJJ and grappling through accessible and well-organized competitions.

- Impact: NAGA provides opportunities for practitioners of all levels to compete and gain experience in a supportive environment.

### 4. Abu Dhabi Combat Club (ADCC)

- Overview: ADCC is renowned for its no-gi submission grappling tournaments, attracting elite competitors from various grappling disciplines.

- Roles and Responsibilities:

- Organizing the ADCC Submission Fighting World Championship, often considered the most prestigious no-gi event in the world.

- Establishing rules that emphasize submissions and aggressive grappling.

- Impact: ADCC has significantly influenced the evolution of no-gi grappling and raised the competitive standard in submission wrestling.

## B. Prestigious BJJ Competitions

### 1. World Jiu-Jitsu Championship (Mundials)

- Organizer: IBJJF

- Overview: The Mundials is the most prestigious gi tournament in BJJ, held annually and attracting the best competitors from around the globe.

- Significance: Winning a gold medal at the Mundials is considered one of the highest achievements in the sport.

## *2. Pan Jiu-Jitsu Championship*

- Organizer: IBJJF

- Overview: The Pan Jiu-Jitsu Championship is one of the largest and most important tournaments in the BJJ calendar, held annually in the United States.

- Significance: The Pan Championship is a key event for competitors seeking to establish themselves on the international stage.

## *3. Abu Dhabi World Professional Jiu-Jitsu Championship (ADWPJJC)*

- Organizer: UAEJJF

- Overview: The ADWPJJC is known for its significant prize money and high-level competition, attracting top athletes from around the world.

- Significance: The event has helped elevate the status of BJJ by offering substantial financial rewards and global exposure.

## *4. ADCC Submission Fighting World Championship*

- Organizer: ADCC

- Overview: The ADCC World Championship is the most prestigious no-gi grappling event, held every two years and featuring elite competitors from various grappling disciplines.

- Significance: Winning an ADCC title is considered the pinnacle of success in no-gi submission grappling.

## *5. European Open Jiu-Jitsu Championship*

- Organizer: IBJJF

- Overview: The European Open is one of the largest BJJ tournaments outside of Brazil and the United States, attracting a diverse group of competitors.

- Significance: The event provides a platform for European athletes to compete at a high level and gain international recognition.

## *6. Brasileiro (Brazilian National Jiu-Jitsu Championship)*

- Organizer: IBJJF

- Overview: The Brasileiro is a major tournament held in Brazil, showcasing the country's top talent and serving as a stepping stone for international competitions.

- Significance: The event is a critical part of the Brazilian BJJ circuit, with many competitors using it as a benchmark for their skills.

By participating in these organizations and competitions, BJJ practitioners can test their skills, gain valuable experience, and achieve recognition in the sport. These platforms not only promote the growth of BJJ but also help maintain high standards of competition and sportsmanship.

# Chapter 30: Conclusion

As we conclude "HowExpert Guide to Brazilian Jiu-Jitsu," it is important to reflect on the journey through the rich history, fundamental principles, techniques, and the vibrant culture that defines BJJ. This guide has aimed to provide a comprehensive overview for practitioners at all levels, from beginners to advanced students, and to serve as a valuable resource for continuous learning and improvement.

## *Key Takeaways*

### *1. Foundations of BJJ:*

- Understanding the roots of BJJ, from its Japanese Jujutsu origins to the innovations by the Gracie family, provides a solid historical context for practitioners.

- Core principles such as leverage, technique, and the philosophy of continuous growth and respect are fundamental to mastering BJJ.

### *2. Techniques and Strategies:*

- Mastery of basic and advanced techniques, including various guard positions, submissions, and sweeps, is essential for progression in BJJ.

- The importance of physical conditioning, mental preparation, and effective training methods cannot be overstated.

### *3. Practical Applications:*

- BJJ is not just a sport but a practical self-defense system that empowers individuals, including specific techniques for real-world scenarios and law enforcement applications.

- The empowerment of women through BJJ, building confidence, and self-awareness highlights the inclusive nature of the martial art.

## *4. Cultural Impact:*

- BJJ's influence extends beyond the mats, impacting popular culture through movies, media, and literature. The stories of famous practitioners inspire and motivate new generations.

- Participation in global competitions and adherence to the rules and traditions foster a sense of community and respect among practitioners worldwide.

## *5. Continuous Learning:*

- Engaging with recommended readings, viewings, and online resources enhances understanding and keeps practitioners updated on the latest developments in BJJ.

- Being part of organizations and competitions not only tests skills but also promotes growth and camaraderie within the BJJ community.

# *Final Thoughts*

Brazilian Jiu-Jitsu is a dynamic and evolving martial art that offers immense benefits beyond physical fitness. It teaches discipline, resilience, and the importance of continuous self-improvement. Whether you are stepping onto the mats for the first time or are an experienced practitioner, the journey of learning and growth in BJJ is a lifelong endeavor.

We hope that "HowExpert Guide to Brazilian Jiu-Jitsu" has provided you with valuable insights and practical knowledge to enhance your BJJ journey. Embrace the challenges, celebrate the victories, and continue to evolve both on and off the mats. Thank you for choosing this guide as your companion in mastering the art of Brazilian Jiu-Jitsu.

Oss!

# About the Author

HowExpert publishes how to guides on all topics from A to Z. Visit [HowExpert.com](HowExpert.com) to learn more.

# About the Publisher

Byungjoon "BJ" Min is an author, publisher, entrepreneur, and the founder of HowExpert. He started off as a once broke convenience store clerk to eventually becoming a fulltime internet marketer and finding his niche in publishing. He is the founder and publisher of HowExpert where the mission is to discover, empower, and maximize everyday people's talents to ultimately make a positive impact in the world for all topics from A to Z. Visit BJMin.com and HowExpert.com to learn more. John 14:6

# Recommended Resources

- HowExpert.com – How To Guides on All Topics from A to Z by Everyday Experts.
- HowExpert.com/free – Free HowExpert Email Newsletter.
- HowExpert.com/books – HowExpert Books
- HowExpert.com/courses – HowExpert Courses
- HowExpert.com/clothing – HowExpert Clothing
- HowExpert.com/membership – HowExpert Membership Site
- HowExpert.com/affiliates – HowExpert Affiliate Program
- HowExpert.com/jobs – HowExpert Jobs
- HowExpert.com/writers – Write About Your #1 Passion/Knowledge/Expertise & Become a HowExpert Author.
- HowExpert.com/resources – Additional HowExpert Recommended Resources
- YouTube.com/HowExpert – Subscribe to HowExpert YouTube.
- Instagram.com/HowExpert – Follow HowExpert on Instagram.
- Facebook.com/HowExpert – Follow HowExpert on Facebook.
- TikTok.com/@HowExpert – Follow HowExpert on TikTok.